Training in
Library & Information Science

Training in
Library & Information Science

Dr Anand Ballabh

2006

SBS Publishers & Distributors Pvt. Ltd.
New Delhi

ISBN : 81-89741-03-9

Price - Rs 995

First Published in India in 2006

Published by:
SBS PUBLISHERS & DISTRIBUTORS PVT. LTD.
2/9, Ground Floor, Ansari Road, Darya Ganj,
New Delhi - 110002, INDIA
Tel: 23289119, 41563911
Email: mail@sbspublishers.com

Contents

Preface

To get proficiency in any profession, education and proper training play pivotal role. This enhances the skill as well as facilitates the smooth everyday functioning. After entering a profession, on the job training, attending advance courses, seminars, workshops, referesher courses is prerequisite to be a fully equipped professional.

Librarianship is a gentle and dignified profession, equally venerated as a university professorship or a director in government and a lecturer or teacher at a junior level. Library education and training is also gaining popularity. As a professional he has to interact with many publics, the government, teachers, students, readers, booksellers and publishers etc. As such he has to play the role of an academician, an administrator and a manager. Though with the emergence of computer, internet and other sophisticated tools of information technology, this education has become modern, yet learning about traditional system is equally important.

This book consists of the following chapters: Continuing Education and Librarianship; Librarian, Bookseller and Publisher; Recent Trends in Information Science Training; Job Training Plans: Some Models; Library Staff Management; Librarianship Education; Student Assistants; Teaching Services; Library Service Interpretation etc.

This book compiles the articles which put ample light on some vital issues pertaining to training aspect in library and information science. To make the book informative and authoritative we have liberally drawn the material from various secondary sources e.g. books, journals, reports etc. As such no claim of originality.

The editor expresses his deep sense of gratitude to all those leading scholars and library professionals in the field. Different institutional libraries and librarians therein have helped us while gathering the requisite information. He is thankful to them. He is equally grateful to his friends and colleagues for their inspiration and moral support. Finally he is thankful to his publisher for materializing the present endeavour superbly in the present shape.

–Editor

1

Continuing Education and Librarianship

Professional Library Associations have to play a prominent role in the development of libraries in a country. The broad sweep of library development is more and more dependent on professional planning, foresight, understanding and activity which are usually fostered by the Associations. The professional Associations can play a vital role in continuing education. It should act as an agency to carry out the continuing education programme of librarians.

Continuing education is of great importance in all rapidly changing professions especially in library profession. "Continuing education is a process by which library personnel (alone, in groups, or in institutional settings) purposefully seek to improve themselves or their profession by changing their knowledge, attitudes or skills." In order to meet the new developments in the field of information technology the librarians have to equip themselves adequately with the developments. For achieving this goal librarians need continuing education.

As a professional body, the library association provides a common forum to bring together all persons engaged in library activities or interested in library development. It should urge the government to enact library legislation for strengthening of library movement and for providing better library services. It should arrange, as often as possible, conferences, seminars, lectures, discussions, study circles, workshops etc. as part of the continuing education programme. This the professionals will get opportunity to meet and exchange ideas among themselves. It can impart professional education supplementing the university education and also act as an accrediting body for maintaining proper standards of library education. It can conduct study and research for the advancement of library and information science and enhance professional education by establishing proper training institutes or research centres. It can bring out bibliographical compilations, reference and other publications including journals as the organ of the association. It can strive for the standardisation of some of the library equipment, techniques and practices. It can offer consultancy services on any aspect of library planning. It can foster reading habit among children, neo-literates and others by organising competitions, book-fairs etc. The library association should maintain cooperation with other state, national, international and other organisations with similar objectives.

Associations in Western Countries

The American Library Association, the oldest and the largest national library association in the world, was established on 6th Oct. 1876 by a band of enthusiastic American librarians with multi-dimensional professional activities.

The Library Association of the United Kingdom was established on 5th Oct. 1877 with similar objectives and activities that of the American Library Association.

National Library Association in India

There are several National Library Associations which helped the development of libraries and the library profession.

India Library Association (ILA)

ILA was formed as a result of the All India Library

Conference which was conducted at Calcutta on 13th Sept. 1933. It is a permanent body established for the achievement of promoting the library movement and development of library services and library science education in India. It represents all types of libraries and librarians.

ILA is publishing a quarterly journal 'ILA Bulletin' and a monthly "ILA NEWSLETTER." Besides these periodical publications, from time to time ILA is publishing proceedings of their conferences and seminars. Other publications include Directory of Indian Librarians (1938), Union Catalogue of Periodical Publications (1952) etc.

ILA was conducting a diploma course in librarianship.

ILA organises national seminars and conferences at different parts of the country. The XXV All India Library Conference was held in Trivandrum in 1979. ILA organised a national seminar on continuing education for librarians in Delhi on 13th February 1984. In all the conferences and seminars latest developments in the profession are discussed.

Government of India Librarians Association (GILA)

It is a professional association of librarians working in the government departments, established in 1933 in Delhi.

GILA has started publishing a journal called "GILA Bulletin."

GILA conducted In-service Post-Graduate Diploma courses in Library Science for the graduates in the Government of India libraries. Five such courses were held between 1951-1960.

Indian Association of Special Libraries and Information Centres (IASLIC)

It was established on 3rd Sept. 1955 with the effort of a handful of enthusiastic librarians with the object of promoting and coordinating the activities among special libraries of scientific, technological and research institutions and other information and documentation centres. It acts as a centre of research and study in special librarianship, documentation and information science.

IASLIC is publishing a quarterly journal "IASLIC Bulletin," a quarterly abstracting journal "Indian Library Science Abstracts" and a monthly "IASLIC Newsletter." Besides these periodical publications, the association is publishing proceedings of its conferences, seminars and other publications.

IASLIC conducted a post-graduate B. Lib. Sc. course in special Librarianship and Documentation from 1966 till 1970. Now it is conducting occasional refresher courses on select topics of documentation and information science.

IASLIC is conducting annual conferences at different research and academic institutions in various parts of the country. So far the association conducted twelve national conferences. The XIIth Annual Conference is being held in the Banaras Hindu University during the last week of December 1986. Another significant activity of IASLIC in continuing education is its "Study Circle." It completed the 100th study circle with a two-day seminar on February 26-27, 1977. Various issues concerning special librarianship and latest developments in the field of Information Science and Documentation are discussed on all these occasions.

Indian Academic Library Association (IALA)

It was established in 1964 at Jaipur Wheat Loan Library Workshop to bring the university and college librarians together. But it has not done any remarkable activity.

Indian Association of Teachers of Library and Information Science (IATLIS)

It was established at a meeting of the teachers of Library and Information Science held at the DRTC in 1969. The association is publishing its organ 'IATLIS

Communication.' As part of the continuing education programme the association is holding periodical seminars on various aspects in Library and Information Science teaching.

State Level Library Associations

Majority of the states in India have their own Library Associations. They are (1) Andhra Pradesh Library Association (1914), (2) Maharashtra Library Association (1921), (3) Baroda Library Association, (1924), (4) West Bengal Library Association (1925), (5) Madras Library Association (1928), (6) Punjab Library Association (1929), (7) Bihar Rajya Pustakalaya Sangh (1936), (8) Assam Library Association (1939), (9) The Utkal Library Association (Orissa) (1944), (10) Gujarat Library Association (1939), (11) Delhi Library Association (1953), (12) Uttar Pradesh Library Association (1956), (13) Madhya Pradesh Library Association (157), (14) Mysore Library Association (1962), (16) Haryana Library Association (1962), (17) Jammu and Kashmir Library Association (1966) and the Chandigarh Library Association (1969).

Almost all the state level associations are conducting certificate course in Library Science. Delhi Library Association started a Post-Graduate Diploma course in 1972. Andhra Pradesh, West Bengal, Delhi, Uttar Pradesh, Madhya Pradesh, and Rajasthan Public Library Associations are publishing 'Granthalaya Sarvaswamu,' 'Granthagar,' 'Library Herald,' 'Lucknow Librarian', 'Pusthakalaya Sandesh,' 'RLA Bulletin,' respectively.

Library Associations in Kerala

There was a 'Public Library Society' organised in Trivandrum in 1829 which was responsible for the starting of the Trivandrum Public Library in the same year. The activities of the Society were confined to Trivandrum City. In 1898 the Trivandrum Public Library Society handed over the Trivandrum Public Library to the Government.

In 1931 the 'Samastha Kerala Pusthakalaya Samithi was started in Trichur in Cochin state. The Samithi started a quarterly magazine 'Grandha Vichar.' The 'All-Travancore Library Association' formed in 1933 existed for about 3 years without any significant achievement, to its credit. The 'Malabar Vayanasala Sanghom' was formed in 1937. In 1943 this was registered as 'Kerala Granthalaya Sanghom.' It did a lot of work until 1953 for establishment and development of libraries in the Malabar area. This Sanghom merged with the Kerala Granthasala Sanghom in 1957.

Kerala Granthasala Sanghom (KGS)

KGS was established in 1945 as the "All-Travancore Granthasala Sanghom" with a membership of 47 libraries. In 1949 the Sanghom was renamed as "Travancore-Cochin Granthasala Sanghom' with the integration of Travancore and Cochin States. Later, after the formation of Kerala State in 1956 it assumed its present name as "Kerala Granthasala Sanghom." In 1977 the Sanghom was taken over by the Government and is being run under a Control Board. There are now about 4883 libraries (Nov. 1886) affiliated to the Sanghom. In its constitution and its functioning the Sanghom differs from other library associations. It can more appropriately be described as a federation of libraries. It has done valuable contributions for the establishment and development of public libraries in Kerala.

In 1948 the Sanghom started publication of its official organ 'Granthalokam' in Malayalam as a monthly. The Sanghom has also published a library manual in 1947 and a directory in 1964. Another work 'Nam Munnott' (We march on) by K.P. Kesava Menon was published by the Sanghom in 1966. A fortnightly known as "Sakshara Keralam" started its publication on 15.8.1972.

The Sanghom conducted a three months training course

for its workers in 1958. Another short term training course lasting for three weeks was also offered to the library workers from 1938 onwards. Now it is conducting a certificate course in library science of four months duration occasionally. So far, the Sanghom conducted 5 courses at different places in the state and produced 175 trained persons. The Sanghom has regularly been conducting conferences and seminars at various parts of the state. In all the conferences and seminars, several subjects of general interest are discussed.

Library Associations in Kerala

Professional Library Associations were late to emerge in Kerala. The first attempt at funding a professional association took place in 1958 when a handful of trained librarians met at Ernakulam. Thus the All Kerala College Librarians Association was formed. The association's activity mainly concentrated on the improvement of qualifications, pay scales, status and service conditions of librarians in colleges.

Kerala Librarian Association: It was formed in 1964 at Trivandrum and the All Kerala College Librarians Association merged with this. The Association functioned very actively for some years and proved to be very effective in projecting a proper image of the library profession. The main achievements include the recognition obtained for professional qualifications as essential for appointments in libraries, the recognition 'given by the two successive pay commissions to the library personnel as a special category, the improvement in the status and pay scale of the State Librarian etc. In 1971 the Kerala Librarians Association was redesignated to form the Kerala Library Association.

Kerala Library Association: KLA is a state-wide organisation of professionally qualified librarians which is registered under the Societies Act of 1955. Its basic objective is to work for the overall improvement of libraries and library services in the state.

It is publishing the "KLA Newsletter" periodically and published a National Library Week Souvenir in 1976 and a XXV All India Library Conference Volume in 1979. Published a book, "Canons of Library Classification "under the series "Kerala Library Association Publication Series."

The association is organising a series of study circles, seminars, discussions for exchange of information among professionals and to keep them abreast of the latest developments in the field of Library and Information Science and to discuss the problems facing them in their day-to-day work. The associations in collaboration with other professional associations (ILA, KCLA, etc.) and research organisations conducted seminars and conferences at different places in the state. The association conducted classes on user education for the post-graduate and research students of different institutions.

Kerala College Librarians Association (KCLA): It is a professional association of College Librarians in Kerala, founded in 1969 and is affiliated to the Kerala Library Association. Its activities mainly concentrate on the improvement of pay scales, status, grading of college libraries and librarians and other service conditions of college librarians. The Association in collaboration with KLA conducted a series of seminars, discussions etc. on library education.

*Academy of Library and Information Services (ALIS):*ALIS was established in 1975 and registered as a non-profit making, educational and cultural society. Services to the people of all nations by selfless conscientious library activity will be the chief motive behind all the programmes of the Academy of Library and Information Services.

"ALIS News and Notes" is published occasionally. Started the publication of the bi-annual journal "ALIS

Bulletin" in 1976 and it has completed volume 10. It contains learned contributions on various aspects of library and information science. It is worthwhile to mention that ALIS Bulletin had brought out a special volume on Library and Information Science Education. ALIS concentrated on extension activities, conducted public lecturers, group discussions with various library professionals for communicating ideas among professionals.

All Kerala College Qualified Librarians' Association: It is an association of professionally qualified college librarians established in 1986. The association submitted a memorandum to the Education Minister for academic status to College Librarians. It is hoped that this association will act. enthusiastically for the development of the library profession.

Problems

The associations face several problems which restrict their healthy activities.

(i) Inadequacy of Finance: The only source of getting finance is the annual subscription from the members.

(ii) Lack of Active Participation Among Members: Active participation and cooperation among the members are most important factors for the success of any programme conducted by the associations.

(iii) Lack of Proper Planing: The associations have to develop long term plans for the continuing education programme for librarians.

(iv) Lack of well-defined Objectives: The associations should lay down well-defined objectives for continuing education.

Summing Up

It is a fact that the Professional Library Associations in Kerala could not yet make any real impact in the library situation, except from the point of view of the staff. Among the associations, KGS, KLA, KCLA and ALIS are conducting continuing education programmes occasionally. But the present activities are not at all sufficient to attain the target.

In order to facilitate continuing education for librarians the Professional Associations have to take initiative for establishing a Research Centre for Library and Information Science and Documentation as a centre for continuing education programme in each state. The Associations should conduct refresher courses for working librarians all over Kerala at least once in every 5 to 7 years because formal training programme of one or two years duration is not sufficient for a professional who has to work in the field for thirty or forty years. Before starting the continuing education programmes the association should constitute a committee to finanlise specific topics of relevance for specific user groups. Continuing education is necessary in all the areas of library and information development. Like teachers, academic librarians may also have to be included in the faculty improvement programme of UGC to provide them facilities for attending conferences, short-term training courses and also for higher education and research. In order to meet the financial crisis of the association in conducting educational programmes, organisations such as universities, research institutions, UGC, ICSSR, CSIR, etc. can be contacted for sponsoring the programmes. The Library Association should emerge to the level of an accrediting body (like the Medical Council or Bar Council) and every professional librarian in the state should register his/her name in the Association. Thus the association can keep a common profile for the coordination of all the professionals in Kerala.

Exchange of Personnel and Inservice Training

A Library is a store-house of inherited knowledge and wisdom of the world systematically stacked and made available for the use of any individual. The librarian is a technocrat who operates the libra-material-machinery for the benefit of the society. He holds the key to the material that generally evades the lay aspirant for knowledge and it is he who is to open up the wealth of information lying piled up in the form of books and periodicals, accessible only to a few who belong to the intellectual aristocracy. The technique of the Librarian lies in locating the wanted information and retailing it out to the genuine consumer, with the least delay and at the shortest notice. When we call the library machinery, and the Librarian a technocrat, it is necessary to emphasise the fact that this technocrat ought to know how to work the machinery. Otherwise he finds himself in the predicament of the Pakistani technocrat in the recent Indo-Pakistan war, operating the most sophisticated American air-craft without knowing how to do it. One arduous task before our democracy is to educate its masses. It is the responsibility of a democratic state to carry knowledge to the common man so that he, thus enlightened, might turn out to be a bulwark of its ideals.

There is no gainsaying that in a democracy opportunities for acquiring knowledge should be within the reach of every aspirant, whatever the disparity in the levels of intelligence. In this context libraries and librarians have a unique role to play. Life has been complex in the modern world which is gradually shrinking into a small place. Nothing in the world seems to have an absolute and independent entity as such. Every day we are getting aware of the inter-dependence and the inter-relatedness of the various fields of human activity.

It may sound odd to any that a knowledge of the rudiments of Physics, Astronomy Anthropology and Psychology and various other branches of learning is essential for the full understanding and appreciation of say, a modern poem, or a modern novel. All the same it is true. "All knowledge, all our knowledge, has been built up communally." Real progress is possible only when knowledge is pooled together and shared equally. Thus, a library is a pool wherein lies knowledge flowing into it from various sources in the form of books and periodicals. The librarians is a responsible individual who is to classify the confusion of material that flows in constantly and give it at least a semblance of order and system. As a custodian of knowledge great responsibility lies on his shoulders. Unless he is well equipped for the ask he cannot be of any use to the society. The problem before us now is to explore by what means a state of society can equip a librarian to play his key role efficiently and proposefully. The responsibility of the state or society does not end when it starts a library and keeps it in-charge of a librarian. It is also the responsibility of the society to create ideal conditions for the working of the machinery as well. Two things that can go a long way in improving the maintenance and working of the libraries, two things that necessarily add to the efficiency of the librarian are: (1) Library personnel exchange, and (2) Inservice training of the personnel, countries that are for advance in the techniques of library maintenance have experimented with them with remarkable results.

Library personnel exchange programme has innumerable merits that cannot easily be overlooked. Experience in various places and situation will sharpen the mental facilities of the librarians and thus the whole society would stand to gain. Weak spots shall have a wave of occasional change when the librarians get transferred and the likes and dislikes, academic and political, with the ambition and the expectation of the management. The whole library takes into a new line of arrangement, new acquisition programme, thereby forging on interdocumentary relationship, more and more complex penumbral relationship developing as tool and instrumental discipline, because of regrouped placement of books personnel and periodicals. The sense of complacency dampens the vigour and vitality which it is result of prolonged stay at the one and the same place. Not only the society loses the enthusiasm for new learning and benefits likely to accrue to the society but also the vices that can likely crop up such as Identifying personnel likes and dislikes, interests and bias with the Institution itself thereby allowing a perverted development advocating a particular angle or view point. I do not like to speak of alliances between the Book suppliers and the bill clearance etc. So far we have dealt with the exchange of the personnel Now let us have a peep into the exchange of thought content. Periodical conferences of this type, seminars, meetings occasional visits to the neighbouring libraries will develop the exchange of thoughts and mutual consultations on the day to day problems of identical interests will be there for increasing the technical efficiency of the library personnel. Librarians should be deputed to attend national and state level Library Conferences, seminars and symposia, and made free to ventilate the lessons drawn out of their experiences. For all those purposes the management should give them practical encouragement by meeting their T.A. and D.A. To eradicate the inherent drawbakcs of inefficiency arising out of ill-equipped and unqualified libraries and improper services rendered by mere replicas of librarians who are giving room to incessant complaints, the resources funds space and co-operation amongst libraries and shortage of well qualified and intelligent workers are to be improved. By achieving this goal of rendering services to the readers the scope and status of the Library profession will be improved.

Then inservice training has two nuances. In the primary sense it means training a non-trained person. In the secondary sense it means bringing his knowledge upto date so as to equip him to utilise the latest developing techniques and devices and exploit them for the benefit of the society. This service training or orientation not only wipes out the feeling that the librarians even when they are better in status and paid decent salaries are not serving to the satisfaction of the clientele.

Such of the clerks and other unqualified and under-qualified persons who are posted as librarians in some of the colleges may be given training in library science if they are inadequately equipped.

Inservice training helps the librarians both qualified and under-qualified gain effectiveness in their work. Therefore, such orientation programmes are to be organised and systamatic instructions and practices are to be given to the employee so that he can know the way to apply the body of knowledge gained in pre-entry education and training to the concrete duties of a specific job. In service training also develops the appropriate habits of thought and action skill and knowledge essential to effective performances. Staff members are expected to have a basic knowledge of library objectives, operation and techniques. Each library has a certain number of individual aims and procedures. Providing professional literature, instituting planned reading courses encouraging meetings of special groups, sponsering group discussions, conferences, arranging special studies of library problems to staff members offering intermittant or occasional professional courses, participating in co-operative programmes etc., shall ensure not only continuity of their objective policies and services of a particular library but also help material in stimulating morale and reducing turnover among the more capable members of the staff.

In-Service Training

The post-independence period in India which has seen tremendous progress in developmental activities of the country has also seen tremendous explosion in the field of education. The library which is one of the important agencies of education has also got its share of progress in a remarkable proportion. Public libraries have been spread in rural parts of the country also. The library has become an inevitable and inseparable part of a university or college from the time of their inception to impart education through printed word of the book along with the spoken word of the teacher. This expansion in the educational values and activities of the library has created some problems. The most important problem is as how to render maximum library service to the reader in minimum time in an efficient way. It is true that a library should have a well-planned and neatly furnished building with good selection of books, journals and other recorded material and trained staff to cater to the needs of the readers. The organisation, development, utilisation and maintenance of the library on sound and modern lines depend on the skill, technical competence and academic attainments of the library staff. In addition to huge growth in the number of School, College and University going students people are going for advanced studies and research work in a large scale in every field of knowledge.

In their educational pursuits and quest for more and more knowledge their dependence on the library has become immense. So to meet these demands of the readers the library personnel should adopt all means in their profession. They can do so by attaining proficiency in the library techniques which improve from time to time so as to help the readers to get the requisite information. To bring them in touch with latest developments and techniques in the field of library science and to serve the reader best in-service Training is necessary.

In-service training means a programme by which all persons in the profession learn and grow together but not a programme to fill the vacancies with trained personnel. Such programs will help to bring together the birds of the same feather and create a climate for 'emotional integration' amongst them (when these programmes take lace on national level these will help for National Integration also). This will help for mutual exchange of ideas regarding their profession and thus mutual co-operation also in the solution of organisational and other problems of the profession. Conflicts between administrative values and goal values are more easily solved when discussed frankly. So not only the librarian but the administrative head of the library should also participate in in-service programme.

"In-service education training is a basic need of any professional worker and facilities ought to be provided by those responsible in this field." Universities can extend their services to Colleges and Colleges to schools. In-service programmes in schools should be so planned as to train the untrained staff who are incharge of libraries. Extention of services can be done even outside of their premises either through the visits of the staff for consultations, lectures or through conducting courses. These programmes may be of temporary or of regular nature. These would be in-service courses because those participating in them does so along with their regular job work.

The improvement in the techniques of library service should be taken up on national scale. It should not be limited to a particular region or state. Then only the libraries can work on new and efficient lines. Then only the libraries can become the potential agency of education in the country. So in order to take up this responsibility of infusing new spirit into the library personnel and revitalising the libraries to serve the cause of education there should be one National Agency on the lines of NCERT or a separate permanent cell in the NCERT. This agency should be staffed with people who have both academic and administrative experience in the field of Library Science. This should attach one Extension Department to every university to give in-service training not only to College Librarians and professional personnel working in public libraries in that university area. A monthly journal should be published and adequate literature on in-service education in this field should also be produced. In-service training will yield good results only when the trainees have professional consciousness. This agency should also provide for the training of University Library personnel and College Librarians in special subjects like Documentation and Study

Programmes in National Libraries during summer vacation. These study visits National Libraries and well developed University libraries will help a lot to observe and learn the progress made in methods and techniques of Library service. These can be applied and tried in the libraries when they go back to their institutes. Provision should be made by the Universities to the in-service personnel, especially to College librarians who are insisted of higher academic or professional qualifications by the U.G.C. to do Masters course in library science as part time students. University Grants Commission should give financial assistance to take up research Projects.

Encouragement should be given by the U.G.C. by granting scholarships liberally to those librarians who are interested in research work which is very much lacking in the field in our country. Exchange of library personnel is not existent in India. It is a novel issue. This will take place where there is surplus of trained staff on one side and death of it on the other side and between the personnel who are technically well trained according to time-to-time-improvements and the personnel who are not abrest of changes and developments in the field. The services of trained College Librarians may be lent to the newly started Colleges or Universities till adequate trained staff is appointed. The assistance of librarians of foreign countries who are working in India under some programme or other may be taken by local librarians since the former have certainly new methods and techniques to be learnt by us. We should not feel shy to learn from the learnt and to follow the path which leads to progress.

REFERENCES

Bennett, Mary A. Microfilm and its use in giving instruction in the use of the library. Spec. lib. assoc. proc, 1938, 1:97-8, July, 1938.

Clatworthy, Linda M. Library test for college students. Denver, Col., University of Denver, 1932. Forms A-B.

Denise, Sister M. Librarian's contribution to freshmen orientation. Catholic lib. world 8:3-6, September, 1936.

Feagley, Ethel M. Teachers. In National society for the study of education. Forty-second yearbook. Part II. The library in general education., ed. by N. B. Henry. Chicago, University of Chicago press, 1943, p. 301-11.

Hurt, Peyton. The need of college and university instruction in the use of the library. Lib. quar. 4:436-48, July, 1934.

Lowell, Mildred H. Reading and the training school library. Col. and research lib. 2:226-30, June, 1941.

Meyering, H. R. and Pierson, Stella. Introducing the library to college students. Jour., of higher educ. 10:447-9, November, 1939.

Pierson, Stella and Gilbert, A. W. Comprehensive examination in the use of the library. Kansas City, Mo., Teachers College, 1939.

Reed, Lulu R. Do colleges need reference service? Lib. quar. 13:232-40, July, 1943.

Reed, Lulu R. Test on the use of the library for the elementary school library. Chicago, Chicago Planograph corp., 1937.

Shores, Louis and Moore, Joseph E. Peabody Library information tests. Nashville, Tenn., Education Test Bureau, Educational publisher; inc., 1940. Unit at college level.

Smith, Xenophon. Streamlining library instruction. Lib. jour. 65:521-2, June 15, 1940.

Standford, E. B. Freshman library orientation. Lib. jour. 64:47-9, January 5, 1939.

Triggs, F. O. Remedial reading programs. Jour, of educ. psychol. 33:678- 85, December, 1942.

Webb, Helmer L. Bibliographic course for the pre-graduate student. Lib. jour. 63:402-4, May 15, 1938.

Wilson, Louis R. Tentative prospectus of a course in the college library in general education for teachers and prospective teachers. Chicago, 1940, (mimeographed)

Young, A. Beatrice. Let us teach library science in college. Sch. and soc. % 50:837, December 23, 1939.

2

Librarian, Bookseller and Publisher

How much do we know beyond generalities and how do we know what could be of specific interest to Indian librarians? How much do we know about India and the needs of its academic community?

1. The Indian Academic Market is--economically--of greatest importance to our company;
2. The contribution of Indian researchers to our STM journal and book publications are considerable;
3. Our second largest book customer in the world is an Indian bookseller; and
4. Without the help of this bookseller and his numerous colleagues our service to you and our knowledge of your needs would be a fraction of what it is now.

And now let us come to the point. The question as we understand it is whether the triangular relationship is necessary and whether it works to all our satisfaction.

We can answer two simple questions immediately:

Do we need libraries and librarians? Of course, as academic research and teaching would come to a complete stand still without them.

Do we need publisher? We feel that even at the dawn of document delivery, electronic publishing and publishing on demand its role as a disseminator of scientific knowledge is immeasurable.

Which leaves us with the question whether the booktrade still plays a crucial role in our trinity. We know that many publishers--in a time of scarcity and constantly increasing overheads--are forced to ask themselves whether a direct link publisher: end-customer would not be more effective and more economical? My answer is, that today both publisher and library need the booktrade as the go-between more than ever before.

For the publisher it is easy to sum up the reasons for his point of view:

> Without a healthy and well-organised booktrade: the publisher would be forced to increase the number of accounts he would have to handle to a proportion which would increase administrative problems--and therefore overheads, for beyond economically feasible proportions. Elsevier in Amsterdam alone maintains about 150,000 customers delivery addresses world-wide in its files. However, invoicing is done to about 2,200 customers only; reducing problems of proforma invoicing or credit risk and credit control to a reasonable proportion.

To serve the need of its academic customers properly the publisher depends to a great extent upon the bookseller's practical knowledge of the market and his willingness and capability to act as a fire-brigade.

Last but not least, the bookseller acts as the publisher's translator. Not everywhere in the academic world is English the lingua frànca as it is in India.

To put down what should be the librarian's point of view--providing the golden eggs for the publisher and the meagre bowl of rice for the bookseller--is more difficult for me:

> Using the booksellers is *cheaper* as he reduce the librarians overhead considerably. Instead of ordering from, paying to, claiming from and corresponding with a minimum of at least 150 different international publishers and organisations he might/should have only a handful of reliable suppliers.

Using booksellers is more *effective* as the personal relations a good bookseller maintains with most of his suppliers guarantees fast and reliable service. The good personal relations a bookseller will maintain with his customers makes communication faster and easier. The international relations a good bookseller has enables him to place his orders at the right moment at the correct place (just think of the numerous sole agents/sole distribution arrangements, territorial restrictions and continuous mergers in the publisher's world).

A good stock-holding bookseller can very often supply titles faster form stock and--if required--on a see-safe basis; a service a publisher would most probably refuse.

A good bookseller knows the requirements (subject specialisation) of his customers and will gladly supplement publisher's promotion materials by providing additional information; mainly for smaller--but not less important--specialised publishers.

Last but not least, my most important argument--and you will agree with me--is that very often the poor bookseller is--gently--forced to finance the library by extending credit terms in times of scarcity. Very often far beyond financial/economical feasibility.

During the last few years the economic situation has forced the publishers to review their terms of trade and to become as cost-conscious as possible. On average we can say that publisher of STM literature deliver at 30% discount. In India, with its special structure of stock-holding importers and booksellers, these terms are slightly better and may even go up to 35% in some glorious cases. Is this profitable? Statistics compliled in Western Europe prove that a *well-organised* bookseller has average overheads of around 29% of total turnover.

An STM bookseller dealing mainly with imported material has to think of an additional cost factor: transport costs are usually higher and he might have to cover special import charges, taxes and foreign currency transfers are usually more expensive than local payment. Stock-keeping and on approval service usually add to his overheads and if in addition to all this the bookseller is forced to pass on discount to his customers, to cover postage, packing and handling charges and to finance his customers I wonder whether his bowl of rice will be full every day?

We have to take this into consideration and for the sake of argument we will have to assume that in India libraries have reasonable annual increases in budgets and that the budgets are supplied properly and in time. Only then will may *Golden Rules* make sense:

Therefore, Dear Librarians, please select your supplier(s):

according to their ability to give you maximum service;
according to their specialisation in STM publications;
according to their financial credibility.
(Publishers tend to stop deliveries if they are not being paid properly.)

Do not select your supplier(s):

because he promises higher discounts and extended credit terms.

If you have more than one supplier:

please do not give all the easy-to-obtain orders to one (who might be "cheap") and the difficult ones to the other (who might be "better");
please invite suppliers-together-from time to time to discuss your changing needs. In this way they will be able to avoid unnecessary duplication in service and deliveries and unhealthy competition;
please fix terms of delivery, payments, returns, rates in advance;
you deserve a fair correct price-also covering the service granted to the library;
the--good bookseller deserves to make a profit;
do not request discounts. Discounts lead to an unintelligible pricing situation (high mark-ups versus high discounts) and unfair competition. May I recommended published

price, converted according to local regulations, plus a reasonable service charge if necessary;

please pay your invoices--UGC permitting--within the time limit agreed upon.

Publishers can be--and are--very harsh if their due-dates are not met.

In case you are bale to provide your supplier not only with the daily bowl of rice, but also with the occasional piece of meat and some pickles you also have the right to become more demanding:

force your supplier to grant you the service you deserve;

force him to be accurate, reliable and fast;

force him to pass on rush orders on the day of receipt. Modern delivery methods like ASP/SAL guarantees a fast and cheap delivery;

force him to pass on subscription orders and renewals immediately with the accurate pre-payment;

force him to adjust his stocking policy according to your changing needs;

and

force him to constantly improve and adjust him internal organisation.

Have I said too much about books? Perhaps. But, it will be easy to translate the above into terms of journals. From my point of view I would like to say:

please order as many new journals as possible;

please maintain all your existing subscriptions;

please renew your subscriptions in August of every year;

please send your new orders all the year around. The publisher is willing to do over-hours if necessary; and

please claim in time.

I have nearly come to the end of my sermon. But, I cannot resist adding a few more lines--even though I have been told so very often by my colleagues "do not constantly mumble to yourself!"

do not forget that it is the international academic community that provides your living;

help your library customers to increase--or at least to maintain--their collections. *Keep your prices down* (Oh, wishful thinking!)

keep your customers well informed without over-flooding them with superfluous material; and

listen to what your customers have to say.

Book Trade and Libraries

The World Book Fair being held in New Delhi every two years has brought the library profession into activity. The Indian Library Association has rightly taken this opportunity of organising a seminar on "Libraries and Book Trade." There have been some occasions when book trade personnel have been involved in discussing their problems with librarians. During 1981 this problem was discussed on the basis of a paper presented at the Regional Seminar held at Gauhati by the North-Eastern Council in March 1981. A number of issues cropped up which needed some consideration and action at the hands of the book trade.

Books for All Activities

Book promotion activities got an impetus during the International Book Year 1972. The Government and the book trade realised that some more steps had to be taken to increase book production and at the same time make the books available and accessible to the reading public. "Books for All" was the slogan of the year as sponsored by UNESCO which had been enunciated and advocated by Dr. S.R. Ranganathan about 40 years ago through the Second Law of Library Science which called for "Books for All" activities. It was good that UNESCO and member countries realised after 40 years of what Ranganathan had advocated in 1931. Thus concerted efforts had to be made to provide facilities for increased book production and their availability and accessibility through libraries and outside. It would have been helpful at that juncture if the Government of India would have brought the thee partners of book promotion activity--Publishers, booksellers, and librarians--together to discuss threadbear some of the issues which needed solution through joint efforts and understanding. Seminars were held not only in this country but in other countries too, some at the international level; but librarians were not adequately represented in such seminars. The sponsors of such seminars did not appreciate the role of librarians in book promotion activities.

Production of Books

India is one of the largest producers of books. Though in relation to its total population and the percentage of literacy, it not a matter on which India can take pride. But taking the other all picture into the consideration, India is a large producer of books and other reading materials. It is also able to export the books that the published within the country. In this activity India imports more books than it is able to take out of the country. In 1968-69, it imported books worth 5.5. While its export of books was 14.1 lakhs. The figures might be different today but it is clear that India imports nearly 5 times more the number of books that it is able to export.

The number of graduates coming out of the universities and colleges in 1976 had been 3.3 million which is expected to double by 1986, while it was 1.1 million in 1961. Thus more books per capita have to be imported to feed the student population in the years to come. The Government of India has been liberal in issuing import licenses to the book trade. But by experience it has been found that the import license suffice only 10% of the total imports within a year.

Implications of High Cost

The cost of book production has gone up substantially recently. The average cost of a book as worked out by the British Library Association, London comes to £6.62. The subscription of periodicals has increased five-fold; the average subscription periodicals has been worked out to be £ 46.81. Even though the book grant to libraries have increased during 1970's but the increase in the book grant has reduced the capacity of libraries to purchase more books due to high cost involved. Some of the university libraries have book budget going beyond 20 lakhs. But their accession registers indicate that within this sum, they are not able to acquire more books than they were able to get in 1960's.

Government has to step in to control the price of books, periodicals and other reading material by providing cheap paper and other facilities. The book trade and libraries are at a loss to understand how to provide more books for the largest number at the least cost which was once the motto of the American Library Association. With the prices of books going up, the impulse for buying has gone down. While the libraries and the reading public have to be very selective and cautious in their book selection, and purchase policy, the book trade has also to be very discriminating, judicious and selective in their publishing and procuring programmes.

Joint Activities

The book industry is more or less in an organised form. There is a Federation of Publishers and Book-sellers at the All India level and Book-sellers association at the state and local levels. The book trade even though being organised, has finances, and is linked up with the acquisition policies of libraries. These organisations have made little efforts to invite librarians in their meetings, seminars and conference to have a total perspective of the book trade in the country. Librarians have got their own associations but some of them have not been very active and due to the non-activity of these organisations and lack of finances available with them, they had little initiative to invite the representatives of the book trade to discuss the issues of mutual interests in meetings, seminars and conferences.

Even the *Indian National Bibliography (INB)* which is sponsored by the Government of India, has not a strong council which is represented both by the book trade and the profession *Unlike* what we find in United Kingdom and other countries. In such a situation any attempt to bring librarians, publishers, and book sellers together is laudible, but it should field some tangible results.

Good Offices Committee

Librarians and the book trade have to come together through the Good Offices Committee which was originally initiated by the book sellers several years back in their own interest. This Good Offices Committee has been revived recently and some of the decisions arrived at for the supply of periodicals àre as under:

- All subscriptions shall be accepted on conversion rates for different currencies and terms and conditions as approved by the GOC from time to time.
- The subscriptions agent shall not offer any discount on the rates of conversion fixed by the GOC even if a library/institution invites quotations nor shall the agent make any charges whatsoever except the actual subscription rates and postal/handling charges, if any, levied by a publisher.

It is obvious that the books are not being supplied to libraries at the foreign exchange conversion rate and this needs reconsideration. Book trade might have its own reason for making the librarians agree to a higher exchange conversion rate. But in view of the high prices of books and limited budgets, such a decision needs reconsideration.

Limitations of Book Trade

It has been experienced that even though the order for the purchase of books are placed with certain bookseller who agree to supply the books within the prescribed time, the experience of librarians in this respect is quite different. Generally 25 to 30% of the book ordered form abroad are only supplied and the library is at a loss as to what it should do for processing the rest of books not supplied. It cannot place order with another bookseller for 70 to 75% of the books unsupplied, so the book trade has to show a little more sense of responsibility when they accept to procure books for the libraries. Under such circumstances the libraries are forced to utilise their grant by purchasing materials which they would not otherwise like to get for the library.

Libraries suffer very much with regard to procurement of periodicals through Indian vendors. A number of subscription agents have come into existence but the experience with the already extablished suppliers has been depressing and it is for that very reason that many libraries prefer to place the subscription of periodicals with foreign agents and suppliers, and in many cases directly with the publishers. The book trade should establish confidence with libraries and assure that the periodicals subscribed through them would in all cases be supplied and in cases where issues are found missing, such issues would be replaced. That is a challenging task for the book trade.

Reduction in Postal and Tariff Rates

Another matter that can be mutually discussed is the high postage involved in the movement of books. The present postal rate inflate the price of a book by 20 to 100% depending upon its size and price. It would therefore be necessary that joint efforts are made with the Government and the postal authorities to charge reduced rates for the movement of books. In Sweden no postage rate is charged for the inter-library loan involving the movement of books and special rate is charged for supply of books to libraries. The Government should be approached that in order to increase the book promotion activity and to make people more interested in procuring books, reduced postal rates should be enforced. Concessional rates in book parcels and concessional tariff rates in book packets should be allowed by the railway and aviation authorities. Already no postal charges are paid for movement of books for physically handicapped in the country.

Unhealthy Practice

There are some other issues which can be talked about particularly relating to the promotion of book trade but it would be worthwhile to point out to book trade to desist and not to resort to some means by which they are able to dump the un-wanted material in libraries which does not bring any credit either to the book trade or to the libraries.

Importance of the Book

Before we discuss the relationship between the librarian, bookseller and the publisher we would like to emphasise the importance of the product, the book, around which the relationship is based. We will also briefly touch on the importance of Indian books not only for our own countrymen but also for sharing of India's rich cultural past and dynamic present with the rest of mankind, a sharing which is enhanced by the fact that an international language is so widely used by Indian writers and publishers. And India's creativity is not confined to the past nor is it restricted to the philosophical, religious, literary, or artistic aspects of human experience. Increasingly, in science and technology, in new approaches to economic, social and political problems found in different societies in the modern world, as well as in contemporary creative expression in literature and other fields, Indian books provide a vital means of enriching the lives of men everywhere.

The social usefulness and creative significance of books as one of the principal means of advancing education, science and culture is recognised by all those who are concerned with the preparation and dissemination of books. This includes not only those professionally, creatively and occupationally involved in books but also those who use books, students of all ages, teachers, scholars, businessmen, government officials ultimately all those who can read. Indeed, the world of books involves many millions of individuals in virtually all countries throughout the world.

Throughout human history and more so in recent times the great ideas which have added new and exciting dimensions to all aspects of our life have almost invariably been communicated through books.

The growth of literacy and the increasing movement of books across international frontiers hold the promise that books will continue to play a significant role in diffusing throughout the world the valuable thoughts, ideas and information which offer hope for man's betterment and progress. We would like to believe that in every good book, read at different times in different places by diverse peoples, there is the genesis of unified consciousness which recognises and accepts the essential unity of making. Frontiers, man-made, are artificial and localised. Knowledge knows no frontiers. Therein lies the greatness of books.

The advance of literacy in Indian languages, the growth of book publishing in several of the more widely used Indian languages over the past three decades, and the notable progress which has been achieved since independence in Indian publishing represent logical and important, indeed, essential, steps in the direction of enlarging the role of books not only in serving Indian society, but also serving the needs of Indians settled abroad in large numbers, supplying text books to the countries of Asia and Africa, and academic books to libraries and research institutes all over the world.

Libraries and Disseminations of Knowledge

Coming to the role of the libraries in the dissemination of knowledge, it would be pertinent to begin with a quote from the *UNESCO Public Library Manifesto:*

> "The Public Library is a practical demonstration of democracy's faith in universal education as a continuing and lifelong process, in the appreciation of the achievement of humanity in knowledge and culture. It is the principal means whereby the record of man's thoughts and ideas, and the expression of his creative imagination, are made freely available to all."

The library system of a country is intimately connected with the task of encouraging people to read. A well organised library system helps publishers directly through its book buying programmes and indirectly by spreading the reading habit. Libraries constitute a decisive channel of distribution as well as dissemination. The strength and advancement of the publishing industries in the developed countries like Japan, UK, USA, France, Germany and the USSR is due to a very strong library movement. In these countries even in the case of children's books 80 to 90% of the books are purchased in the libraries. This has strengthened the publishing industries in these countries and they can meet all the challenges and demands of the society and provide them all types of literature.

The Triangular Relationship

Having talked about the importance of the book and the library movement, I will discuss the relationship between the people who produce books i.e. publishers, the people who distribute them in the farflung areas of our vast country i.e. the bookseller, and the librarian who ultimately buys them and promotes their use. From what I have said before it is evident that we are all doing laudable work and our relationship should be consistent with our objectives. To my mind there are no factors, conditions or circumstances which should hamper, the growth of our cordial relationship. We are so inter-dependent that we cannot afford to be at loggerheads. All the three units have to work together to achieve the ultimate aim of "Books for All."

There are times when there may be a crisis in one of the units and I feel that this is the time when we should all work together to enable that unit to pull out of that situation. If the publishing industry is in crisis the booksellers will automatically be under pressure and with new books not forthcoming the librarians will not be able to fulfil the demands of the readers.

As the ultimate aim of all the three is to serve the needs and demands of the readers we should jointly fight our battle for more funds for our libraries and opening of more and more libraries in the furthermost reaches of the country.

The need of the hour is the introduction of library legislation in the states of India where it is wanted. If the states are able to collect five paisa on each cinema ticket for channelising into the library movement we will have atleast 50 crores rupees every year which can be utilised for the opening of more libraries and for the purchase of books.

This will fortify the publishing industry resulting in a strong bookseller and a confident librarian--having confidence in himself and the books he is providing to the readers.

The librarian, the bookseller and the publisher are thus bound in an indissoluble and unique relationship wherein each support and is supported by the other.

REFERENCES

Agnes Scott College. Hanley, Edna R. Agnes Scott college library. Lib. jour. 62:323-36, April 15, 1937.

Brooklyn College. Dickinson, Asa D. Brooklyn college library building. Lib. jour. 62:757-60, October 15, 1937.

College of Mines and Metallurgy (Texas). Polk, Baxter. New college of mines and metallurgy library. Lib. jour. 64:20-2, January 1, 1939.

College of New Rochelle. Cieri, Anne M. The new library of the college of New Rochelle. Lib. jour. 64:262-4, April 1, 1939; Gertrude, Mother Mary. How a 5400,000 library was planned. Lib. jour. 66:599-601, July, 1941.

Connecticut College for Women. Stewart, Lavina. New library wings of Connecticut college library. Lib. jour. 67:707-10, September 1, 1942.

Eastern Washington College of Education. Blair, Hugh M. College library building opened. Lib. jour. 65:280-2, April 1, 1940.

Georgia State Woman's College. Patterson, Lillian L. Georgia state woman's college library dedicated. Lib. jour. 66:540-2, June 15, 1941.

Goucher College. Goucher college campus competition; preliminary studies. Pencil points 19:735-50, December, 1938.

Linfield College. McKee, Wilbur R. Linfield college library. Lib. jour. 62:762-3, October 15, 1937.

MacMurray College for Women. Creek, Ellen. The Henry Pfeiffer memorial library, MacMurray college for women, Jacksonville, 111. Lib. jour. 67:1087-90, December 15, 1942.

Madison College. Logsdon, Richard H. Madison memorial library. Lib. jour. 65:477-8, June 1, 1940.

Milwaukee-Downer College. Chapman memorial library. Milwaukee-Downer college bull. ser. 21, no. 1, June, 1938.

Mount Holyoke College. Blakely, Bertha E. Mount Holyoke college library. Lib. jour. 60:284-6, April 1, 1935.

Reed College. Unger, Nell A. The new Reed college library. Lib. jour. 56:115-16, February 1, 1931.

Rhode Island State College. Alien, Francis P. Rhode Island state college library. Lib. jour. 62:760-1, October 15, 1937.

Rockford College. Sharpe, Jean M. Rockford college library. Lib. jour. 65:1064-5, December 15, 1940.

3

Recent Trends in Information Science Training

Library as Nodal Information on Centre

Aspects of the training process that require special attention in order to improve training results include communication, training materials, and scheduling of training are the major.

Communication. When effective communication occurs during training, the supervisor will have built a positive foundation for future interactions and interpersonal relations with employees. In considering the many different facets of communication during training, the supervisor needs to recognise that a great deal is being communicated to the trainee both formally and informally. The trainee learns from the instruction provided and also by observing relationships and behaviour within the department. Thus, what is communicated during the actual training process (expectations and standards for performance in particular) should be reinforced in practice among all of the employees. There is no point in emphasising with a new employee that all staff are expected to be on time to work every day if he or she watches other staff regularly come in late without any action being taken. The new employee will accept the norm of the group rather than what he or she has been told. In focusing on specific components of communication during training, the supervisor should not ignore the complex network of communication that proceeds continually in an organisational environment.

Three dimensions of communication are there that are particularly important to focus on during training: feedback, training style and methods, and jargon.

Feedback. Communication is an interactive, multi-dimensional act, not a one-way process. So when supervisors are considering the necessary feedback during training. In addition to identifying who will need to be involved in the communication, it is also necessary to recognise that feedback occurs in both formal and informal ways. Feedback on the trainees' progress occurs during the instruction process as the trainer observes responses and performance. In addition, progress should be reviewed in periodic meetings between the supervisor and the trainer, and between the supervisor and the and the trainee. Periodic review meetings are not often conducted by the supervisor, and yet they are the key to identifying difficulties in training at an early stage and allow the supervisor to provide ongoing support to the trainee. Frequent review meetings allow everyone involved in the training to review progress and any problems. When the training is for a new employee, it is suggested that review meetings be held at least once a week during the first four to six weeks of employment.

For other training situations, a similar review process should be established, though the length of time over which it should be conducted will vary depending on the nature of the training. When structuring review meetings, it is suggested that the supervisor meet separately with the trainer and then with the trainee. This procedure will allow both trainer and trainee to speak frankly without being uncomfortable. It should be noted, however, that the trainer should not discuss learning or performance problems with the supervisor that have not been brought to the attention of the trainee. The focus of the review meetings should be to determine if the training if moving at the

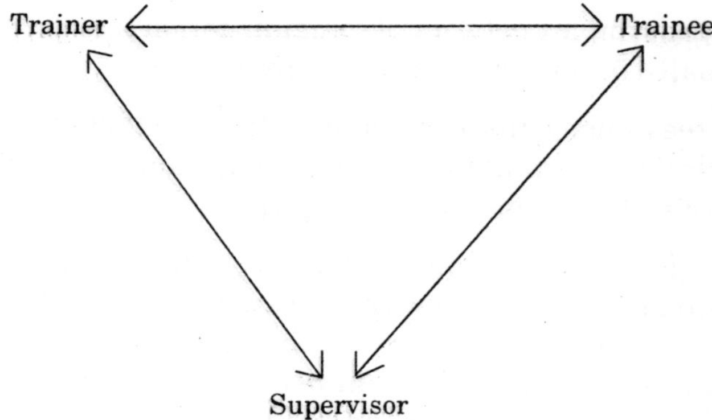

appropriate pace; if the presentation is clear; and if opportunities for practice, review, and asking questions are being allowed. In addition, the review meeting is a time for the trainee to indicate if sufficient support and encouragement are being provided, and for the supervisor to determine if the trainee's relationship with the trainer is constructive and positive. The supervisor wants to find out how the trainee is feeling about the training, the work, and the department.

Despite the supervisor being the trainer, a review meeting is necessary to provide the opportunity to look at an entire week and to evaluate the trainee's progress. Many frustrations with job training, whether for new employees or for employees learning new routines or operations, could be avoided if supervisors and trainers would periodically review the progress of the trainees, and how the trainers are performing. With new employees, this review sometimes does not occur until-several months into their employment or at the end of a probationary period. At that point, it most likely will be too late to correct problems--or at best be very difficult--whereas addressing difficulties early in the training process results more often in positive responses.

In order to achieve constructive and continual feedback, though, more is required than establishing the mechanism for feedback to occur through review meetings. Supervisors and trainers need to recognise what barriers may exist in providing honest and direct feedback to trainees. The difficulties fall into two categories: providing criticism or correction, and providing praise. The reasons tend to relate to concerns about how the trainees will feel about himself or herself and how the trainee will feel about the person providing the correction. Few people feel good if they hurt another person's feelings, nor do they feel good if the person is angry with them. Supervisors need to develop an ability to separate the performance problem from the person; they need to focus the criticism on the desire to see improvement and not cast it in tones that attack the individual. If corrections can be made in this context, the trainee is more likely to accept them in a positive way and not feel defensive or angry. Feedback that may be perceived as negative is also avoided because of a fear that conflict will develop. Unfortunately, conflict is likely to develop if trainees feel they are not provided honest feedback, but the conflict may remain below the surface and as a result not be easy to address. Finally, there is often a concern by supervisors that possibly their criticism is not fair and that their judgment is subjective, and therefore they hesitate to correct a problem or request a change. If supervisors articulate clear performance expectations with trainees, this barrier should be removed or at least reduced.

While providing constructive criticism is difficult to handle effectively, some supervisors also have difficulty in providing praise to staff for good performance. Some of the reasons for this difficult include the following:

High expectations exist, and therefore good or excellent performance is not noted.

Since good performance does not create a problem, it is overlooked.

Supervisors fear over-praising staff because too much praise will have no value.

Supervisors want to avoid a perception that there are favourites on the staff.

The consequences of inadequate feedback may be that employee morale drops; the trainee develops negative feelings about himself of herself and the job to fill the vacuum; small problems become crises; staff worry unnecessarily, which interferes with learning; the trainee assumes that he or she is doing well when this is not the case; and opportunities for staff to improve are lost. Constructive and continual feedback should instead contribute to a healthy work environment in which learning and improvement represent a shared value.

Training Style. Trainers have a primary role in and responsibility for effective communication. The ability to share knowledge and information, to listen, to instruct, and to be supportive are all skills that are required by an effective trainer. The trainers' most important communication comes during the actual training sessions when they are explaining, demonstrating, and correcting. There are a number of communication pitfalls that can lead to ineffective results both in learning and in attitude development. Some of these relate to the "false assumptions about training", that were covered elsewhere. These false assumptions should be reviewed by every trainer before beginning training. Trainers often unwittingly say or do things that are damaging to the training process or to the trainee. Such words or actions may not cause an immediate negative reaction but may contribute to a continuing poor relationship between the trainee and the work setting. Several examples of situations trainers should try to avoid follow.

1. *Minimising the difficulty of learning.* Most trainers want to find a way to put trainees at ease and to reassure them that the material can be learned easily. Often his desire results in the trainer beginning instruction by saying, "This is simple and you shouldn't have any difficulty." The

reaction of the trainee, unfortunately, is not one of being made to feel at ease but one of anxiety. What if trainees do have questions or have not understood?

Does their confusion mean they are incapable of performing the job? While it is important to reassure trainees about their ability to grasp material, this particular approach will likely backfire if used too often. Instead, the trainer might begin by indicating that at first trainees might find the procedure or equipment a little overwhelming because it is new, but once they have learned the basics they should not find it difficult. The trainer might also explain that while trainees may have questions and possibly initial difficulties, the trainer is sure that they will be successful once they have learned the basic operation. The trainer should strive, therefore, to put the operation into the context of the *new* person, not into context of an experienced person. Words of reassurance should be such that they do not discourage questions or belittle the person, albeit accidentally.

2. *Rushing ahead.* The trainer makes assumptions about what trainees already know or have understood, and moves quickly from the explanation of one task or activity to another. Trainees are not likely to alert the trainer if an explanation is not clear or if they are lost. They are more likely to remain quiet and to hope that they will catch up. This situation will undoubtedly create a certain amount of panic for a trainee. Inattentiveness may result because a trainee in this situation is worrying about what has been missed rather than what the trainers is now covering. It is important for trainers to establish a pace that is suitable to the material being covered as well as to the ability of the trainees to grasp the material. Otherwise, a great deal of time is wasted in retraining, and considerable frustration as well as other negative feelings will occur for the trainee.

3. *Praise and correction.* Job training most often occurs

in the work environment, not at some remote location. Training may occur at terminals, at the card catalog, at the reference desk, or in the reception area of the administrative office. Because trainees are instructed in locations where other staff or the public are immediately adjacent, trainers need to be particularly sensitive to ways in which they can instruct and correct without either intimidating or humiliating trainees. For instance, it will be difficult to provide instruction in filing in the card catalog without also pointing out mistakes at the same time.

Even so, the trainer should be sensitive in handling corrections or evaluation of performance when other staff--or the public--can overhear. The general axiom of "praise in public, correct in private" should be the premise on which trainers interact with trainees. Whenever possible, training should be conducted first "behind the scenes." For instance, rather than instructing someone in the basic rules of filing in the public catalog at the catalog, the trainer could have a set of "dummy" cards that could be used to provide initial training with the necessary correction. Once the trainee has demonstrated a grasp of the filing rules, he or she could be taken to the public catalog area to begin to work with actual filing.

The trainer should work next to the trainee and be sensitive to the tone and volume of his or her voice when providing further instruction and correction. In other situations where training cannot occur except in the immediate work area, the trainer should talk with the trainee beforehand to outline how they will approach the training and particularly the correcting of mistakes. The issue of how to correct staff is one that should be given very careful consideration, because pointing out mistakes publicly has a negative impact on the person's self-esteem and sense of worth.

4. *Conflicting messages.* Trainers need to avoid sending

conflicting messages to trainees. They need to be aware of the relationship between verbal and non-verbal behaviour and to recognise that non-verbal behaviour always carries the most powerful message between people. If trainees receive confusing and conflicting messages from trainers, particularly if such communication results in their own embarrassment, their reaction will be anger, discouragement, and low morale.

If a trainer indicates to trainees that it is acceptable to interrupt to ask questions, or to return as often as possible to ask questions, then their expectation will be that the trainer will respond positively. Instead, too often a trainee will get an exasperated response such as "You mean you didn't understand that?," or "This has been clear to everyone else," or "Could you go reread the manual first?" Now the trainee has been told one thing--ask questions--but has received a very different response upon asking questions--don't ask or, worse, bring staff don't need to ask! In this environment, trainees are going to be hurt and angry; they may well have negative feelings about their own abilities, and therefore they will likely not trust the trainer in the future. This situation is often made much worse when the comments are made in front of co-workers or the public. Another typical example of conflicting messages being sent during training occurs when trainers or supervisors indicate that they believe staff "learn from mistakes." When actually practised, this attitude by a supervisor can put employees at ease and can assure them that they can try new activities or tasks without fear of reprisals if a mistake is made. This attitude encourages staff to accept responsibility and to take initiative, and should increase the likelihood that staff will continue to contribute to the library.

Unfortunately, this philosophy is not always followed in practice. When mistakes are made, the employee is "chewed out" and made to feel as through the mistake will certainly bring the department, if not the library, to a grinding halt. Responding to a mistake with comments such as "How could you possibly have done that? It's so easy to followed," or "Well, this has made a lot of work for me now," or "Boy, is this going to make the boss mad!" will not correct the problem nor will it assist the trainee in learning from the mistake.

If indeed the supervisor and trainer want trainees to learn from mistakes, supervisors should see such occurrences as opportunities to analyse with the trainee what went wrong and why. Trainers should use mistakes as a constructive way to assist trainees to develop a better understanding of procedures, or to organise their work more effective, or to communicate when difficulties arise, and so forth. It is unlikely that any one mistake in a library will create an irreversible problem; therefore, supervisors and trainers should not overreact and make trainees feel as though they have jeopardised the department or the library. If a mistake occurs that involves a library user, then the supervisor can explain to the patron that a staff member still being trained had not fully understood a procedure and can do so without humiliating the trainee. Indeed, when staff feel that they will not be punished for making mistakes, they often can and will identify their mistakes and move to correct or resolve them. On the other hand, if they are punished for mistakes, then they will not be likely either to point them out (which can create bigger problems) or make any effort to correct them. While learning from mistakes is important, trainees should also understand the limits for repeating an error. The supervisor might indicate that making a mistake once or even twice is considered part of the learning process, but that making the same mistake repeatedly signals a learning or performance problem.

Further conflicting message that trainees receive occasionally is that they are told to seek assistance from co-workers when the trainer is not available. When they pursue this approach and the trainer indicates displeasure by saying that "Jim doesn't really have a grasp of the specific task," then the trainee has been placed in a difficult position. In this case, the trainee is again not going to trust the trainer and may in fact decide that Jim is more pleasant to deal with and therefore accept his instructions and ignore those of the trainer. If the trainer does not want the trainee to check with other staff, then this should be made clear.

If other staff should be used as resources, then the trainer should be clear about which staff should be checked with on particular issues or problems, and when. The objective is to avoid confusing trainees while they are learning and to avoid creating unnecessary tensions and distractions because of conflicting messages being sent from the trainer to the trainee.

5. *Closed mind.* A trainer who believes that he or she knows everything there is to know about a specific activity, task, or department will create communication problems immediately. Trainers with this view of their own knowledge will find it difficult to accept trainees' questioning and differing views or ideas regarding procedures, policies, or people. Trainers who consider their own knowledge and opinions sufficient tend to react in a negative way when asked "why," responding that "We have always done it this way" or "This is the best way." Closed-minded individuals do not usually like to provide explanations, since they believe that their view of the practice or procedure is a sufficient rationale. In other situations, staff with training responsibility may be unsure of their own abilities but not want to appear so to trainees. Thus, they react to questions in a negative manner, appearing to trainees as resistant to others' ideas or views. Whatever the motivation for trainers, acting in this manner may create an environment in which few questions will be asked.

Training may then evolve into a lecture process as the trainee retreats from active participation. Indeed, the trainee might learn early on to be reticent in trying new skills or in testing new ideas for fear of being judged too harshly by the trainer or supervisor.

Library Jargon. New employees joining an organisation with which they have little or no familiarity must learn a new language. Every profession has its own jargon or terminology, and this jargon becomes a major barrier for the new person to overcome. The problem with language also occurs when certain changes are introduced, such as the installation of an automated system. Frequently, people working with automation use terminology with which few are familiar, and they often do not stop to explain meanings or usage. Terminology can become a problem even for library staff who move from one department to another, or in meetings that involve people from multiple departments. Library staff in one department can rely on specialised terminology and acronyms that are sometimes to esoteric that the original meanings escape even the most experienced library staff from another department. The heavy use of specialised language and acronyms makes library staff appear to be talking "in tongues" to those who are not familiar with the particular vocabulary. An example is the secretary in the administrative office of an academic research library who after two weeks asked in total frustration for someone to please explain ACRL, ALA, ARL, CLA, MLA, OCLC,...and the list went on; this individual had been struggling to make sense out of what to her was gibberish in order to function in her job. In another example, an individual joined the staff of a library that had a collective bargaining agreement and wondered why librarians spent so much time talking about the "union list"; she assumed, of course, that this referred to the list of union members.

To prepare a brief glossary of the most frequently used terms or acronyms is one of the best ways to introduce new staff to library and department jargon. A glossary can be reviewed during that first day so that the trainee can begin to grasp the definition and, more importantly, the use of the terms. Not all library terms can reasonably be put into a glossary. Therefore, the trainer and other staff need to be sensitive to explaining terms and usage. The trainer should ask periodically if there are any words that have not been explained or that are not clear, and the trainee should be encouraged to ask for explanations immediately when uncertain about a term. When a glossary does not exist, the trainee might be asked to keep a list of terms and acronyms with the definitions as they are given.

This list would provide the trainee with a reference as he or she continues to learn library terms. In addition, what the trainee compiles could then be reviewed and edited by the supervisor and used for future trainees. This approach also involves the trainee immediately in contributing to the department by developing a useful tool for later use.

The communication issues that should be addressed during training are ones that require continual attention. When effective communication is used during training, it lays a positive foundation for future interactions.

The following exercise can be performed by the supervisor and trainer together or individually:

1. Consider mechanisms for feedback during training in your department. What needs improvement? Do you feel that you provide honest and constructive feedback on problems? Do you make time to praise staff performance? What difficulties exist, and what are reasonable goals for improving feedback during training?

2. Consider trainers' style, and identify the strengths of current trainers. Are those strengths being used in the best way? How can they be developed? Now consider trainers' weaknesses, and identify ways in which these can be minimised or eliminated.

3. Consider the extent to which jargon used in your department is (a) common to the library and (b) peculiar to your department.

Identify ways in which you can provide information to staff about terminology and usage, and minimise the negative impact of jargon.

Training Materials: Procurement and Organisation

Library training materials are often inadequate; either they do not exist, or what is used is poorly designed. Libraries have demonstrated the effective use of innovative teaching for instructing patrons in the use of library resources and bibliographic tools by developing self-instructional materials, slide-tape shows, and video presentations. Yet these same techniques have been used minimally for training and instructing library staff, even though their use would reduce costs and improve the effectiveness of training. The formats and techniques that can be considered for use in developing training materials include audiovisual aids (slide-tape, filmstrip, video), computer-assisted instruction (particularly the use of microcomputers for simulation training), and written aids (programmed or self-instructional). The appropriate formats and techniques for training materials are determined by the subject or skills to be taught as well as the audience.

Materials can be developed in segments or modules to allow brief and focused presentations and to provide trainees with the flexibility to review or learn a small portion of information at time. For example, rather than developing a half-hour slide-tape show on the library's classification schemes, a more effective approach might be to develop individual contained segments on each classification system. The development of training materials in alternative formats should allow for an improvement in the quality of training. At the same time, it will free the supervisor or other staff from having to rely exclusively on time-consuming individual instruction.

Types of Materials. Materials are needed to support the orientation activity as well as skill and knowledge training. Supervisors need to identify materials that are required for new employees and those that are needed for current employees who will be working with new systems or new programmes. The complexity of developing orientation materials is usually not as great as that required for developing training materials; but, nonetheless, to be effective in the orientation effort, equality materials are essential.

Orientation materials appropriate for new employees might include the following:

Brief description of the parent organisations (objectives, organisational structure, size, activities, etc.) and its relationship to the Library Description of primary politics and benefits, and information on how to obtain more details.

Library organisation chart, and description of basic activities of library departments.

Explanation of library mission and goals, policies, procedures, resources, services, and staff directory.

Department organisation chart, and description of objectives and basic activities, names and positions of staff, and location of materials and supplies.

It is often helpful to have an orientation checklist that supervisors can use as a reminder of the topics, issues, and information that should be covered during the orientation period.

Supervisors also need to consider what background information or materials would be appropriate for staff who will participate in a new project or new assignment. For instance, what descriptive general materials might be helpful to staff when implementing a database search service, or implementing an online circulation system, or altering the cataloging requirements. The purpose of orientation is to provide a work context and thus contribute to an employee's understanding of and commitment to the activities of the library. Therefore, it is important that orientation materials not focus soley on new employees, but that they recognise the needs of continuing staff as well.

Some libraries have put effort into developing more sophisticated orientation materials, such as slide-tape or video presentations explaining the library organisation for new staff. Such materials can be very effective when well presented, because they not only provide information, they contribute to positive feelings about the library. Other types of orientation materials are often available for library supervisors to use. The parent organisation (such as the college, business, or special foundation) may have developed introductory materials to the organisation for fundraising purposes, and these might be appropriate to show to new employees as well. Certain other materials may be available to provide staff orientation to specific equipment or systems. For instance, the local telephone company may have a film that could be borrowed by the library on the use of the phone system and phone courtesy. Vendours and utilities serving libraries may have materials that could be used to introduce staff to the system and services prior to the skills training. Library supervisors should also determine whether materials produced for library users would be useful for staff in learning the library organisation and in developing an appreciation for the range and scope of activities and services.

Instructional materials are even more critical to effective training and therefore demand attention from supervisors. As library operations become more complex, particularly with the expansion of automated systems, the difficulties faced in training with non-existence or inadequate materials only confound the problem of implementing change.

The process of developing training materials is difficult, and a considerable level of skill to produce quality materials is required. Supervisors should begin by acknowledge that a manual is not an instructional or training material; at best, it is a source document. Too often in libraries, trainees are given an operations or department manual to read. If the trainees have no opportunity to apply what they read, they are unlikely to retain the information and may indeed be confused by a great deal of what is contained in the manual. Instead, a trainer can use sections of a manual as the or she trains for a specific function or task so that trainees know that there is a source to go back to in order to check details once instruction is concluded.

Supervisors should recognise the problems that exist with the use of manuals, particularly with the use of outdated manuals. The training process can be seriously impeded if trainees are instructed to read a manual that is partially outdated or inaccurate. If trainees are aware that the manual is inaccurate, they will not be inclined to put much energy into the activity, will see it as a futile exercise, and will wonder why the supervisor wants them to waste time. All of these concerns could result in the trainees' losing respect for the supervisor and trust in the accuracy of future materials given during the training process. Therefore, outdated sections should be deleted or clearly marked. Again, manuals should not be seen as instructional materials but as source that can be referred to during training.

Training materials should *complement* personal instruction but should not replace it entirely. Personal interaction is needed to clarify, to test knowledge and ability, and to support and encourage.

The following criteria should be considered in developing materials for skills training: (1) materials should be designed to provide information about a single knowledge area or task at a time, (2) trainees should be able to use materials independently or as part of training sessions, and (3) trainees should have a means for self-testing so that they will know if the information has been absorbed or the skill has been acquired.

In addition to using training materials developed by library staff, materials developed by other sources should be identified and reviewed for use. Materials developed by other libraries, library associations, utilities or vendours, and commercial producers should all be investigated. It is a good idea to preview materials with staff before purchasing or using them on a regular basis so that the materials are appropriate and likely to contribute to training results. One final comment about training materials: library professionals need to begin to exert more pressure and demands on vendours of automated systems to improve the quality of the materials they provide with their systems. Specifically, vendors should be expected to develop well-written and comprehensive training materials that library supervisors will be able to use in the implementation of an automated system. This request should be part of the process of negotiating a contract with a vendour. Unless library professionals are willing to make more demands in this area, they will continue to have to absorb all of the requirements for developing and testing training materials for these systems.

An agenda can be drawn up by the supervisor and trainer together or individually. It is one in which it would be useful to involve other department staff.

1. List the orientation materials that are provided to the new employee by the parent institution, by the library, and by the department. What other materials should be included? How can you acquire these additional materials? If someone in your department has to prepare material, such as a glossary, who would be qualified to do this?

2. List the training materials that are available in your department and what functions or activities they

service. What other training materials would be a high priority to develop or acquire? Who would be qualified to develop training materials in your department?

3. Finally, what training materials are currently being used in the department that are outdated or inappropriate, such as manuals? What actions must be taken to update materials or to eliminate the use of inappropriate materials?

Calender and Time-table

The final consideration in implementing training is setting the actual schedule for the date, time, and location of the training activities. The supervisor and trainer should have already identified the order for training segments, but immediately before training begins, a specific schedule should be developed. Scheduling should not be done too far in advance in order to avoid having to make numerous changes in the schedule because of other intervening time demands on the trainer or equipment. Two primary considerations should be reviewed when establishing a schedule: department needs and the needs of the trainee.

Department and Trainer Considerations. In considering departmental requirements, the supervisor should be concerned with minimising disruptions to normal work flow, the availability of resources such as equipment, and the schedule of or demands placed on the trainer. Most library training occurs in the immediate workplace, and thus the likelihood of some disruptions to other staff or to the public must be considered. The supervisor needs to consider what the best time for training will be so that other staff's work or the ability of the public to use library facilities is not seriously disrupted. For instance, if the supervisor knows that patrons use the public catalog most heavily starting at about 11:00 A.M., then scheduling training for new filers during this same time period would not be wise.

In planning training for an online system, the supervisor

should consider the off-peak time and the least expensive time to use the system. Based on this information, a schedule can be set up that takes advantage of the availability of the equipment in relation to production work and costs.

Too often, training just happens without reference to how the schedule affects the department. The trainer's time and attention are other considerations in determining the best schedule for training. The training should be able to give full attention to the training activity and not be diverted with reference questions from patrons or interruptions from other staff.

Trainee Needs. Another component to consider when scheduling training is the needs of the trainee. If several employees are to be trained at one time, it becomes more difficult to consider their individual needs. Some review of the trainee's needs, however, is worthwhile in order to maximise the training effort. In particularly, supervisor might consider the following normal attention span in relation to a particular subject or activity, and the energy levels of individual trainees. With a highly technical subject, a trainee's attention is likely to wander after thirty or forty minutes because of difficulty in absorbing too much material. Most people know whether they are more alert and attentive in the morning or in the afternoon. The idea is to schedule training in such a way as not to exceed a normal attention span for the subject matter and, when possible, to capitalise on the individual's high energy periods for particularly difficult instruction. While a supervisor may not always have sufficient flexibility to take all of these factors into account (particularly individual trainee needs), they are worth considering. The supervisor primarily needs to build variety into the training process to avoid overload and boredom.

If the trainees are lectured at for several hours, their attention may drift, and their ability to translate the information into action will be low. Trainees need a mixture of lecture, presentation or demonstration, observation, practice, and reading. This mixture will not only be more likely to keep their attention at a peak level, but it will provide trainees with a number of ways both to learn and to test what they have learned. Using a variety of approaches makes the training more interesting and sets a reasonable pace for the person. It is difficult to sustain attention and interest if trainees are asked to absorb a lecture on a very complex procedure or routine late in the day. Although supervisors will not always be able to tailor the training scheduling to fit all of the needs of individual trainees, they should at least review the needs of the people to be trained as part of the scheduling activity.

By combining both the departmental and trainee needs, the supervisor should arrive at a balance that will be likely to increase the results from the training effort. It is necessary at this stage to:

1. Consider the way in which training has been scheduled for departmental trainees in the past, and identify what problems may have occurred with disruptions to operations and with the trainees. Have there been any difficulties in getting access to materials or equipment for the training function?

2. What steps can be taken to improve the training schedule in relation to department and trainer needs?

HRD Evaluation in Information Science

In fact, 'Evaluation' is the final planning component in job training. Although this segments is presented as a separate chapter, the actual activity of planning for evaluation should occur when training objectives and content are being established. The process and purpose of evaluating job training are similar to other evaluative responsibilities of a supervisor: to gather and analyse information in order to justify past actions, and to project the future use of departmental resources--staff and materials. When job training has been treated informally, the evaluation of this function has also been informal or non-existent. Once a supervisor invests significant time and energy into improving the job training activity, an informal approach to evaluation diminishes the potential for future effectiveness and efficiency. The evaluation step allows the supervisor to seek improvements in training while building on the strengths that exist.

Conroy suggests that the following goals can be achieved through the evaluation of training:

Furnish accurate information to assist further planning, to improve decision-making, and to document achievements

Determine to what extent a programme and/or activity is accomplishing its goals and objectives, and what results are being achieved

Identify programme strengths and weaknesses and the reasons for specific successes and failures.

Assure more consistent quality in learning activities and efforts

Reinforce learning and develop an awareness of growth and change

Determine the cost and benefits of the programmes and its activities

Justify the investment and answer demands for accountability

Produce documentation that allows information to be shared with others.

Though Conroy is focusing on the evaluation of organisation-wide training efforts, these points have validity for evaluating departmental job training efforts as well. This list can serve as a set of broad objectives for the evaluation of job training.

While it is true that all job training should be evaluated, there will need to be differences in approach to evaluation and methodology based on the position for which the job training is provided. The methodology and amount of effort devoted to the evaluation of job training will vary for different training situations. Certain positions require more extensive training in depth, scope, and length of training time, and these training efforts should receive more thorough attention in the evaluation of the training. In other situations, large numbers of staff may be trained at one time for the same task or operation, and this will require modification in the approach to evaluation. Supervisors will therefore need to make adjustments in approaches for both training and evaluation of training not because some positions are worth less or more than others, but because of the nature of the positions and the training context.

The evaluation of job training for a large number of hourly employees at the beginning of a semester in a college library would be structured somewhat differently than for a single clerical or professional position. In the former situation, the supervisor might decide to evaluate training by using a simple questionnaire to obtain feedback from the student employees, or to evaluate training on a semester basis when most new student assistants are hired. In establishing mechanisms for obtaining feedback about the training a person in a supervisory position receives, the manager may determine that meetings to assess progress in training will be held less often than for other positions, because more time is needed to acquire the necessary knowledge and skill for a supervisory position. In every situation, the supervisor planning the training will need to make decisions regarding appropriate methods for evaluation within the context of the training.

Trainers' Trainer

The first question to be addressed for evaluation is who will have responsibility for actually evaluating the job training. Several staff usually participate in job training activities; these same people should have a role in the evaluation as well. Specifically, the supervisor, the trainer(s) and the trainee(s) all have a role in evalauting the job training activity. In some situations, it might be appropriate to have a third-party evaluation, such as by co-workers who either know specifies of the job well and can comment on training or who interact with some aspect of the trainee's performance.

Everyone who is involved in the evaluation of job training should share a common goal to determine if the training "worked." Did the trainee learn what was taught? Can the trainee perform job duties and tasks as required? Each individual evaluating the job training will be influenced by his or her own role and positive in relation to the training activity, and this bias must be weighted by the supervisor when analysing the information provided by those who are doing the evaluating. The supervisor has the responsibility for outlining how the evaluation will be accomplished and for analysing the information in order to make future decisions. In addition, through observation and discussions with the staff involved in the training process, the supervisor will be in a position to evaluate results from his or her perspective.

The supervisor has to be concerned with both effectiveness (quality) and efficiency (cost) in evaluating training. The supervisor will focus on the specifics of the training, as well as on the overall impact of training on departmental performance--work flow, services, and relationships among staff. The trainee will be most concerned with whether everything that will be required in knowledge and sill has been presented and learned before independent performance is expected. The trainee will be very attuned to the learning environment, relationships with co-workers and the trainer.

Finally, the trainee can evaluate the schedule and pace of training in relation to his or her own abilities. The perspective of the trainer is whether the end result of the training has been achieved. Indeed, the trainer focuses on whether success has been achieved with the trainee and therefore if the training process is concluded. The trainer is also likely to be concerned with his or her own performance in the training process.

Assessment Agenda

There are two broad objectives in evaluation of job training: (1) an assessment of the trainee's performance as a result of training and (2) the effectiveness and efficiency of the training. It will not be sufficient to focus only on the performance of the trainee without considering whether the desired performance is a result of the training itself. At the same time, there has to be a consideration of whether the training was conducted in the most efficient manner in using staff time, materials, and equipment.

The best evaluation results will occur if performance objectives have been clearly stated as part of the training plan. As each segment of the training plan is being developed, the supervisor should ask "What should the trainee have learned?" and "What do we want to result from the training?" By focusing on evaluation as part of the initial planning process, the supervisor will ensure that the evaluation is integrated into the overall training plan and also that the objectives and content of training are appropriate to meet job and departmental needs.

Kearsley describes the points that evaluation should cover in the following way:

Improved efficiency--same results with fewer costs.

Improved effectiveness--better results with same costs.

Improved productivity--better results with lower costs.

In order to conduct training evaluation to meet these broad categories, specific information on the following topics needs to be gathered:

Trainee performance

Trainee reaction to the training

Training process, content, and learning environment

Trainer strengths and weaknesses

Costs (staff, materials, and equipment).

Trainee Performance. Certainly, the most obvious place to focus evaluation is on the performance of the trainee and on the desired change in behaviour. Is the trainee able to perform tasks and activities at the level of expectation. Does the trainee exhibit the preferred behaviour and attitudes? Since job training should be evaluated throughout the training process, there will need to be "benchmarks" for performance as the trainee acquire knowledge and skill. These benchmarks should be articulated as part of the training objectives. For example, database searching may have multiple criteria for performance evaluation, and these would be applied differentially to a reference librarian as he or she moved through the training process. The criteria might include the ability to apply search strategies, knowledge of descriptors, formulation time, interview time, search costs and number of searches that are rerun, and degree to which the search is handled independently.

If training objectives have been defined against these performance criteria or expectations, then evaluation of the training will be straightforward. Since individual trainees bring different skills and experiences to the training situation for a particular job, these should be taken into account when evaluating the results of training. If these differences are over-looked, the supervisor might view the training process as achieving the desired results when actually the performance was based on the trainee's previous knowledge and ability.

Training Process, Content, and Learning Environment. It is important to evaluate specific aspects of the training, not just the end product. By doing so, the supervisor can be more certain of what is successful and what needs improvement. The process, content, and learning environment should be evaluated, with the trainee being a key person to provide this evaluation; thus, the trainee's reaction to training is obtained. The trainee should be able to comment on whether the content was appropriate (was more or less needed), whether it was provided in a clear manner, whether the relationship among the topics was logical for the purpose of learning, whether the schedule was reasonable, and whether a sufficient variety of activities was presented. Did the trainee feel that there was adequate support and direction from the trainer and co-workers during the training process? Were questions encouraged and answered fully and in a constructive manner? In addition, the trainee can be asked whether communication with the supervisor was adequate and timely.

Finally, the trainee can be asked what might be done to improve the training process. The trainee might be asked to suggest whether anything was overlooked or given insufficient attention during training, or what materials might have been useful, such as a glossary.

The aim of evaluation is to assess the overall process of training as well as the specific modules and units within the training plan. The supervisor wants to focus on the total outcome, particularly keeping in mind the need to address issues of motivation, job satisfaction, commitment, and loyalty that should be developed as part of the training process.

Trainer's Strengths and Weaknesses. In order to support successful training efforts in a department, the supervisor will need feedback on the trainer(s). When this information is sought from the trainee, it should be handled carefully in order not to create tensions between the trainer and the trainee. Indeed, new employees are likely to be reluctant to be candid in this regard for fear of alienating co-workers. The supervisor should find a way to acquire information from the trainee in a manner that does not threaten the trainee or embarrass the trainer. The trainee can provide feedback on the trainer's instructional style, the clarity of his or her communication, and the support and guidance the trainer provided. The trainer also has a valuable role in evaluating his or her own performance as a trainer.

This role is particularly important if the trainer's responsibility is a new one. Indeed, all trainers should be expected to evaluate all aspects of the training in which they are involved: the process, content, schedule, pace, and the individual trainee's abilities, as well as the trainer's own abilities. If the supervisor presents the evaluation process as a means of strengthening the training activity, then the trainer will likely be open to assessing his or her own performance and accepting suggestions for improvement. Finally, the supervisor has a responsibility to assess the trainer's performance through observation.

Cost. It is necessary to identify all of the various costs related to the designing, implementing, and monitoring of the job training. An improvement in the efficiency of training is another motivating research to improve library training activities. While the employee is still being trained, he or she is not a fully contributing member of the organisation; indeed, the person is a drain on the organisation's resources as other staff train him or her. Thus, the supervisor should evaluate the trainer effort in order to determine whether job training is as efficient as it might be. In this regard, costs should be determined for the following:

Staff resources to:

develop a training plan;

organise and prepare related materials, such as manuals and hand-outs;

design workbooks and instructional materials;

conduct training (trainer and trainee time);

retrain (trainer and trainee time);

evaluate training.

Materials and equipment:

written materials (paper, printing, or photocopying);
audio-visual materials (purchase, rental, or production);
telecommunication time; and
equipment rental.

There has not been much attempt in libraries to assess the cost for training. In addition, there is no information available on costs of inadequate training--costs in wasted time, error rates, and higher equipment or telecommunications rates (such as for database searching, online cataloging, etc.). At the very least, supervisors should begin to assess costs related to training. This assessment provides them with the information needed to determine whether improvements should be made to reduce costs or to realise increased quality for the dollars already expended on training.

Assessment Process

The process of evaluation should be integrated into the training plan, not be performed as a separate activity that is grafted on at some point after training is completed. In addition, the evaluation process will be most effective if it is approached in a number of different ways and conducted both formally and informally. The following section suggests different points at which evaluation might occur and mechanisms for evaluation.

Before Training Starts. Supervisors need to assess the level and extent of a staff member's abilities in relation to the requirements of the job. In some environments, this may involve a pre-test in order to determine specific knowledge that the individual possesses. In most cases, though, assessment is more informal. For a new employee, the supervisor has information obtained through the interview and reference process. This information can be supplemented with a discussion regarding job requirements and the training plan on the very first day of employment in order to check assumptions about the person's knowledge and skill.

Information about current staff should be available through past performance evaluation, observations, and discussions, and this information provides the basis for assessing where the staff member might begin in the training process. With new staff, though, it may be worthwhile to ask in individual before training begins to assess his or her strengths and weaknesses in relation to the planned training.

The point to remember is that some mechanism should be used to determine the abilities of staff before beginning a training process so that the plan can be modified where appropriate.

During Training. Job training should be flexible enough to be modified and adjusted as the training is occurring. In order to achieve flexibility, information will need to be available to the supervisor and to the trainer throughout the process, not just at the conclusion of training. One of the most effective ways to monitor training is for review meetings to be established throughout the training period. When training a *new* employee, it is suggested that review meetings be held weekly during the first four to eight weeks of employment, depending on the complexity and length of the training process. A weekly review meeting should be held between the trainer and the trainee, between the trainee and the supervisor, and between the supervisor and the trainer. This approach can be modified, of course, depending on the level of the position. For instance, with temporary or hourly employees, such as student assistants, it is probably not reasonable to hold such frequent review sessions, particularly if their training is very task specific and completed in a short time frame. On the other hand, for an individual filling a department head position, bi-weekly meetings might be sufficient. The intent here is to suggest a guideline that can be modified to suit the particular situation, taking a guideline that can be modified to suit the particular situation, taking into account the experience of the person being trained and the complexity of the position and of the environment.

Review meetings between *trainer* and *trainee* are suggested when there is a primary rather than a number of staff training in very specific tasks or duties. The focus of this review should be on what has been learned, where problems occurred and why, what may need to be repeated, and whether the training can be accelerated. Further, the trainer and trainee should discuss the pace and mix of training activities, as well as whether communication in instruction is clear. The trainer should provide the trainee with an overall assessment of his or her progress, as well as with comments on what was accomplished within each segment of the week's training. This assessment should be honest so that the trainee does not assume that progress is being made when it is not. If the trainee is not informed about problems early on, then correction will be impossible, and such problems are usually compounded as the training progresses. In these review meetings, both the trainer and the trainee benefit from a frank discussion regarding the entire training for the week.

Also, at this weekly meeting, the trainer and trainee review the plans for the next week of training. The supervisor needs an update from the trainer on the progress of the trainee, on any problems encountered that disrupted training, and on plans for the next week. A meeting between trainer and supervisor is an opportunity for the supervisor to determine whether the trainee is progressing within the objectives of the training plan and, if not, to determine what corrective action might be taken. Secondly, it is an opportunity for the supervisor to assess how the trainer is handling the training responsibilities and to provide support and direction. Finally, the supervisor must assert his or her continued interest in and responsibility for all staff even though the training is being conducted by someone else.

A review meeting between supervisor and trainee provides a chance for the supervisor to interact directly with the trainee to determine this person's view of the training process and his or her progress. This meeting allows the supervisor to continue to establish a presence with the staff in the vital area of training and to determine if values and expectations are being adequately represented. This meeting with the supervisor also allows the trainee to express any difficulties or frustrations with the training process including with the trainer. While it is unlikely that a new employee is going to be very forthright in criticising an experienced staff member, this meeting at least provides an opportunity for the supervisor and staff member to talk.

There will be some situations in which other library staff should be asked to contribute to the evaluation of training. For instance, some reference departments use an evaluation process that involves the librarians in evaluating one another using specific criteria. Young reports that at the University of Arizona Library's Central Reference Department, a checklist representing reference standards and behaviour within these standards was developed to provided an evaluation tool. He describes the five major reference skills that are included in this checklist: communication style (verbal and non-verbal) with users, user interaction at the reference desk, co-worker interaction at the reference desk, knowledge of collections, and personal qualities or traits exhibited at the desk toward co-workers and users. Within each of these reference standards are desired behaviour that form the basis of evaluation. This method of evaluation could be used for the reference librarian during the training process as well to allow colleagues at the desk the opportunity to provide feedback to the supervisor. Young also describes a similarly system at the State University of New York at Oswego, Penfield Library. Schwartz and Eakin similarly describe a colleague evaluation process at the Taubman Medical Library,

University of Michigan. A set of standards for performance at the reference desk have been developed. Periodically, the reference librarians are asked to complete a checklist of reference skills for their colleagues, evaluating performance in the categories of attitude and demeanor; interviewing, listening, and referring; search strategy; knowledge of resources and collections; and knowledge of services and policies. These examples indicate that there are situations in which evaluation or review by colleagues may be appropriate, and this review process can be used equally effectively during training as well as for continuing performance evaluation. The trainee should always be aware when this approach will be used and understand the process and the basis of the evaluation. During the training process, a variety of checks or tests are conducted to monitor the trainee's progress. In some jobs revision is done to correct mistakes and to identify further training needs. Oftentimes, a trainee is asked to demonstrate a particular tasks or is observed when performing some aspect of the job assignment.

For instance, stacks supervisors may tag books in order to determine accuracy of shelving by new shelvers. The concept of checking specific tasks or activities is not unusual in libraries. It should be recognised that this traditional process of checking performance is also a way to evaluate training. What needs to be added to this task approach for checking or revising work is a review of the trainee's overall progress and performance in relation to the training plan.

Conclusion of Training. A mechanism for evaluating the results of training at the end of the process should be established. This mechanism might involve several components, such as a final review meeting similar to the periodic meetings, a questionnaire for the trainee to complete to evaluate the entire training process, or a "quiz" for the Trainee to test some specific aspects of knowledge and skills. What is important is to wrap up the training by evaluating results and not simply allow it to trail off into the dust. This review is also important so that the trainee recognise that the formal training, at least, is completed. At this time, it should also be clear whether follow-up evaluation of performance related to what was provided during training will be conducted. A review should also be considered at some point after the trainee is working independently to determine if the training "took" and whether the person can indeed perform all of the job activities at the level of defined expectations or standards.

Post-Training Analysis

The supervisor will be making decisions regarding the training as evaluation is conducted throughout the training process. At the completion of the formal training process the supervisor should then consider all of the information obtained and determine what future changes might be made in the training process, such as the content, approach, pace, and trainers. The supervisor will need to sort out what was specifically related to a particular trainee or to a situation within the department that is unlikely to reoccur, and what occurred that suggests that permanent modifications are needed. As evaluation information is collected over a period of time, the supervisor will be able to assess trends and be able to obtain an overview of specific and general aspects of job training. The supervisor can use the evaluation data to identify future training needs for trainers, the need for improved training materials, and possible ways to reduce staff costs related to training.

As the supervisor considers the responses to departmental training, he or she may gain insights into other aspects of the department that might be improved, such as communication and cooperation among staff. The supervisor might also gain information related to high turnover or continuing performance problems. Finally, the supervisor may develop ideas on how to continue to prepare the department staff for future changes in work routines, work flow, job assignments, and skill requirements. In general, job training evaluation is another important source of information to assist the supervisor in considering ways to improve the use of the most valuable resources--the staff.

An exercise can be conducted by the supervisor and the trainer together or working alone.

1. Review each segment of the training plan and determine the method(s) for the evaluation of trainee performance and progress. How will these evaluation points be described and conducted?

2. Determine the methods for acquiring feedback from the trainee on his or her views and suggestions about the training.

3. Describe your expectations for trainer performance, and develop standards to evaluate effectiveness.

4. Identify the costs that you will monitor, and describe how this monitoring will be accomplished.

5. What follow-up will be done on training after it has been completed, when, and how?

Communicator's Training Plan

Libraries, as information service organisations, have a large proportion of jobs that fall into the category defined by Drucker as "knowledge work." Drucker indicates that managing the knowledge worker will be the challenge of tomorrow. Difficulties in managing lie in trying to define productivity and accomplishments for knowledge workers, since the results of their work are not always observable or at least not for some time. Library staff are highly representative of knowledge workers, consisting as they do of supervisors, managers, reference librarians, selectors, and catalogers--hereafter referred to as professional staff. These professional positions involve the coordination of human resources, and the organisation of and provision of information, all of which are responsibilities involving a range of intellectual activities.

The knowledge work environment with all of its attendant complexities also requires greater demands in training staff that fill these positions. Therefore, supervisors need to go beyond the training plan to identify multiple approaches for staff learning and development. A longer time span (one to three years) will be required both to train staff and to measure results from training efforts. This is not to suggest that a training plan is not in fact useful for all library positions at all levels of the organisation but that more may be required for many library positions.

Psychology of Development

Two of the most important vehicles for training and development are the coaching and role modeling that an experienced supervisor or colleague can provide to a more junior person. While coaching and role modeling cannot be structured into a training plan, they are still valuable as means to train and should be recognised as such.

Coaching is the responsibility that a supervisor has to provide ongoing direction, support, and correction to staff. It goes beyond merely correcting mistakes, and instead focuses on assisting the person to see opportunities, consider alternatives, and develop strategies. Coaching should focus on the individual in a broad sense: the person's needs for growth and development beyond a specific position. Coaching suggests to the junior individual that the supervisor has a commitment to his or her success and learning. Supervisors who coach staff recognise that their experience and perspective are a valuable resource to other staff, and they share their expertise willingly. Further, coaching is not always provided solely by the immediate supervisor, nor should it be. Supervisors should encourage professional staff to accept coaching from other members of the library staff or in the profession, because one can benefit from a broad spectrum of views and opinions. While the amount of coaching cannot be prescribed and will vary based on the individuals involved, supervisors should be alert to the opportunities that this informal approach to training allows. It can be a far less threatening and more relaxed environment in which to discuss particularly sensitive issues of personal development.

Role modeling is another way that staff learn, although it is subtle and often not' recognised at all as part of training. A manager of a department or division needs to recognise that his or her approach to supervisor sets the example for those supervisors and staff who report to him or her. The alert manager recognises that "actions speak louder than words" and that no matter what philosophy is espoused, supervisors under him or her are more likely to believe and emulate behaviour not philosophy. Thus, when a manager describes expectations for communication, participation, and staff development, the supervisor will naturally (though not necessarily consciously) look to the manager as an example. Therefore, much of what the manager wants the supervisor to learn must be set by example as well as by directive. If a manager indicates that performance evaluation is important to the health of the organisation and that time and effort should be devoted to it, then the supervisor will rightly expect support and recognition for this effort. If support is not forthcoming, and indeed if the manager provides little to the supervisor in the way of a performance evaluation, the supervisor will "learn" that this activity is not a priority after all and respond accordingly with his or her own staff. Acting as a role model occurs of the seniority of one's position and experience not because of choice. The recognition of this fact may offer opportunities for the supervisor that may not have been tapped previously. The supervisor can look for situations in which a person's participation or observation might provide a learning experience, and also be sensitive to how his or her own behaviour is providing indictors of priorities and acceptable behaviour.

Goal Identification

One more method for training and developing professional staff is through goal setting. Establishing performance goals provides a future-oriented and result-oriented basis of communication between the manager and the professional. Although the supervisor defines the initial performance goals when developing the training plan, these goals will have to be revised and updated as the person becomes more capable and confident in the position, and as department priorities change. Through the process of focusing on the performance results that are wanted, the supervisor is assisting the professional in identifying gaps in knowledge, skill, and ability and in finding ways to close the gaps.

This process also allows the supervisor and staff member to identify new activities that might be undertaken and new skills that might be acquired. The focus should be on the growth and development of the individual, which in turn benefits the organisation. Goal setting, when used in a constructive way, should encourage personal development. If unrealistic goals are set, the process can be frustrating to the individual; or if punishment results from setting high goals that are not achieved, the individual may be discouraged and in the future show little initiative or willingness to take a risk.

Goal setting provides a comfortable format for ongoing communication between the supervisor and the professional; it is this dialogue and discussion that is most valuable. The actual writing of goals is simply a tool that provides the context for constructive discussion. To be useful, goals need to be reviewed and updated at least twice a year.

Other Training Sources

While supervisors have the primary responsibility for training and developing staff, not all training can occur within the department, particularly for professional positions that require a broad range of knowledge, skills, and abilities. Although staff filling these positions will often bring to the job many of the competencies required, they will need to enhance, refine, alter, or expand these skills as they adapt to a new environment or to changes within that environment. Primary sources for professional development include participation on library committees and in system-wide meetings, participation in workshops, and attendance at conferences.

Library Committees and Meetings. Professional staff should be encouraged to be actively involved in a variety of committee activities or meetings that allow for participation in projects outside of their specific job assignments. Staff learn from these opportunities by acquiring information, as well as by exposure to the perspectives and opinions of other staff.

Committees tend to foster cooperation and the development of skills in deliberation, negotiation, and compromise. Committee responsibilities can also foster a recognition of the role of leadership and the development of leadership skills. Other library meetings can be used as a means to provide staff with the chance to discuss questions or problems, and to share ideas and experiences. For instance, periodic meetings among supervisory staff of a library would provide an opportunity for this group of staff to discuss specific topics (such as delegating responsibilities, controlling absenteeism, and conducting performance evaluations) and to draw on the ideas and viewpoints of one another. In a large library system, for example, reference librarians from the various divisions might benefit from periodic meetings to exchange ideas on bibliographic instruction and database searching.

Besides holding job focused meetings, the library can encourage the professional staff to meet periodically to discuss broader topics, issues or trends that are likely to affect the library or the profession. In many libraries, the professional staff meet periodically to discuss professional conferences they attended or research projects they are conducting. While it is difficult to measure the relationship of such meetings to improved job performance, they do provide opportunities from which potential learning and development may occur. These types of meetings do not have to be organised by the library administration, although the administration should encourage and support such meetings as a recognised means of continuing learning among professional staff and crating organisational cohesiveness.

Workshops. Supervisors are seeking to formal workshops offered by various associations and agencies to complement departmental training. In many cases, these workshops are needed to provide both basic and advanced training for supervisory and other professional staff because of the complexity and variety of knowledge, skills, and abilities needed by these individuals. Depending on the size of the library and on the expertise that exists in specific areas, internal staff may be able to provide workshops on a range of subjects.

When funds are available, trainers may be brought to the library to conduct workshops. It is also possible that several smaller libraries in a region could organise together to offer a workshops for their combined staff. Library managers can also draw on other resources to supplement job training, such as library schools that offer workshops on professional or managerial topics; library associations--local, regional, and national; and commercial organisations. The use of these resources can be integrated into a job training plan when the supervisor knows about scheduled workshops, or topics can be identified for long-range development.

Library supervisors should be alert to training opportunities that exist outside of the job setting and that support identified performance goals and department and library objectives. It is necessary, however, to be critical in assessing workshops in order to judge the appropriateness and the quality of programmes. Supervisors should guard against the staff's viewing attendance at a workshops as a reward; this attitude does not contribute to a climate for learning or a commitment to a change in performance. To establish a mechanism for determining what workshops would be potentially useful, criteria should be developed against which supervisors and staff can judge the potential value of any workshop.

The criteria might include the following questions:

> What is the specific content of the session, and how does it relate to the current and future needs and demands of the job department, or library?
>
> What are the goals for the person who will attend? What will the person be expected to do differently as a result of attendance at the workshop?
>
> What changes or resources will be required to support the implementation of what the person learns?

Many more similar questions allow the supervisor and the professional to determine the relevance and timeliness of the workshop in relation to the needs of the library, and they ensure a greater likelihood of transferring what is learned from the workshop to the job setting. There is also a need for supervisors and staff to evaluate the quality of the organisation or person presenting the workshop.

Some guidelines that might be brought to the evaluation include the following:

- Background, experience, and reputation of workshop leaders.
- The formal of the workshop. Is variety offered in the workshop, such as lecture, discussion, case studies, role play, and films?
- Who is the target audience, and how many participants will there be?

- What do evaluations from previous workshops (if available) indicate about the quality of the programme?

Conclusively, costs should be weighed, including the fee for the workshop, the time spent by the person attending the workshop, and related costs such as transportation, meals, and hotel, if applicable.

Shortly after the workshop is concluded, the supervisor and staff member should meet to discuss the workshop and determine what steps the person will now take to implement what has been learned. The supervisor should encourage the individual to use the newly acquired knowledge and skills, and provide positive rewards when the person is successful. Once it has been determined that a staff member would benefit from participation in a workshop, then the supervisor needs to consider how he or she will reinforce the learning opportunity once the person returns from the workshop.

Conferences

Attendance at conferences and participation in professional association activities add valuable dimensions to the professional's development. While libraries differ in the funding available to support staff attendance at conferences, they all can provide the time for such attendance. Attending conferences provide with a broader view of the library profession, establishes valuable contracts with colleagues from other organisations, and contributes to a pride in librarianship.

The experienced professionals in a library should take responsibility for assisting the new professionals with learning the ropes in regard to professional association activities. Librarians also should consider the value of participating in professional associations in other fields that relate to their library responsibility. For instance, the academic librarian may benefit from attendance at the

Modern Language Association or the American Historical Association conferences. Librarians who work in a media center may benefit from participation at a conference that focuses on new technology and software. Although it may be more difficult to "measure" the effectiveness of participation in professional conference in relation to job responsibilities, it is reasonable to expect that librarians who actively engage in conference activities will gain knowledge that will be useful to the library.

Challenge of Information Technology

As libraries become increasingly automated, will staff training have to alter? Will there be new requirements and considerations for training? Will training be more demanding and difficult for supervisors? The answer to all of these is a resounding *yes.*

The following are major training issues that supervisors will need to face in the electronic library:

1. Quality training will be even more critical.
2. New work patterns and new work will require new training approaches within the context of accelerated change.
3. Training will have to accommodate both the traditional and automated environments.
4. An increasingly diverse staff will require greater flexibility and imagination in training.
5. Training must include more than skills training for staff to be effective in the automated environment.
6. To increase training efficiency, new techniques and approaches to training will be required, and far more training may be centralised in the automated environment.

As Mason has stated, "Technology is bringing about

an order of magnitude of change. To put it bluntly, the stakes are higher, much higher." Information has become a valued commodity, and there will be an increase in the number and variety of organisations that wish to be the information providers. There are numerous commercial vendours providing access to a variety of databases, and they will increase in the future. On university campuses, the computer center is expanding and may be competing with library services in providing access to online systems. Libraries are going to have to be far more competitive; they will have to be on the "cutting edge" of technology in order to maintain a central role in the information society. This goal cannot be achieved without skilled and knowledgeable staff.

Librarians who are comfortable with last year's technology and who are not current and innovative in the use of technology will quickly fall behind, and with them will fall the library. This means that the commitment to training must improve. Training cannot take a back seat to the multitude of other demands placed on the time and energy of supervisors. As jobs are defined for supervisors and staff, training should be identified as a component of the duties and tasks for which staff will be responsible. Unless there is recognition from this pointed forward, training will continue to get relegated to the "when we have time" category. In addition, increased funding will be needed to support the quality of training that will be required.

Currently, training is usually a hidden cost in libraries; as major automation projects are implemented, funding for training will need to increase in order to support the development of training materials, to provide for trainer positions, and to insure that adequate time is available for staff to learn.

Second, as the work itself changes (e.g., content, patterns, flow, relationships, location), training must shift to relate to the new work. To date, most staff have perceived their work as moving from step to step in a linear fashion until completion, and training has followed this same approach. In the electronic environment this approach is likely not realistic. In some situations, work may be more interactive, such as staff and users communicating online via electronic mail; and in other situations, work may have to be batched, with steps accomplished as different intervals. Training approaches should reflect the differences in work patterns and work flow, as well as develop skills to facilitate the new working relationships that will rely increasingly on interaction via a terminal. Another major change in work in the automated environment is that the work itself becomes more abstract.

Zuboff states that "when information technology reorganises a job it fundamentally alters the individual's relation to the task." She refers to this new relationship as "computer-mediated" work. She goes on to say that "with computer-mediated work, employees get feedback about the task object only as symbols through the medium of the information system. Very often, from the point of view of the workers, the object of the task seems to have disappeared `behind the screen' and into the information system.... Computer-mediated work is the electronic manipulation of symbols. Instead of a sensual activity, it is an abstract one." A result of the abstract nature of automated work is that staff can become distant from the objective of their work, lose sight of the importance of the work they perform, and become too focused on technical skills and output. The training process will have to address this potential liability. The movement to a highly automated work environment may be accompanied by a sense of loss of control over the work, because physically the work will be in the system, not in a stack of papers or cards on the desk.

Besides, the language or protocol of a system is very specific, and staff may feel limited because they have no flexibility with the system. Staff have to adapt to the system, and this can lead to frustration and a feeling of loss of creativity in accomplishing work. Staff also have to adapt to time when the system is slow or down. Preparation should be built into training so that staff are able to handle the normal disruptions that occur in an online system. Supervisors should think about what staff might do to remain productive during slow times and should prepare still emotionally to handle occasional system sluggishness or even a "crash." As change continues at an accelerated pace, the response time available to plan and implement training will be shorter. In the past, change may have been introduced in a more leisurely fashion, and thus the process of adaptation and training was accomplished over a longer time period.

The figure does not offer this luxury. Training and retraining will have to occur more frequently in the electronic library.

Third, training will be complicated by the fact that for the immediate future, supervisors will have to be prepared to train staff for both the traditional and the automated environments. It is likely that a library will be neither one nor the other, but a mixture of environments as integrated systems are implemented function by function and as new activities and services emerge to co-exist with certain traditional services that remain vital to library services. Supervisors will have to be knowledgeable in both the traditional and the automated environments, and be capable of training staff in both.

Fourth, most libraries will require an increasingly diverse staff in order to obtain the range of knowledge and skills needed in the high-tech environment. This need is likely to create, in the future, a more heterogeneous library staff, which, in turn, will require flexibility from supervisors in both training and supervision. It is possible that more staff who lack library experience or a master's degree in library science will be recruited. Thus, supervisors may have to expend more time providing basic information about library operations and services than in the past. At the same time, it is inevitable that some library work will be performed by staff in their own homes, thus creating a library cottage industry. Supervisors will have to develop mechanisms for training and retraining these individuals as well, and for maintaining them as members of the organisation even though they physically are not in the library.

In the online library environment, it will be necessary for training to include far more than a focus on learning skills. While this new emphasis should be the case also in the traditional library, it becomes even more imperative in the automated environment. Sokol and Bulyk describe a programme for training in an integrated information environment as having three components:

- Sensitisation--activities that emotionally prepare prospective users for automation.
- Education--activities that intellectually prepare users for using automated tools and further learning.
- Training--activities that actively prepare users to employ new automated tools proficiently.

In the electronic library, as staff focus more on the database and on the terminal, it will become more important for training to include the broad picture and for staff to develop an understanding of the relationship of their work to the whole. At the same time, the tissue of meeting personal and social needs in a highly automated environment requires attention in order to prevent a sense of alienation from the work and from the organisation.

Staff attitudes toward the process of change and specifically toward the new technology will need to be recognised and addressed. In the automated setting, psychological factors will be more important than ever because of each individual's reactions to the technology and to the impact it will have on his or her work life. It will be important to determine ways to introduce new technology in a positive way and, whenever ways to introduce new technology in a positive way and, whenever possible, to introduce it gradually so that learning is accomplished with minimal difficulty.

Ultimately, training in the electronic library will require the exploration of new approaches and techniques and very likely the centralising of a good deal of job training. It will not make sense if a library fully automates and yet does not use the technology to enhance training. Opportunities for computer-assisted instruction (referred to in chapter 3) will be more readily available. As microcomputers are used more broadly in libraries, programmes should be developed to provide interactive learning modules. The development of learning modules using computer technology will be important as a way of familiarising staff with the technology and of increasing cost efficiency in training by encouraging independent and self-paced learning. Related to this issue is one that will have far-reaching effects on library training--the need to centralise a great deal of job training for automated systems. Because of the sophistication required for training in the high-tech environment, the need to use the technology to design training modules and materials, and the frequency of training and retraining as modifications to systems or new systems are introduced, it will be likely that more job training will occur in a centralised manner.

This centralisation might be accomplished in several ways, such as through periodic classes being offered by a trainer from a central office as system changes are announced or as staff turnover dictates; or through trainers from a central office who will provide the basic introduction to and skills training for the online system to department staff on an "as needed basis"; or through certain departments that will assume responsibility for training all staff on specific system functions. For instance, if cataloging is distributed to various branch libraries, the training for the cataloging on the system may still be provided by the central cataloging department. The same approach could be used for training staff in the circulation function. In these situations, staff requiring training would spend time in the "training" department before assuming their job duties in the "home" department. The main point is that the way in which training has been accomplished in the past may not be reasonable in the new environment where all staff will have to follow the same requirements in working on an automated system.

Greater efficiency and improved quality might also be achieved if training responsibility were centralised, with adequate resources being developed to support the activity and accountability from the training resource being established for quality. Whatever the specific arrangement, it is likely that more skills training will occur outside of the department. The supervisor, though, will still have to be concerned with establishing a working relationship with the staff member, setting performance goals and expectations, and insuring that the person understands more than just functional skills.

Supervisors will also have to remain involved and concerned with any centrally developed training materials and sessions, and then will have to adapt their own training to fit what is provided in this other setting. All of these factors suggest that training in the electronic library should be vastly different from what exists today. More will be required and expected; supervisors will have to become more sophisticated in their understanding of the relationship between learning and performance, and will have to devote the time and energy needed to respond to training needs in the electronic library.

REFERENCES

Branscomb, Harvie. Teaching with books. Chicago, Association of American colleges and A.L.A., 1940. How large should the college library be? p. 166-75.

Carnovsky, Leon. Self-evaluation; or, how good is my library? Col. and research lib. 3:304-10, September, 1942.

Coney, Donald, and others. A survey of the Indiana University library. Chicago, A.L.A., 1940. (mimeographed).

Laing, Alexander. Library for the undergraduate college. Col. and research lib. 1:314-21, September, 1940.

Ludington, Flora B. Evaluating the adequacy of the book collection. Col. and research lib. 1:305-13, September, 1940.

Lund, John J. Undergraduate in the university library. American association of university professors. Bull. 28:480-8, October, 1942.

McCrum, Blanche P. Estimate of standards for a college library, rev. ed. Lexington, Va., Journalism laboratory, Washington and Lee University, 1937. Purpose, scope, content of book collection and other materials, p. 20-42; 104-17.

Mohrhardt, Foster E., comp. List of books for junior college libraries Chicago, A.LA., 1937.

Mudge, Isadore G. Guide to reference books. 6th ed. Chicago, A.L.A, 1936; Supplement, 1935-37; Supplement, 1938-40; Supplement, 1941 43. Chicago, A.L.A., 1939-44.

Rider, Fremont. Growth of American college and university libraries-- ,and of Wesleyan's. Wesleyan university. Library. About books 11:1-11, September, 1940.

Shaw, Charles B., comp. List of books for college libraries. 2d preliminary ed. Chicago, A.LA., 1931; Supplement, 1931-38. Chicago, A.L.A., 1940.

Shores, Louis. Basic reference books. 2d ed. Chicago, A.L.A., 1939. Core collection, p. 415-46.

Stanford, E. B. Honors work and the college library. Lib. quar. 12:221-45, April, 1942.

Stieg, Lewis. Technique for evaluating the college library book collection. Lib. quar. 13:34-44, January, 1943.

Walling, Ruth. Book requirements of survey courses. Lib. quar. 12:75-93, January, 1942.

4

Job Training Plans: Some Models

The job training plans included here are intended to assist supervisors as they begin to construct their own plans. The job training plans cover different types of positions and are from a variety of libraries. Because of the length of the training plans, only portions of each are provided, mainly those sections that were felt to suggest a useful structure or approach.

The training plans are grouped by job families that should be standard to all libraries: clerical (including student assistant positions), technical, and professional. It is suggested, though, that the reader review all of the training plans in order to benefit from the different approaches and ideas presented in these examples.

Clerical Positions

STUDENT ASSISTANTS

Documents Center
National State University
Central Library.

[This training plan is developed in a modular format and is an example of self-instructional material. The employee would receive only those training plans for responsibilities assigned.]

Below is a list of your job responsibilities as well as a

training plan for each. It is your responsibility to organise you time to complete each training plan. They are listed in general priority order. However, the sequence does not have to be strictly followed. If you need to skip one training plan and pick it up later you may. All training plans should be completed within the first three weeks of employment.

Job Responsibility	*Training Plan*	*Check Off When Done*
1. Shelf Reading	How to shelf read	--
2. File microfiche	How to file microfiche	--
3. Process Congressional Publications	How to process Congressional pubs	--
4. Shelving New Publications	How to shelve new publications	--

Training Plan: How to Shelve New Publications

Job Responsibility: You will shelve all new issues and titles within one week from the time they are put on your shelves.

Training Time: 4 hours

Job Task	*Training Task*
1. Obtain and sort publications from shelves by superv.'s desk	1. Read written instructions
2. File a new title	1. Read and follow instructions Set A
	2. Review work with superv.
3. File a new issue	1. Read and follow instructions Set B
	2. Review work with a superv
4. File microfiche (other than ASI, IIS, SRI microfiche)	1. Read and follow instructions Set C
	2. Review work with superv

Instructions for Shelving New Material: These instruction will explain the different types of new materials and how to shelve them. You will find the material on the shelves behind your supervisor's desk. It should be divided into different types of materials, but don't be afraid to question if something is on the wrong shelf. Sometimes mistakes occur.

Page #1

If the material is	Then go to instruction set
new title	A
new issues	B
microfiche	C
serial set	D
Arab World File	E
any other publication	notify. supervisor

Page #2

Instruction Set A: How to File a New Title

1. Check shelf lists to make sure it is a new title. (New titles will not have cards in the shelf lists.)
2. Type 2 cards--one for title file; one for shelf list.
3. Put cards box marked "new cards."
4. Place publication on proper shelf.

Page #3

Instruction Set B: How to File a New Issue

If there is	*then*
a call number	go to Step A
no call number	go to Step B

STEP A

1. Look in shelf list and record new issues on any holdings card you find.

2. Follow any special notes on cards.

If the card reads	*then*
latest ed. in Documents Center	1. record latest ed. 2. place new ed. on shelf 3. pull old ed. from shelf 4. cross location off call # on old ed. 5. place on "stacks" cart by reference desk
latest edition only	1. pull old ed. and throw away 2. put new ed. on shelf
has no special notes	place publication on shelf

STEP B

Look in dictionary title for card.

If	*then*
you find a card	go to Step A
you don't' find a card	check alternate locations 1. newsletter drawer 2. census drawer 3. supervisor

PART-TIME PAGE

Circulation
Deer Park Public Library
Deer Park, New Zealand

Training Period: Six Weeks

The following is a training schedule for part-time pages at the Deer Park Public Library, a small municipal library where everyone does everything. As each section of the training is introduced, the new employee receives the appropriate section of the procedures manual explaining the specific policy or task. In addition, the page has a file at the circulation desk for his or her training materials so reference as needed. Pages are never left alone at the desk until they have completed the six-week training period.

I. *First Week*

Introductory material

Opening and closing responsibilities

Patron complaints

Shelf reading

How to use the public catalog

Shelving

II. *Second Week*

Practice skills learned during first week; ask questions

III. *Third Week*

Patron count

Operation of the telephone

Answering patrons questions

Handling money from patrons

Matching returning books with the proper cards

Training Objectives

I. After Two Weeks Training is completed, the employee should be:

Familiar with policies and procedures as outlined.

Able to shelve all materials in the library.

Able to shelf read in his or her section.

Able to use the public catalog.

II. After Four Weeks training is completed, the employee should be able to:

Match all returned items with the proper book card (slip).

Collect money for all purposes.

Answer the phone.

Handle simple directional questions.

STUDENT ASSISTANT

Interlibrary Loan Office
First City Library
State University, Tasmania

Welcome to Interlibrary Loan! As when learning any new job, you are about to be bombarded with new information, concepts, and procedures. Don't Panic! Working together with your supervisor, you will follow a training programme designed to help you learn the ropes of your new job. The training programme will last approximately one month. The first weeks will focus on providing basic information related to the initial activities that you will be responsible for assuming and will help to familiarise you with the services provided by the Interlibrary Loan Office. You and your supervisor will review your training on a regular basis to assess your progress and smooth out any areas where you may be experiencing difficulty. The training plan is not inclusive--other information identified during the training will be included. Your questions, comments, and suggestions will be welcomed at any time. We're glad to have you here!

Objectives

Familiarise the student assistant with the tools and techniques necessary for the successful completion of tasks listed in the job description.

(1) Orient student to the physical location of departments in library;

(2) Introduce other students and staff with whom he or she will work;

(3) Establish working patterns for most efficient handling of work loads:

(4) Set guidelines for behaviour; and

(5) Outline expectations in regard to amount of work to be completed each day.

Working Tools	*Date of Expected Proficiency Met*
OLLI	2 weeks
COM catalog	2
Card catalog	2
Shelf list	1
Opening packages	1
Periodical list	1
Circulation print out	1
OCLC terminal	2 months
Files	1
Truck house	1 week
AAUC microfiche	2
Microform printer	3
Photocopy machine	1
[A daily training schedule follows.]	

Training Plan: Second Week

During the second week of training, you and your supervisor will work together to help you refine the skills and techniques you acquired during the early part of your training. Please question, comment, suggest about procedures--if something seems difficult, perhaps there is a better way, and your comments will help. The objective of your training is to enable you to do your job successfully and efficiency. Each day you will be responsible for completing the following tasks:

(1) get call numbers for the requests

(2) pull books and periodicals

(3) do photocopy

(4) open packages.

The number of requests received varies from day to day, so it is difficult to predict the length of time required for each of the above tasks. In order to assess an average time for these tasks and as a way for you to assess your own progress, please record the following information daily for the remaining three weeks of your training period:

# of Requests ALA	Amt Time OCLC	Amt Time to get call #	Amt Time pulling books	Remarks photocopy

Sample questions from a questionnaire given to student assistants during their training:

1. Do you feel the training thus far has prepared you to successfully complete assigned tasks?
2. Have you been given enough information? Are explanations adequate?
3. Have your trainers been well-prepared? Knowledgeable? Helpful? Difficult to work with? Confusing?
4. Do you feel comfortable asking questions and are your questions answered satisfactorily?
5. Generally has the training each day been a positive or a negative experience? Why?

SECRETARY

Library Administration Office
University of Panama, Library, Panama.

The training for the secretary position will cover approximately 4 to 6 months. The first 2 to 4 weeks will focus on providing basic information on the initial activities that the incumbent is responsible for and to provide an introduction to the services of the Library Personnel Office.

This plan outlines the areas of information that should be covered. It is not expected to be inclusive, and other information will be added as identified.

The incumbent will meet with the supervisor on a weekly basis for review during the first four weeks. These meetings will allow for a review of the secretary's progress and any problems with the training, as well as identifying any area(s) that need further attention or clarification.

Recruitment and Hiring of Regular Support Staff

During the first two weeks, the secretary will be trained to assume responsibility for all the routines involved in this function including:

preparing, distributing, and posting vacancy announcements,

scheduling interviews, and typing tests as requested,

providing reference checks as requested,

preparing appointment activity records,

making the job offer,

scheduling orientation with University Personnel.

Eventually as the secretary becomes more knowledgeable about the University's affirmative action and employment policies as well as special needs in the Library, she will be able to assist supervisors in all facets of recruitment and hiring of regular support staff, including:

- Provide information about preparation of job descriptions and selection criteria,
- Assist in determining if affirmative action, reduction-in-force, and promotional opportunities programme policies have been adhered to,
- Assist in determining if fair employment practices have been met.

Once the routines for support of employment activities for regular support staff are learned, the secretary will assume responsibility for support of Librarian employment activities as well.

Files, Records

During the first two weeks, the secretary will be trained to maintain personnel office files. As she becomes familiar with the files and related procedures, she will be responsible for organising and weeding of files.

The secretary will be supported to attend the University's training session on organisation of files.

Personal Contacts

Contact with staff and visitors to the Library Personnel Office is a primary role in this position. It is the goal of the Library Personnel Office to offer accurate and timely information in a pleasant and courteous manner. Training for this will involve:

> learning to answer the phone in a pleasant and courteous manner and taking appropriate messages,
> becoming familiar with Library organisation and staff,
> being familiar with the typical questions asked of the LPO,
> being familiar with forms and other materials requested by staff and/or applicants.

TECHNICAL POSITIONS

LIBRARY ASSISTANT
Acquisition Department
Central Tech University
Technology Park, Durham (UK).

Training Objective. To have the new employee learn all library procedures necessary to perform duties required for this position.

Content. Work involves order and payment of subscriptions, single issues, and back runs. Orders are placed with both domestic and foreign vendours. This work requires the ability to learn invoice processing, machine readable and manual serial holding files, use of OCLC terminals, filing, and other related tasks. This position requires judgment, and the ability to cope with varying work flow patterns.

Sequence of Training and Time Allowed to Learn Tasks

1st Week:
1. Tour of Library
   Time Allowed: 1 hour
2. Explanation of procedure manual
   Time Allowed: 1½ hours
3. Explanation of how subscription interacts with the serials work flow
   Time Allowed: 1 hour
4. Sorting 1st Class mail and checking invoices
   Time Allowed: 1 week
5. Processing of invoices and accounting procedures
   Time Allowed: 2 weeks
6. Correspondence and Filing
   Time Allowed: 1 month
7. Responding to payment problems
   Time Allowed: 1 month

Although we have gone through the training procedures in only two weeks, we do not expect this person to be fully trained without continued supervision. Within 3 months items 1-5, 8, 11 should be totally understood and carried through without supervision. Within 6 months items 6, 7, 9, 10 should be understood and carried through without supervision unless a problem is unusual and cannot be solved with the usual steps learned in training.

LIBRARY TECHNICAL ASSISTANT

Serials Unit
State Library
University of Zaire,

Introduction: The objectives of this plan are to train you in the skills and knowledge required to catalog serials independently in accordance with standards and local requirements.

This plan is not intended to be rigid nor to include everything. The time frames suggested may be adjusted depending on your pace in learning or the quantity and kind of materials receives for cataloging. Components may be rescheduled or rearranged, and additional topics may be introduced as the need for them is identified during the process of training.

Training Feedback, and Evaluation. Approximately the first nine months or so will be a period of intensive training, followed by a period of some three months or so of increasing independence in straightforward cataloging alone with continued instruction in original and member library cataloging and in various serial cataloging processes.

It is expected that by the end of the first year you will be working fairly independently, and that you will be able to meet the quantitative norms defined in the Minimum Output Standards for Serials Catalogers. Our expectations for paraprofessionals in the Serials Unit are outlined in detail in the departmental administrative manual.

Primary responsibility for training and evaluation will rest with the supervisor, but there will be occasions when other staff will be involved in the training process. We will meet frequently at first, and at least weekly during the first six to nine months. You are encouraged to submit your work with notes on questions, uncertainties, your interpretation of the cataloging rules, etc. You may always propose additional discussion sessions beyond what we schedule. Besides the informal meetings mentioned above, there will be formal evaluations held after two months, at the end of the first six months, and at six-month intervals thereafter.

[An explanation of the revision process followed.]

Training Schedule

I. General Orientation

   A. Read Library Administrative Manual

   B. Read Catalog Department Administrative Manual

   C. Read Serials Cataloging Manual, Section 1

   D. Read Periodicals Cataloging Manual, Section 1

   E. Read Osburn's Serial Publications, pp. 3-19, 193-228

   F. Read Wynar's *Introduction to Cataloging and Classification,* pp. 184-185

II. Progression of Cataloging Assignments

   A. Shelf list revision

      1. Read GCM, Section 28

      2. Read PM, Section 11

   B. Periodical added volumes which do not need updates

      1. Read GCM, Section 16, 21, 49

      2. Read PM, Section 4, 6, 7, 12

Requirements for Paraprofessionals in he Serials Unit

By the end of the first three months of work:

Be able to catalog with a minimum of difficulty periodical and serial added volumes which involve no cataloging changes and to recognise changes of entry.

Be able to revise satisfactorily the periodicals shelf list.

By the end of the first six months of work:

Be able to catalog without revision and at the minimum rate of speed periodical added volumes which involve no cataloging changes.

Be able to catalog satisfactorily and at the minimum rate of speed monographic and serial added volumes and to recognise cataloging problems and irregularities that come to light when volumes are added.

Be able to revise satisfactorily the serials shelf list.

[Continues through first year. Also included are quantity and minimum output standards.]

REFERENCE DESK ASSISTANT
College Reference Department
University of Ashton Library
Ashton

This training plan will be used to guide your orientation in the College Library Reference Department. The orientation will consist of lectures, reading assignments, exercises, observations, and practice. All members of the Department will participate in the training programme.

At the end of each week, you will meet with the Head of the Reference Department to discuss your progress and observations of the training programme.

The training programme is designed to provide continuous feedback on your performance. At the end of the first month, the Head of Reference will provide an informal review of your progress in advance of the formal probationary review.

The objectives of the training plan are:

1. To develop a knowledge of the bibliographic record, the public card catalog, and the online bibliographic search system.
2. To develop a knowledge of information sources.

3. To develop basic public service communication skills for reference service, such as reference interviewing, search strategies, problem patrons.
4. To develop an understanding of the role of the Technical Library Assistant in the philosophy and practice of reference service.

Initial Discussion of Service Desk Skills

Objective: To provide a general introduction to attitudes and skills necessary for effective public service desk work.

Contents/Sequence:

Basic Reference Interviewing Concepts

Attitudes Toward User

Courtesy

Professionalism

Problem Patrons

Teaching Function of public services staff

Length of Time: 1½ hours for presentation/discussion.

1 to 2 hours for trainee to read articles.

Suggested Materials:

Reference Interview:

Bunge, Charles A., "Interpersonal Dimensions of the Reference Interview: A Historical Review of the Literature," *Drexel Library Quarterly* 20, pp. 4-23.

"The Reference Interview" in Davinson, D.E., and Bingley, C., *Reference Services*. London Clive Bingley, 1980, pp. 77-92.

Problem Patrons:

Vocino, Michael, "The Library and the Problem Patron," *Wilson Library Bulletin* (January 1976), pp. 372-73.

Reference Desk II: Reference Interview

Objectives: To assist in developing a question negotiation ability that is able to define and encourage inquiry for reference service.

Contents/Sequence: Using specific selections from the literature that are read prior to the session(s), discuss the following:

definition of the reference interview

the reference process (definition, components)

reference interview style (personality of person at desk, nonverbal communication)

reference techniques ("step interview")

Length of Time: 4 hours for each section.

Suggested Materials: [Specific articles are provided.]

Reference Desk III: Telephone Service

Objective: To explain the philosophy, mechanics, and etiquette of telephone reference service.

Contents/Sequence:

Outline the philosophy of telephone reference service: differences and similarities with in-person reference work.

Explain the mechanics of telephone service: putting someone on hold, transferring a call, use of local extension, etc.

Describe good telephone etiquette: how to answer, the appropriate length of time to leave someone on hold, returning a call, etc. Length of Time: 30 minutes

Public Card Catalog I: Introduction

Objective: To serve as a general introduction to the Graduate Library Public Card Catalog outlining its special characteristics, in addition to providing instruction in the basic knowledge of the Catalog Card and the Computer Card formats.

Contents/Sequence:

Catalog Card
Catalog Card Set (main entry, subject, added entries)
References
Practice Exercise
Pre-AACR2/AACR2 Computer-Produced Card Format
Practice Exercise
Union Catalog Concept
How to Determine Locations in Public Card Catalog

Length of Time: 2 hours with a 15-minute break

Suggested Materials:

Oversize visual aids of catalog card
Transparencies of samples from Michigan card catalog

Public Card Catalog II: Filing Rules

Objective: To bring into focus the arrangement of entries in the public card catalog describing the concept of a dictionary catalog and the basic filing rules on which to build on one's understanding of the catalog arrangement.

Contents/Sequence:

Definition of Dictionary Catalog
Publications Not Included in Public Catalog
Publications Only Partially Represented

General Rules for Filing:

Author:

Length of Time: 2 half-days with time for review

Suggested Materials:

Shakespeare drawer
Michigan drawer
U.S. government drawer
Filing Rules Handout

[This training plan has many more components relating to the reference tasks and reference sources. In addition, a specific training schedule has been developed for the first 25 days of training.]

Professional Positions

MONOGRAPH CATALOGER

Processing Division/Original Cataloging Department
Coolidge Library
Dale Humanities University
College Station.

Training Objectives: To train entry-level monographic catalogers:

to search for appropriate cooperative cataloging copy on OCLC,

to describe a monograph according to AACR2 standards,

to assign LC subject headings and call numbers to the described materials,

to prepare OCLC work forms for input by the terminal processors in the Copy Cataloging Department.

Length of Training:

1st quarter: departmental background, LCSH, and call

number assignment familiarisation

2nd quarter: original cataloging, including AACR2 descriptive, OCLC search techniques

3rd quarter: OCLC searching and input editing

4th quarter: sharpening skills obtained in the first three quarters.

Schedule

Time Period: 1st Month

Trainer:

Objectives: To become familiar with processing procedures and policies relative to the operation of the Original Cataloging Department.

Departmental Overview:

Scheduled Meetings: [Completed in Plan]
Specific Tasks
Background Readings
Attachments

Time Period: 2nd Month

Trainer:

Objectives: To become familiar with:

the technique of subject analysis
the use of the LC Subject Headings list
the use of the LC classification schedules for call number assignment.

Training Overview:

The month will be spent in one-on-one training sessions with the trainer, learning the necessary skills for adequate subject analysis and assignment of classification numbers.

Scheduled Meetings:

Weekly meetings for the first two weeks with the Head

of Original Cataloging Department and the trainer for updating and planning.

Specific Tasks:

Become familiar with handling cooperative cataloging copy referrals from Copy Cataloging Department.

Become familiar with the LC Subject Headings list and manual, as well as explanatory texts used by the department.

Become familiar with using the LC classification schedules, as well as explanatory texts used by the department.

Background Readings:

Procedures manuals

Cataloger's Bookshelf

[Training Plan has similar outline through 12 months.]

SELECTORS

Manfred Gotleib Medical Library
University of Nebraska
Nebraska.

Objectives: When training has been completed, the selector should:

1. Be familiar with basic principles of collection development.
2. Know the general structure of the UM programmes in each field of selection responsibility: instructional programmes, research emphasis, clinical services.
3. Be broadly familiar with current emphasis and major issues or controversies in research, diagnosis, or treatment. Know who the leaders in the field are.
4. Be able to identify the major professional organisations in the field.

5. Know the key journals in the field, the best sources for book reviews, and the primary texts and review publications.
6. Understand current collecting criteria for the Taubman Medical Library and be able to apply them to selection of new books in the field.
7. Understand and be able to carry out selection responsibilities.

REFERENCES

Botden A: K. College librarian and research. A.L.A. bull. 29:41 2-1 6, July, 1935.

Borden, A. K. Reference work in a college library. Libraries 35 33-4, January, 1930.

Branscomb, Harvie. Teaching with books. Chicago, Association of *American* colleges and A.L.A., 1940. Reference service, 201-9.

Brown, C. H. Alumni education and its relation to the library of the A.L.A. bull. 25:22-31, January, 1931.

Dimmitt, LeNoir. Extension work by means of package libraries. Lib. Jour 57:984-6, December 1, 1932.

Fenton, D. M. Reference librarian. Jour. of higher educ. 9:153-6, March 1938.

Fussler, H. H. Microphotography and the future of inter-library loans. Jour. of documentary reproduction 2:3-10, March, 1939.

Gerould, J. T. Alumni and the college library. A.L.A. bull. 30:13-17, January, 1936.

Hanks, R. M. Bibliography of printed aids. Lib. jour. 67:235-6, March 13, 1942.

Henry, E. A. Judging reference service. Lib. jour. 64:358-9, May 1, 1939

Hurt, Peyton. Staff specialization: a possible substitute for departmentalisation. A.L.A. bull. 29:417-22, July, 1935.

Kelly, C. J. Reference work with periodicals. A.L.A. bull. 33:193-5 October 15,1939.

Keys, T. E. Practical hints for reference librarians. Special lib. 33:15-12 January, 1942.

Lowell, Mildred H. The centralized libraries of the Oregon state system of higher education. Col. and research lib. 2:136-41, March, 1941.

McCrurh, Blanche P. Estimate of standards for a college library, rev. Lexington, Va., Journalism laboratory press, Washington and Lee University, 1937. Reference and bibliographic service, 110-12.

Michigan. University. Library. What to read; alumni reading lists: third series. Ann Arbor, Midi., University of Michigan press, 1939.

Perry, Warren L. Small colleges organize. PNLA quar. 3:115, January, 1939.

Reed, Lulu R. Do colleges need reference service? Lib. quar. 13:232-42 July, 1943.

Revised code. Lib. jour. 65:802-3, October 1, 1940; *also in* Interlibrary loan code--1940. Col. and research lib. 2:318-19, 376, September 1941.

Rogers, R. D. Undergraduate reference work. Col. and research lib. 3:248-51, June, 1942.

Tochman, Fred B. and Ditzion, Sidney. Prevailing practices in handling serials. Col. and research lib. 1:161-9, March, 1940.

Trylor, K. L. Inter-library loans. Lib. jour. 66:470-1, June 1, 1941.

5

Library Staff Management

The effective participation of the college library in the instruction of students in the use of library tools and bibliography, in defining and carrying out the objectives of the college in collaboration with the faculty, and in extending the use of library materials in education requires a well-qualified and numerically adequate staff of trained librarians. The position of the staff in library service is pivotal. The student body, faculty, and public using the library are peculiarly sensitive to its oversight, judgment, and enterprise.

Selection and Appointment of the Staff

Using practice as an actual criterion, it has been that the college librarian is primarily responsible for the selector and nomination of the staff, and the president for the approval of appointments. The president's approval, of course, is subject to the: final approval of the board of trustees. In this chapter the processes which the librarian goes through in selecting a candidate for a staff position are discussed. While the treatment is from the point of view of the administrator, the information concerns every staff member indirectly, and sometimes directly.

The fundamental basis of selection is an obvious one: to secure the best person for the salary the library is able to afford. Some of the qualifications taken into account in the attempt to secure the best person are these:

1. *Experience:* The amount of professional training and experience required depends in the last analysis upon the position to be filled. The A.L.A. *Classification and pay plans* suggests the principal prerequisites for different positions in varying types and sizes of college libraries. As a general rule, librarians prefer experienced staff members for the more advanced positions and for types of work involving instructional duties with students and faculty. Should all librarians insist upon this preference, it would be impossible for the inexperienced library school graduate to get a position As it is, the deficiency in library salary budgets and the under-supply of librarians usually results in a majority of appointments being made from the immature and inexperienced librarians. There is little danger that they will lack for a chance to gain experience. In the long run, it is to the advantage of the library to fill the larger number of its professional positions with superior library school graduates rather than to employ less able librarians whose chief claim for consideration is a year or so of experience. College librarians seem to prefer staff members between the ages of twenty and thirty in the initial appointments. The age limit in the original appointment may be extended to thirty-five for the more important positions, but in general, librarians are reluctant to make such appointments beyond this age group.

2. *Education:* The minimum training required of a person who is planning a professional career in college library work is graduation from a recognized college or university and one year of library training from a library school accredited by the American Library Association. Consideration is given to the undergraduate institution from which the candidate has received a degree and the quality of the work he did there. If the work to be performed falls somewhere between the classification of professional and clerical duties and yet calls for a broader educational background than is expected of a clerical assistant, it is customary for the librarian to make his choice from the

college's own graduates. The term "subprofessional" is sometimes applied to a position classification of this nature. The position of reserve librarian, for example, may be filled in some libraries by a competent college graduate without library training, or a graduate of a college or university which offers accredited library instruction in the final year of the undergraduate programme.

3. *Personal qualifications:* There is a wide variation in the personal qualifications desired in staff members, although some effort in the direction of standardizing certain general traits is indicated in the A.L.A. *Classification and pay plans.* These are given as follows: intelligence, integrity, good health, pleasing voice and manner attractive appearance, pleasing personality, interest in people, imagination, dependability, courtesy, physical and mental energy, dignity, ability to do team work and forcefulness. 'Personal traits for specific positions are also suggested. Miss Clara Herbert stresses for such positions the importance of a distinctive cultural background, physical health as a personal attraction, spiritual comprehension and taste and genuine interest in the profession. "Some line on these qualities," she points out, "may be secured from information as to the extracurricular activities and social life at college; some from the personal interview and some from the recommendations of college and library school officers."

Methods of Selection

The college librarian selects and nominates the library staff for appointment and that staff members are selected on the basis of their training, experience, and personal qualifications, there remains for consideration the matter of how the library personnel is employed and what methods are used for insuring the best selection possible for a given position. Intelligent procedure in the employment of personnel obviously demands accurate knowledge of the position to be filled. When a vacancy occurs for which there is no eligible candidate within the library system, the librarian prepares a description of the position for submission to the placement officers of library schools and to other sources of recruitment. The description gives a realistic picture of the position in terms of the education and experience required, personal qualifications, the character of the work to be performed, the conditions under which it is done, and preferably a statement of the living conditions in the community. Specific information should be given regarding the time when the position will be filled, the beginning salary or salary range, the wishes of the librarian, in respect to individual applications, recommendations, photographs of candidates applying, and whether or not an interview is contemplated.

This amounts to what, in some professions and in industry is called an occupational description. When completed, it is transmitted in the form of a letter to the library schools and other sources of recruitment. It may be sent to all library schools on the accredited American Library Association list, or it may, in the event the position is specialized rather than general, be sent only to library schools which offer instruction in the particular field. For recruitment in the higher grades of service where experience is important, the librarian may visit library schools for personal interviews, or he may seek contacts through university and large reference libraries or at library meetings, and he may also ask for recommendations from the placement bureau of the American Library Association. This latter service is open to librarians at no expense, as well as to members who are seeking better positions or a change in position. In most college libraries, where the turnover in staff is comparatively small, there is no urgent need for application forms. When the librarian has selected tentatively what he considers the best possible candidate or candidates from the recommendations of library schools and other placement agencies, he writes them for an expression of their interests, and, if they are interested, for details of their qualifications. There are certain advantages, however, in having an application form if the college library staff is large enough to have a fairly large turnover, in personnel and if the library receives many direct requests each year from persons who are interested in working there.

The application form can be sent to those who make inquiries about positions whether there are vacancies or not. The information about prospective candidates is then conveniently at hand and in a form that can be readily scrutinized in the event there arises an unexpected vacancy. The data generally called for in application forms used in public libraries may be adapted to college library use. Miss Herbert mentions among other items; the name, address, age, full information as to education with names of institutions attended and general standing, subjects of special study, professional training and experience, the position or work preferred, specific skills, and references. Each librarian will vary his form to meet his particular attitude toward library work.

One librarian will stress training and ask many questions relevant to the preparation of the candidate, another will emphasize experience, or breadth of interest, or some other aspect of personal qualification and will ask more questions about each of these. When the applications and recommendations have been sifted and narrowed down to the top candidate of candidates for a particular position, the library may ask for an interview if distance does not make this impractical or impossible. The personal interview, properly conducted, is an important method for getting a line or personal qualities which are difficult to judge on paper. Ordinal one thinks of the interview as a device of use to the employer only but the interchange which takes place in the course of the interview and the opportunity for visiting and seeing the library and library staff are also of considerable advantage to the person being interviewed.

If the interview is well conducted, it serves both parties, whatever the final decision may be.

Its technique is discussed in detail by Bingham and Moore in *How to interview.* The average library interview is a less complicated affair, but it is nevertheless susceptible of deliberate planning. It should be easy, never hurried, and should elicit information on such questions as: Is the candidate a negative, neutral, or positive type of person? Is he frank and sincere? Is he mentally alert and observant? Miss Herbert wisely cautions that "it is most important to exercise care that the dreams for the development of the position or the idealism of the appointing officer should not innocently misrepresent the situation."

Appointment of the Staff

The final steps in the appointment will vary in different institutions, depending on who exercises the final authority. Generally speaking, however, the process of selection is completed when the librarian's nomination is approved and the chief executive officer of the college has notified the candidate of his appointment to the library staff. The notification may be made by wire, but it should be confirmed in a letter stating the date of the appointment, the position, the salary, and whether the appointment is temporary or permanent after a period of probation. Ordinarily all first-year appointments are for one year only, with" the hope and expectation that if the candidate's services are satisfactory and he or she is content the contract will be renewed. In one library, the librarian informs the candidate of his appointment immediately after a decision has been made, and states that the confirmation will be sent by the president of the college. This has the advantage of making sure of the services of a candidate who might be considering other opportunities, and it enables the librarian to confirm the arrangements regarding vacations and other matters which are sometimes omitted from the president's appointment letter. When the final appointment is made, it is common courtesy to inform the other applicants that the position has been filled. The librarian should also inform the library schools that an appointment has been made whether or not it was one of their candidates who was chosen.

By such cooperation between librarians and the placement officers, the efficiency of the library school's placement service can be materially increased. After a library staff member has been appointed and comfortably, located in suitable lodgings, he should be introduced to the college administrative officers, members of the faculty, and his associates. He should be instructed in the general policies of the library and be given specific instruction regarding his special duties by the librarian or his immediate supervisor. Not only is the adjustment of the member to his position necessary, but he should be given a go deal of help, encouragement, and direction during the first months of his work.

Size of the Staff

Donald Coney, librarian of the University of Texas, has suggested certain variables which determine the size of the staff in a particular institution: (*i*) the rate of acquisition; (*ii*) the number of students and faculty members; (*iii*) the nature of the teaching programme; (*iv*) the hours of opening, the number of service units, and the organization of procedures in the library; and (*v*) the nature of the building programme. When the libraries selected for comparison are chosen with an eye to their similarity in type and size, it is evident that the factors of enrolment, number of faculty and rate of acquisition would afford an approximate basis for estimating staff size.

In the past the usual method of determining staff size has been the student enrolment. The *Land-grant survey* recommended five full-time trained librarians for the first five hundred students, ten for one thousand students, and four additional staff members for each additional five hundred students. A more scientific approach to the estimate of staff size is contained in a recent report previously mentioned, the A.L.A. *Classification and play plans.* In this report there are designated six classes of libraries for four-year degree-conferring institutions. For each, there is a set of minimum standards which includes an estimate of staff size. The problem for each librarian, then, is to determine in which of the six classes his library belongs. This is done by establishing the library's service unit load according to a formula given in the report. Each underclass (under graduate) student other than an honours student is counted as on unit, each upperclass (undergraduate) student other than an honour student as two units, each honours student as three units, each graduate student as four units, and each faculty member of the teaching staff as five units. For the purpose of illustration, it may be assumed that a particular library's service unit load totaled 3,998 units.

According to the A.L.A. *Classification and pay plans,* this library would belong in Class 4 and would have a minimum staff of three professional positions for the first 800 service units, plus one more for each additional 500 units, plus the chief librarian. The number of professional positions in the example used, therefore, would be nine or possibly nine and one-half in full-time equivalent. The number of clerical staff positions recommended in the report ranges from a minimum of 40% of the number of the professional positions to a maximum of 60%. Student assistants are counted in terms of their full-time equivalent in the clerical force. In the preparation of the A.L.A. formula, tests were made with a large number of institutions of varying types and sizes to insure its validity. In using it as a basis for estimating staff size, however it is important to keep two things in mind. In the first place the recommendations are minimum. It is expected that average libraries and better than average libraries will exceed the estimates and requirements. In the second place it is recognized that no computation of a library's service load can be precisely estimated.

Status of Staff

"Status" is commonly defined as relative rank or position. Dr. Robert McEwen suggests that a satisfactory status would mean relative position in the situation and community in which he the librarian] lives and works which would express satisfactorily his sense of his relation to that situation and community." At present the academic status of college librarians and library staffs is somewhat confused and uncertain. A contributing cause to the uncertainty lies in the nature of library duties themselves. These are in part technical, in part administrative, and in part instructional. This uncertainty, as Dr. McEwen points out, is illustrated in the state-on status in Randall and Goodrich:

> As a matter of fact, the proper status of the librarian seems to be rather administrative, in the class of the deans, secretary, etc., than pedagogical, in the class of the actual teaching faculty. . . Even though the librarian conducts no classes, his teaching function is very important. If a distinction is rank is to be made, his professional responsibilities should place him with the faculty group rather than the administrative.

The question of staff status should not be thought of in terms of rank alone. Satisfactory status is determined in the last analysis not-only by academic rank but also by such matters as salary, tenure and retirement provisions, vacations, sick leave, membership on college bards and committees, social relations to the faculty, attendance at meetings, and the opportunity for continuing education.

The opinions of a majority of librarians and of many educators are tinged somewhat with the same trend of thought as that ex-pressed by Randall and Goodrich. As early as 1898, President Gilman of Johns Hopkins University made the statement that:

> The librarian's office should rank with that of professor.... The profession of librarian should be distinctly recognized. Men and women should be encouraged to enter it, should be trained to discharge its duties, and should be rewarded, promoted, and honoured in proportion to the services may render.

From another administrator, the president of Brown University, comes this statement:

> The librarian, in summary, despite his administrative duties, is primarily officer of instruction. He should have the scholarly interests and tastes which are expected of other members of the faculty. He should be gives faculty status and should participate in all the committee and other discussions incidental to that status.

The following are typical comments of librarians:

> The problem is different from the business organization.... because the essential connection of the library staff with the teaching and research programme.

> The conclusion seems inescapable that whatever dignity may attach to at "administrative" official is limited to himself, and in the minds of often almost inevitably results in the classification of his assistants as clerks.

The general consensus of library opinion is summed up in A.L.A. *Classification and pay plans* report, which reads in part :

> As all professional staff members contribute to the educational of the institution they are deemed to be of an academic rank corresponding to deans, teaching staff and departmental assistants. They should the academic privileges including participation in retirement plans.

Prevailing Practices

In 1939 Mrs. Miriam C. Maloy addressed an inquiry to lib: on staff status and the results of her summary provide the first factual picture of conditions pertaining to staff status in the college library field. She warns, however, that her figures must be used with caution because "the percentage of non-faculty librarians who asked that their reports be held confidential was more than one and a half times the percentage of faculty librarians making the same request.

The essentially educational character of library work and academic and professional qualifications required for service clear indicate that librarianship can be more logically classified with teaching than with clerical or administrative work. Failure of a college to recognize it as such is to deny the importance of the role of library in modern education. The important functions of librarian as teacher cannot be disputed. They are definite and becoming more pronounced in modern library practice. Yet in the many colleges the status of library staffs still remains unsatisfactory Where salaries and working conditions are reasonably satisfactory the attitude of most librarians is to let well enough alone. Other feel that more immediate advantages can be gained by stressing their status as a separate professional group rather than as faculty or administrative employees. In the last analysis, the problem of status terms to hinge on two questions: (*i*) are librarians doing the kind work that demands faculty status because of its importance educationally? and (*ii*) if librarians are doing work of real educational significance, have they the necessary qualifications to do this work properly? When these two questions can be answered affirmatively Status of the library staff will be made the same or the equivalent that of the teacher. If librarians are to make this advancement, by must: (*i*) base their work on a clearly defined philosophy of education; (*ii*) express this philosophy in terms of definite objectives (*iii*) distinguish clearly between the professional and clerical activities designed to carry out these objectives; (*iv*) free the professional staff from all routines, such as charging books, typing and filing, in order that its members may devote their full time to such things as book selection, bibliographical instruction, and reading guidance; and (*v*) require of their staffs the equivalent in academe and professional qualifications of the teaching faculty.

Professional and Clerical Duties

Besides the head of the college library, the typical library staff consists of professional and clerical assistants, with considerable student help. The A.L.A. *Classification and pay plans* sets up two types of services only, omitting subprofessional employees who are included in the public library classification plans and combining student service with clerical.

In the prefatory statement of standards of education in the pay plans, the two types of services are defined as follows:

> 1. Positions in the *professional service* usually fall into one of groupings: executive, bibliographical and those requiring contact of a professional nature with the public. Thus a knowledge of library work as taught in a library school is considered essential. When certain positions require *unusual* subjects or language background, it may, on rare occasions, be very difficult or impossible to find someone who has this required back- ground plus library school education. In such instances the subject back-ground may be deemed more essential to the specific position and the person possessing it be chosen for the position with the understanding he complete his library education within a specific period.
>
> 2. Positions in the library's *clerical service* are similar to clerical positions in the business and other offices of the institution. To hold a position in this service the incumbent is not required to have had prior library eduction or experience.

To be classed in the professional service, the person must have these minimum qualifications for the lowest grade:

Graduation from a college or university approved by an accrediting association of more than state-wide standing, including one year of training in a library school accredited by the A.L.A.; or equivalent qualifications.

To be classed in the clerical service, the person must

have these minimum qualifications for the lowest grade:

> Graduation from an accredited high school; or equivalent qualifications.

A great deal of the work in any college library is of a clerical or routine nature. If the professional staff is to provide the services needed in carrying out the instructional work of the faculty, it must be relieved as much as possible from work of a purely routine or clerical nature. It must have the time and opportunity to become acquainted with the students, to become familiar with their problems and needs, as well as to know the materials which are available for aiding their study. While it is impossible to separate these tasks completely, there are good reasons why each library should attempt to outline and analyze the professional and clerical duties in its own service. They may be stated briefly as follows:

> 1. A clear distinction between professional and clerical duties enables the professional staff to give more time to work of an instructional character and thereby to improve the quality of library service. It frequently, results in a reclassification of duties in which many tasks of a routine nature are transferred to competent, clerical assistants. As a consequence, it helps to raise the professional standing and prestige of the staff in the eyes of the faculty.
>
> 2. If there are certain duties which are clearly set apart as clerical, and if the librarian can demonstrate the need for help to perform these duties, his chances of securing this help are greatly increased even though college personnel funds are limited. The business-minded college president is impressed by the possible economies; the president who measures costs in terms of the educational value received will readily recognize that a librarian who has been freed from such requirements as typing and filing will have more time to study the instructional needs of the individual student and to give direction and guidance in the use of books. This fact cannot be stressed too" strongly. College libraries are perhaps more seriously handicapped by the lack of sufficient full-time clerical assistants than by any other single factor.

> 3. A classification of duties provides a basis for clarifying and in improving organization, for placing responsibility, and for the intelligent treatment of salary problems.

Evidently in practice there are serious difficulties in separating completely professional and clerical tasks. The time during which a college library is open is long, and it is generally impossible to provide professional assistants at the loan and reference desks at all hours of the day and evening. As a consequence there are clerical and student assistants doing professional work and professional staff members doing clerical tasks. Moreover, the varying nature of duties at the loan desk does not easily permit a hard and fast distinction between professional and clerical duties. In the technical processes, where the distinction is more readily made, the professional staff is often obliged to do a great deal of routine work in order to keep abreast of individual duties. In spite of these obstacles, and others, however, the attempt to distinguish between professional and clerical activities in the college library is strongly recommended as vital to effective service and recognized academic status. Obviously there are types of work in the college library which are purely clerical and to which full-time clerical and part time student help can be assigned. Unless a clear distinction is made in these positions, there is danger that all library assistants will be classified as clerks by the administrative officers.

Qualifications of the Librarian

In discussing the role of the library in higher education, Dr. Louis R. Wilson has this to say about the librarian:

> The modern college exacts higher qualifications of its librarian than formerly. It no longer considers the possession of an A.B. degree and the completion of one year of training in a library school sufficient equipment for the librarian who is to become a successful administrator, a wise counselor in the use of books, and a force in shaping college instructional policies. It insists that the librarian must be a person of imagination and initiative, that he mast have

> a sound understanding of library administration and some subject field, and that he must know how to relate the use of the library to the educational programme of the college.

The emphasis in this quotation is on the training, progressiveness, and mental attainments of the college librarian. One might add that if he is to be a leader in the college community, he must be person of character, integrity, and professional idealism--qualities sometimes overlooked in the filling of important teaching and administrative posts on college faculties today. Few enter--or should enter the library profession to make money; ideals for the most part must be the determinant. A devotion to one's profession goes a long way in establishing feelings of trust and confidence among the library staff and faculty.

Administrative Ability

It would appear an obvious truism to declare the college librarian should have the qualities of a good administrator; yet so important are the librarian's instructional relations to the faculty that this requirement is not so generally nor so permanently borne in mind as it should be. Dr. Harvie Branscomb correctly states that the administrative problems of the university librarian are more complex, but it must be stressed that so far as the realities of college library work are concerned, one of the best services of the librarian is to be a good administrator and leader in the library. It is essential that the librarian assume a large measure of administrative responsibility, including the supervision of the staff, the proper budgeting and expenditure of library funds, and the oversight of the library building. These functions require frequent consultations and close relationships with the president, the business officers, and department heads, and the librarian must impress them with his should business judgment and innate ability to manage the library's affairs. He must also hold the confidence of the library staff by his ability to develop a systematic organization of library work, to conduct the many types of transactions involving the administration and faculty, and to administer personnel, budgets, and services in a satisfactory manner.

In many books and articles, the qualities of the executive are given. One of the best brief summaries is contained in Randall and Goodrich, who state that administrative ability consists generally of four things: (*i*) the power to see clearly the significance and the implications of a problem; (*ii*) the ability to analyze a known problem in such a way as to identify the important parts of its structure; (*iii*) the genius to put facts side by side, to consider their combined significance, and thus to come to a conclusion and (*iv*) the faculty to secure cooperation from others. To attain even to an approximation of these qualities, the librarian first must understand thoroughly the objectives of the library in the particular college programme, the functional organization of library materials and the problems and needs of those he serves. One who has not the personal ability to work with others and to secure their co-operation will not make a good administrator, but he may improve his chances for success considerably by making a serious effort in understand the psychological factors involved in personnel relations.

Mutual confidence is an important factor in satisfactory personnel management. If the librarian is to have confidence in the staff, he must first have confidence in his own judgment, Indecision is fatal to good administration," write Randall and Goodrich but "self-confidence must not develop into obstinacy." Staff members are attracted by a librarian who will take responsibility; conversely they are likely to be wary of one who hesitates because of lack of confidence in his own judgment or who tries to "pass the buck." Mutual confidence implies also that the librarian should have full confidence in the staff. The best evidence of his trust is the degree to which he is willing and able to delegate authority in work to be done. To be given a particular job to do and to have the satisfaction of seeing its final accomplishment is a great motivator. On the other hand, always to be doing something patently as a subordinate and under constant supervision and checking and to see nothing of personal accomplishment in what is done has a very debilitating effect. The librarian is also responsible for cultivating and maintaining an *esprit de corps.* In plain language, this amounts to giving everyone on the staff a square deal in matters of promotion and salary, in providing for the physical comfort of workers, in showing appreciation of satisfactory performance, and in being fair and impartial in criticism. Sometimes grievances and friction will show up in the staff for reasons which have nothing to do with the librarian's personal administration. It is then his job to determine the cause of the friction and to eliminate it firmly and openly. He cannot hope to do this unless he knows each staff member well and has the courage to deal firmly with older and experienced members of the staff as well as with the new members. One other factor, even in a brief summary, merits careful consideration. The attitude of the librarian in administration should be democratic. The greatest danger to satisfactory personnel relations and effective library service is represented by the librarian who is domineering, autocratic, and reprehensible in his attitude in handling people in subordinate positions. As President Mildred H. McAfee of Wellesley College once pointed out in a talk to college librarians:

> It is easy to forget how really unimportant we are in our own right. A president has less reason for existence apart from the institution than; library does, but not much less. You know the danger signals for me and my presidential colleagues. While I was a teacher, I asked my college president for some advice about my office, and he said, "Don't bother me with that. That's what I hired you for." "I hired you"--a bad symptom then the college president begins to think of himself as the boss, his Colleagues as his employees.

The librarian is the one to take the initiative in formulating administrative policies, but he should see to it that his policies do not constitute dictatorship. Consideration for subordinates is not only essential for maintaining an *esprit de corps;* it is also the best way for securing good work.

Scholarly Interest and Understanding

Practically all writers stress the importance of an understanding and appreciation of scholarship on the part of the college librarian, John D. Russell, presenting the point of view of the college professor, writes:

> In order to maintain effectively his position in this community of scholars. . . , the librarian must himself qualify as a scholar. He must be broadly acquainted with the manifold fields of human knowledge. He must be able to speak the language of scholars. He must know the ways in which scholars and specialists in various fields derive their knowledge and apply it to practical situations. Under modern conditions one can scarcely qualify as a scholar unless, in addition to the general types of knowledge already indicated, one has penetrated fairly deeply into one or more specialized fields. This last characteristic, however, is sometimes unfortunately over emphasized, I believe, almost to the exclusion of the grasp of the broader types of knowledge which in former generations was the predominant characteristic of the scholar.

It if worth while to dwell a moment on the meaning of this quotation, for it is a fact that unless the college librarian can develop sympathetic understanding of the book needs of the scholars who teach and do the research work in the college, he cannot fully enter into the possibilities of his calling.

It is not the intent of Professor Russell, or of others within the library profession who write about the scholarly requirements of college librarianship, that the librarian should be a scholar is the sense of an eminent specialist or research man. There is one very practical reason why he cannot be. His work allows him no time for the continuous application to a single subject which is essential for the specialist. His working hours are long, he is interrupted at every turn, and his administrative and instructional duties in the library require him to switch his attention at a moment's notice to a new subject. As a librarian his function is not primarily to engage in teaching or research; he exists, rather, to aid those who are teaching, investigating, or writing. He certainly must have the instincts and sympathies of a scholar, and yet be able to think independently while attending to the interests of others. He should be familiar with the methods of research; he should be competent to impart his knowledge in the training of young people in the proper use of bibliographical tools and in offering counsel in problems of research. As a librarian of scholarly interests and instincts, he should know thoroughly the organization and curriculum of the college and should be able to select and evaluate books in relation to the courses of instruction. Above all, he should be a person of broad interests with the intelligence and ability to appreciate and understand the problems of others. Sir Frederic Kenyon, at one time librarian of the British Museum, stresses this quality in these words: "The moral basis of both the capacity and the willingness to help others in their several pursuits is Sympathy. . . It is the capacity of entering into the mind of another, of being able to see interest where he sees it, and thereby of being able to cooperate genuinely in the search which he has in hand." A broad academic background and professional training should give direction to these qualities; experience should provide practical judgment.

Ability to Work with Students

The ability of the librarian to work with students is a requirement so widely recognized by the profession and so frequently emphasized that it calls for no extended mention here. One word of caution may be in order, however. So sharply have modern methods of teaching focused attention upon library relations with the faculty that there is danger the librarian may not fully appreciate the fact that the library is primarily designed to be of service to the college student.

The library fails to fulfill its complete function unless the librarian knows the students' needs, how they may be met, and what students expect of the library. The adaptation of library service to student needs must necessarily be developed in terms of a particular college serving a specific student body. There are three general factors, however, while will greatly affect the success with which the librarian carries or his work with the students. These are discussed briefly in the following:

Personal Contacts With Students : In a college library the librarian has a good many personal contacts with students. The may range from the recommendation of supplementary reading for a class assignment to the explanation of library policy and regulations. They may, and often do, include the giving of lectures it the use of the library, the provision of books for some special class or extra-curricular project, the arrangement of an exhibit to illustrate some subject of instruction, or the recommendation of books on careers for a particular student. The successful librarian, is it the service of each student who needs help in his studies, guidance in outside reading, or advice on personal problems. He need not be all things to all men, nor be unremitting in industry, but he must have wide intellectual interests and a sympathetic understanding of the problems of young people. The quality of sympathy is the least dispensable.

Student Opinion of the Library Staff : As one writer has wisely pointed out, the best test of the real usefulness of a library is the composite attitude of the library staff toward the student. What ever demands a body of undergraduates may make upon the library, they do not wish to be treated as so many automatons'. The have little respect for a servile, smirking type of service, and they resent the begrudging, hostile attitude which sometimes characterizes loan desk service. What they want first and foremost is sympathy, an understanding of themselves as well as of their needs By virtue of his responsibility for the selection and guidance of library personnel, the librarian must see to it that the staff develops a real understanding and appreciation of the human aspects of its work.

Faculty Opinion of the Librarian : The way in which the librarian is regarded by the faculty; and the interpretation he encourages students to put upon his place in the college will greatly evidence the success with which he carries on his work with students. Is he regarded simply as a caretaker of the books, as a technician as an administrator, *or* is he regarded as a helpful friend and adviser, as a librarian-teacher, and as the leader of a staff competent and willing to aid the teacher? In a librarian who evidence the second set of qualities, there is a definiteness and forthrightness which inspire the confidence of teachers.

Academic and Professional Training

Two major criticisms have been levelled at college librarians, and professional training for librarianship. It is often said that college librarians are expert in the making of catalogues and in the technical processes of the library, but that they lack the educational, and scholarly experience of those whose colleagues they ought to the second criticism applies particularly to the chief librarian, who it is claimed, often lack's the vision and ability to play an active part in the formulation of college policy. There is, no doubt, a great deal of truth in both criticisms and they deserve to be sought out into the open, though it is questionable whether every newly fledged holder of the doctorate is doing his profession a service by discussing the weaknesses of his colleagues at every opportunity he is given to speak or write. A reasonable amount of criticism is healthful, but it can be carried to the point where it is either profitable nor wise.

Comprehension before Criticism

Before discussing trends in education for librarianship which are designed to eliminate the weaknesses cited in the criticisms above, it is worth while to mention four things which the student and critic of librarianship should keep in mind in evaluating library training and librarian performance.

1. The field of modern college librarianship is comparatively young. The librarian and his staff, in the development of educational processes in which they have had an increasingly active part have had to change their entire concept of the library function Some of the difficulties incident to this change, particularly as regards the librarian's relationship to faculty members and instruction, are still with the profession.

2. Library service is not to be judged exclusively on the technical aspects of its work. For example, the limitations of the card catalogue are sometimes attached to the work of the library and its staff as a whole. No librarian will deny that card catalogues are awkward to use, costly, and inadequate; but to appraise the whole of library service in terms of the technical cataloguing is to overlook the many-sided character of a library. Success in college library administration, or in reference work, or in instruction in the use of the library, or in readers' advisory service--to mention only four important aspects of the library job--depends less on technical skill than on broad cultural knowledge, wide reading, and versatility in aiding readers. By and large, college librarians have shown themselves to be more successful in these phases of their work than they have in producing a usable and practical catalogue.

3. There is, as Dr. William Warner Bishop points out,

some misunderstanding regarding a "supposed basic contradiction between scholarship and librarianship.'" In the last analysis scholarship is dependent upon books and books are the stock in trade of libraries. "It is equally obvious," Dr. Bishop continues, that in the organization of books and library materials for scholarly use "there has been a working combination of librarian, library staff, and the university's several faculties." The same is true in the college library. The librarian is naturally dependent on the various members of the teaching staff, each of whom is an authority on the literature of his subject, for the development of the collections in aid of instruction and scholarship. It is obvious that the librarian cannot be a specialist in all fields. It is at least open to question whether he would prove a letter librarian by becoming an expert in one field rather than by cultivating a diversity of interests in several. His job, in this one aspect of library work, is to maintain a proper balance in the collections and to see that they fit the needs of students. The difficulty sometimes is to get the specialist to take sufficient trouble to submit de*siderata* to the library, whereas in other cases the enthusiasm of the professor produces wholesale recommendations in his own special field, out of all proportion to its importance in the college or to the requirements of undergraduate students. In the development of a college library, therefore, it would seem that each group--the librarian, library staff, and professor--has its own role to play.

4. Finally, although it is all too true that the librarian has not played an active part in the formulation of college policy, there is at least some reason to doubt whether this is as much a defect of his professional training as certain other factors over which he has no control. The trouble lies at least half the time in the fact that the library is still a relatively unknown factor in college education to most faculty members and administrators. It is unknown in the sense, of course, that its potential contribution is not realized.

In the formal organization of the college, its relationship to instruction is often left to the initiative of the librarian, whose best efforts will prove abortive if he is too aggressive, or to a committee for whose members the library is only a sideline. The president, under pressure from all sides, is frequently too busy to see that the right relationships are provided even though he may be interested and sympathetic with what the library is trying to do. In other words, a greater degree of personality and mental attainment is required for appointment on the part of the librarian and the library staff to membership on the educational and policy-making committees of the college than for the faculty who have already an accepted place in the academic circle. It is an anomaly of the educational world that librarians everywhere should be actuated by such genuinely high motives of service and yet should so often fail to find an opportunity to contribute their best.

The above is not an attempt to justify present library practices or library school teaching programmes. As was said at the outset, there is a certain amount of disquieting truth in the weakness these criticisms typify. It is, therefore, of interest to inquire what has been done in recent years to remedy the faults and to raise the level of scholarship in the profession. The most noticeable trends so far as they affect the training of college librarians, are in the selection and recruitment of personnel, in the library training programme itself, and in the continuing education of librarians in-service. The discussion of the last of these trends is deferred to a later section of this chapter.

Trends in Professional Library Education

So far as recruitment is concerned, there has been a determined effort to improve the quality of candidates entering the profession. The American Library Association through publication and through its board, on education for librarianship has sought to interest most promising graduates, particularly men, in entering the profession.

All library schools have developed comprehensive plans for selective admission, usually based on college scholarship records, interviews and counseling procedures, and intelligence and aptitude tests. Higher standards of admission are required for entrance library schools. A much greater emphasis than formerly is placed on personal qualities of leadership. The responsibility of the colleges librarian and his staff in discovering students with unusual abilities for library service has been stressed. This is a matter which is of real concern to college librarians because their institutions send a larger proportion of students to library schools in comparison with their enrolments than do the universities. The college librarian moreover, has many personal contacts with students which enable him to weigh not only their scholarly, ability but the more intangible factors of personality.

The improvement in the quality of library school graduates by better methods of passing upon the fitness of applicants for admission and by creating greater interest in library service as a career for college graduates of exceptional ability has been accompanied by a more precise definition of the requirements for pre-professional training. Fundamentally, this training should consist of a general education leading to a knowledge of broad fields of learning and a real understanding of the relevance of this knowledge to the intellectual and social structure of the world. For this reason the intensive type of survey course in broad fields of knowledge has been recommended as highly desirable during the underclass college years. Specialization in the upperclass years has largely been, sought in the humanities in the past. It is now urged that more students should choose for their final collegiate specialization work in the social, biological, and physical sciences. In addition to a major field of study, the student is expected to have a good reading knowledge of at least two foreign languages.

Leadership in college library work requires training

in educational aims, statistical methods, and in the general principles of administration. A very promising trend in education for librarianship has been the change in emphasis from the study of techniques to the study of principles in the first-year professional curriculum. Most college librarians and library school faculties now agree that the first-year library school student should concentrate less on specific skills and more on the fundamental knowledge and principles of librarianship. this is evident in the provision for "courses which seek to orient libraries and librarianship..., which stress the reasons and requirements underlying technical operations, and which present books with a view to mastery rather than manipulation." It is evident also in the statement of the major objectives of first-year library school courses as set forth by library school directors and faculties.

Professor Reece of Columbia suggests six objectives:

> (*i*) To give students all the knowledge possible about the materials and conditions relating to their duties; (*ii*) to imbue them with understanding of the purposes of their calling; (*iii*) to put them in command of the principles involved in organizing and conducting libraries; (*iv*) to make dear that these purposes, principles, and knowledge are to be the controlling factors in their work; (*v*) to enable them to see the enterprise in which they are about to engage both as an entity and as a part of the social mechanism; and (*vi*) to make the student so familiar with means and devices that he will be able to select and employ them or to direct their employ when the need comes.

Courses in college library administration begin with a consideration of the American college, its objectives, types, and services, its support, government, and administrative organization. The student is made to set that the library is not something which operates independently or in isolation from the teaching faculty but rather that its effectiveness depends on a realization of the function of the college and an under standing of curricular programmes.

The change in emphasis from technical knowledge and efficiency to the broader aspects of librarianship, as noted above, is probably the most significant trend in recent instructional methods in library schools. Without minimizing the importance of technical knowledge and skill, an effort is being made to lay a broader foundation for technical training and, at the same time, to give the prospective librarian a more scholarly background for his work. Some attention has also been given to distinguishing between the potential abilities of students in library school for different levels of library work. The system of course syllabi and comprehensive examination at Columbia enables the incoming student to begin his work at the level on which a year's study will yield the greatest returns, and to base his professional degree not upon a certain number of credits accumulated by the process of taking courses but upon evidence obtained through objective, comprehensive examinations. The syllabi-place a greater responsibility upon the student and provide for a larger share of independent study. They have also helped to eliminate unnecessary overlapping in the content of library school courses, and they have provided the basis for the comprehensive examinations.

For work beyond the first year of library school, there are also noticeable improvements in the curricular offerings for librarians. One established practice is illustrated by the extent to which the facilities and resources of many departments are brought into the educational programme of the librarian. At the University of Illinois, for example, a student may combine a major in library science with a minor in any special subject for which he is adequately prepared. The practice quite properly recognizes the close relationship that exists between librarianship and instruction in the various subject fields, and it emphasizes one way in which the subject field departments can contribute to the education of the superior librarian. As a further aid to the development of the librarian's critical ability and his understanding of faculty research work, courses are being introduced in methods of research and investigation. Dr. Wilson calls attention to this in his statement of the four objectives for the student at the second year level of library training:

> At the M.A. level he should be expected : (*i*) to become acquainted with the methods and spirit of graduate study and research in the fields of library science; (*ii*) to extend his knowledge of library science generally; (*iii*) to increase considerably his knowledge of the special field of university (one might insert *college* here) librarianship and related subject fields; and (*iv*) to demonstrate his ability to use research methods in the preparation of a report or thesis in the field of his specialization.

Finally, there is a strong trend toward taking graduate courses in the academic and professional fields which will lead to the doctor's degree. There is no general agreement that the Ph.D. is essential in the work of the librarian, but it is 'recommended on the ground that if the librarian is to work effectively with a group of scholars, he should have a scholarly training equal to theirs. The opinions of the leading university librarians support this thesis for the university librarian, and the fact that many of the recent graduates of the Chicago Graduate Library school have filled the top positions in college libraries argues strongly in its favour. In the A.L.A. *Classification and pay plans* the minimum qualifications for the positions of chief librarian, associate librarian, department heads, and certain other persons occupying places of importance in college libraries recommend the doctorate degree in librarianship or in a special subject field. All these statements mount up to a very strong argument for advanced training, indeed, and they can be supported by the practical argument that the higher degree commands a higher salary and greater prestige. On the other hand, it is equally necessary to point out that graduate work at the present time suffers from an overemphasis on narrow specialization, and that for the college librarian, at least, there is little doubt that breadth of learning in many fields is more important than narrow concentration. It is not the intention here, however, to debate the question. It is enough to note that there is a distinct trend in favour of the doctor's degree and that the opportunities are improving for the librarian to pursue advanced training without having to confine himself to the narrowing effects of specialization.

These illustrations in library programmes are only a few examples of the many changes that are taking place and are now under consideration in the preparation of librarians. *Programmes for library schools,* by Professor Ernest J. Reece, contains a summary of the defects in present training practices and suggests possible remedies. Efforts are being made to improve recruitment methods and to attract a higher grade of college graduate to the profession. The pre-professional training of prospective librarians is being emphasized and more specifically defined. The educational programme in the first two years of library school work is placing more emphasis on the broader aspects of librarianship and less on the training of specific skills, on the acquisition of educational and social understanding on the part of librarians, and on the training of librarians in methods of research. There is considerable pressure on younger librarians to seek higher academic and professional training leading to the doctorate. All these efforts have improved the quality of librarians and are helping to make librarianship a more integral part of college education than it has been in the past.

Remuneration

Formal status and appropriate ranking are important factors in raising the level of staff efficiency, quality, and morale. But formal "listing with the faculty in the college catalogue" or assignment to the somewhat anomalous status of faculty membership will not solve the problems of library personnel unless status is accompanied by full faculty privileges. These include comparable provision for salaries appropriate to training and responsibilities, tenure and retirement provisions, vacations, membership on faculty committees, social privileges, and opportunity for advancement and study. Of all various aspects of faculty status, none is more important to the librarian than salary. In almost all colleges there is need for strengthening the library staff.

Generally speaking, this can be accomplished only by making available additional funds for increasing salaries. During the past few decades library salaries have been increasing, and what is more important, they appear to be increasing at a more rapid rate than the salaries of the teaching faculty. In spite of this favourable progress, the salaries of librarians, particularly those in the staff ranks, are not high enough to attract and hold persons as efficient in librarianship as those in teaching. A for leading librarians and educators have held that the position of the librarian is fairly comparable to that of the dean or the head of major department, the position of head of a department in the library to that of the associate or assistant professor, and so on.

There appears to be a direct relationship between the salaries paid to librarians in the higher positions and the size of the student enrolment. The median salary for the chief librarian it the large college and university class is almost 100 per cent larger than it is in the other two classes. Attention is also called to the fact that the salaries in the teachers colleges are somewhat higher for all grades of library service than those in the small liberal arts colleges. Significantly, there is a considerable difference between the salary paid to professional assistants and to librarians in the highest brackets in the large college and university class.

This variation is greater than in either the small college or teachers college class. It is true of course, that the same variation seems to hold true for the salaries of the instructor and professor in the large college and university class, but library staffs are numerically small and there is less opportunity for individual advancement. This is not to suggest that the salaries paid to the heads of departments or to the chief librarian in large college and university libraries are too high. The salaries of chief librarians and department heads are not so large as those of their teaching colleagues with comparable responsibilities and training but at the same time it is quite evident that capable people cannot be attracted to and held in the position of professional library assistants by the salaries now in effect. In comparing the salaries of teachers and librarians, it is observed that the greatest discrepancies occur in the ranks of assistant professor and instructor on the one hand and the department head and professional library assistant on the other. The median beginning salary is higher for the teaching faculty, the range in salary is greater for those in each rank. This means that the instructor and assistant professor have a much greater opportunity to advance to a higher salary within their respective ranks than the professional library assistant and department library head have. And as has already been pointed out, the situation is still less favourable to the professional library assistant because he has fewer opportunities to move from one grade of service to the next hi grade. Attention is also called to the fact that instructors have opportunity not open to college library staff members--namely tip receive additional remuneration during summer sessions beyond their annual nine months' salary.

In an effort to provide a plan of classification of library positions with recommendations for salaries based on duties, training, and responsibilities, the board on salaries of the American Library Association has made an intensive study in the last few years of the whole subject of training and salaries.

This plan has now been published in a manual which has been previously referred to as the A.L.A. *Classification and pay plans,* and it may be regarded as one of the most important aids and guides to future efforts for the improvement of salaries. It emphasizes the need for a clear distinction between professional and clerical work in the library, for adequate training in positions which make an important contribution to instruction, for a salary schedule providing advancement on the basis of satisfactory performance, and for a basic salary of $1,620 for the beginning professional assistant.

Working Conditions

The librarian, acting in his capacity as chief of the library staff, is usually directly responsible for, or vitally interested in, a considerable number of other personnel matters in addition to the selection and training of the staff, academic ranking, and salaries. These include such matters as the physical conditions under which staff members work, hours of service, hours of work, vacations and leave, tenure and retirement provision, and other matters having to do with the improvement of the staff in service. It goes without saying that every library staff member is also directly concerned. Each of these topics is discussed briefly in the remainder.

Physical Factors

It is important that every consideration be given to provide the best working conditions possible for the staff. This involves consideration of the layout of the building, building facilities, storage facilities, heating, lighting, ventilation, air conditioning, floors, floor coverings, communication systems, furniture and equipment, as well as office maintenance. But because of their importance in personnel management, they are referred to briefly at this point also. In 1939 Miss Clara Herbert laid down certain" requirement which she regarded as minimum essentials in working conditions in public libraries. The most important of these are summarized briefly as follows:

1. Library work makes heavy demands upon the vitality of its staff. It is of the utmost importance, therefore, that librarians give due regard to such details as will result in the maximum output with the minimum expenditure of nervous energy.
2. Work requiring concentration and accuracy should not be scheduled during the time an assistant is at the loan desk.
3. Workrooms should be planned in detail with an eye to improving efficiency and securing economy of effort. Furniture should be so arranged as to expedite duties without loss of motion or time. In the allocation of space, 100 square feet per person is the usual rough allowance which includes space for files and typewriters. From 3 to 3 feet should be allowed between the back of one desk and the front of another, and 4 feet should be regarded as the minimum width for aisles.
4. Proper conditions of ventilation and heating are important, The optimum atmospheric conditions for the comfort and health of personnel are a temperature of from 68°. to 70° and 40-60 per cent relative humidity.
5. The lighting of workrooms and offices, whether by means of incandescent or fluorescent lights, should be economical in cperation, supply sufficient illumination without glare, and give a uniform and nearly shadowless illumination for desks. As much natural light as possible in offices is desirable.
6. Experience has demonstrated the desirability of individual desks so that each person can have his own outfit of necessary tools. Consideration should be given to the proper selection of chairs, tables, supply closets, and other conveniences in the workrooms.

7. Noise is a contributing element to fatigue and should be minimized as far as possible. Acoustical tiling and noiseless floor coverings are recommended.

Apart from those mentioned above, there are certain other physical factors which have an important bearing on staff efficiency. The most important of these concern the equipment with which the staff has to work. Many scientific inventions not intended primarily for libraries are directly usable or adaptable, and it is well worth the time and expense involved to discover and apply them. They include major equipment items which should be considered at the time of building or remodelling: ventilating and air-conditioning systems, passenger and freight elevators, book lifts and conveyor systems, and telephones and their adaptations. They include also smaller and less expensive but equally necessary types of equipment such as typewriters, duplicating machines -- particularly the mimeograph, calculating machines for office and record work, visible record files, card sorters, charging machines, book marking aids, stapling machines, light meters, and other types of equipment.

Service Hours

There is considerable variation in the number of hours that college libraries are kept open for the use of students and faculty. The size of the staff, the number of rooms to be serviced, and the student enrolment are controlling factors. The hours open for circulation service in a group of twenty-six typical college libraries in 1942, as reported to the American Library Association, ranged from fifty-four to eighty-six, with the median at seventy-seven hours. If to these hours is added the time the library is open for reading and study but not for circulation service, the range increases from fifty-four to one hundred and three, and the median is seventy-eight. Most college libraries are open on Sundays for limited service -- study and reading;

and for shorter hours than during the week -- three to four hours Sunday afternoon. An increasing number of libraries, however, are making available the full services of the library during Sunday afternoon and evening. If the library is playing its part in developing reading habits and in producing the qualities of mind aimed at by the whole educational programme, then it is important that a professional staff member should be on duty all hours during which the building is open.

Work Hours

Hours of work should not exceed thirty-eight a week, although the latest statistics reported to the American Library Association in veal a range of thirty-six to fifty and a median of forty hours per week for college librarians in institutions with a thousand enrolment or less. If thirty-eight hours a week does not cover the library schedule, then the remedy is an extra staff member and not excessive hours of duty--not even occasionally. If Sunday duty is extra, this fact should be made clear to the assistant at the time of "appointment. Randall and Goodrich report that Sunday duty may be voluntary on the part of the staff members, and paid for at a fixed rate per hour, or the time may be considered as part of the weekly schedule with commensurate freedom at other periods.

Vacations and Sick Leave

As in the case of hours of service, the length of vacations; and leaves of absence for illness with pay varies greatly in difference colleges. In 1939 Miss Hazel Timmerman reported that "eighty two per cent of these university and college libraries grant twenty-four or more working days to all or certain members of the professional staffs." In certain institutions she noted some varities in the length of vacations based on length of service and on position. As regards the former, twelve working days were allowed for less than one year of service, eighteen working days for one to five years, and twenty-six working days thereafter. In colleges where the vacation varied with position, the chief librarian and department heads were allowed one month and the professional still eighteen working days.

If there is to be a difference in vacation allowance based on position, then it is logical and equitable to make this distinction on the basis of the contribution of the position to instruction and to scholarship requirements which it entails his Blanche P. McCrum holds to this view in her recommendation :

> That six weeks in summer, with time equal to one week during the winter holidays be granted to the professional staff as a whole. In the case of the head librarian, reference librarian, bibliographer, archivist, curator of special collections, and for the incumbents of the other posts requiring incursing scholarship, that the summer allowance be extended to the full faculty vacation. The same implied requirement as that in force for the faculty should, however, obtain for these librarians, namely, that travel, the study of books and publishers at home and abroad, and at least some contributions to knowledge should give proof of the wise.

Library work does not offer a high financial reward. Therefore, a may be argued that a generous vacation allowance will help to offset the salary deficiency and attract those who might otherwise to into other fields of work. If this is a reasonable assumption, than is questionable whether there should be any distinction in be length of vacations granted to professional members of the library staff. An arrangement of vacations to give the fullest benefit to all members of the professional staff will undoubtedly improve morale and encourage the staff to give compensating service. In all cases, the usual general holidays of the college are in addition to the vacation period. Provision should also be made for persons who change positions in the middle of the year or just before their annual leave is due. The practice will vary in each library but no person can be expected to work for two years at the peak of his efficiency without a vacation.

College libraries apparently make few regulations about sick leave "but make adjustments depending upon the individual case. Among the few that have special rulings on sick leave, the practice seems to be about as follows:

> One library allows three months
> One library allows forty days
> Eleven libraries allow a month's salary in case of illness
> Thirty-seven libraries allow two weeks or thereabouts.
>
> Library regulations on sick leave should in general conform to the college's policy in regard to faculty leaves of absence or sick leave.
>
> Whenever possible, the regulations should be definite and codified.

Retirement Provision

Retirement provision is an important element of faculty status. It is particularly important that the library staff should participate in any form of retirement provision granted to the faculty because library salaries are not adequate to provide for old age and disability. In addition to compensating in part for lower salaries the retirement provision is a strong morale builder and it attracts a higher type of personnel to library work. In state colleges which have a retirement provision for the faculty, the librarians are usually included on the same basis as other employees of the college. In such a system the librarian makes a regular contribution to the retirement fund which is matched by the state. These contributions are credited to him with interest, and his own share, plus interest may be withdrawn in the event of a change in position or resignation. At the time the librarian retires, the sum of the contributions plus the accumulated interest serves as a basis for an annuity based on standard mortality tables. Some form of retirement allowance comparable to that above is in effect at various private institutions such as Antioch, Vassal and Lawrence, but the library staff is not always included. An excellent policy of its kind is offered through the American Library Association retirement plan in which individuals may participate jointly with the library or independently. McCrum points out the advantages of the Teachers' Insurance and Annuity Association of America plan, in which teachers and librarians contribute five per cent of their monthly salary, the college adds a like amount and the whole purchases an annuity at the retirement age."

Promotions, Service Ratings, Tenure, and Dismissal

Although the principles of promotions and dismissal, the methods of measuring personnel efficiency, and the regulations concerting tenure are well understood and applied in business and education, librarians in college libraries have shown remarkably little interest in such matters. At least very few studies have investigated the factors pertaining to these problems. The situation offers a challenge to practicing librarians and an opportunity to advanced students in library schools to make a worthwhile contribution to professional writing.

Promotions

Few college libraries have a definite programme of promotion. The number of positions available and the size of the personnel budget in the average college library are too small to provide for the advancement of staff members who are entitled to promotion on the basis of an excellent service record. Moreover, promotions in salary are all too frequently a matter of individual bargaining-- the librarian with the president for additional salary funds, and the staff members with the librarian for an increase in salary. When promotions in position are made, they are likely to occur as a result of a vacancy on the staff or the creation of a new position in the library. When it is impossible to advance a staff member in position or salary, it is sometimes possible to show recognition for good work by transferring the staff member to another position offering new experience, placing him in charge of a special experiment, giving him some supervisory duties, or putting him in charge of some general library activity.

However, there are objections to these makeshifts because they may detract from the success of the work that the staff member has been doing effectively and for which he is deserving of additional compensation or a promotion to a higher paid position. The policy of granting periodic increments in salary on the basis of efficiency, followed in some libraries, would greatly bolster staff morale and increase the effectiveness of library service if it were more widely adopted by colleges. The three municipal colleges of New York City, administered under the jurisdiction of the Municipal Civil Service Commission, have a definite salary schedule with mandatory increments for assistants in the beginning bracket.

Very few studies have investigated the facts pertaining to promotions in college libraries. In such evidence as the professional writings afford, it would appear that the following principles should govern the administration of promotions:

1. Promotions in position and salary should be made for reasons of merit and not on the basis of years in service. The merit principle is just, stimulates a high performance of work, and encourages the staff member to improve himself in service and through further preparation in order to be eligible for a higher position.
2. Promotions should be based on records of fitness such all service ratings and not alone on the individual judgment of the librarian.
3. When vacancies occur, careful consideration should

be given to the qualifications and experience of the present staff with a view to promoting a qualified person to the vacant position.

4. When new appointments are made to the junior levels of professional service, consideration should be given to persons whose qualifications and record seem likely to entitle them later to motion to more responsible positions.

Service Ratings

Service ratings of the library staff, when they exist at all, are usually informal and are based on the personal opinion of the librarian or the librarian in consultation with the immediate super visor of the staff member. One of the best definitions of the service rating is that given by J.B. Probst, who writes that it is generally "taken to mean the periodical measurement or appraisal of an employee's worth or value to his employer. . . A service rating properly embraces the factors of efficiency, character, and conduct. Some of the advantages of a service rating plan in the college library with a staff of sufficient size to warrant several departments are: (*i*) it assists supervisors in comparing the work of an assistant with the standards set up in the library, which is essential to a fair policy of promotion and salary increase; (*ii*) it i may indicate the need for transferring an assistant from one type of work to another; (*iii*) it helps to reveal weaknesses which can be corrected at the outset; (*iv*) it affords a just basis for dismissal if weaknesses are not corrected and if the assistant continues to do poor work; (*v*) it help's to discover staff talent and enables the librarian to assign special work to those persons who have special capacities; and (*vi*) it stimulates interest in self-improvement be-cause the ratings are impartial and are shown to and discussed with the staff member. Some limitations of a service rating plan fare: (*i*) it is difficult to rate personality, (*ii*) the raters may interpret the traits on the rating sheets differently, and (*iii*) the raters not be wholly aware of certain personal tendencies which colour their judgment of others.

The principles of constructing and using a service rating plan are summarized: by Miss Lucy Buker:

1. Ratings should be clear and simple.
2. Ratings should insure a fair appraisal of. the qualifications and work of each person.
3. Ratings should be uniform for those doing similar work.
4. Ratings should be made at regular intervals, but not too frequently to allow for change.
5. Ratings should be made by three raters when possible, or passed upon by a reviewing board.
6. Ratings which provide for an expression of the rater's opinion in his own words are of more value than those the rater checks or those in which standardized adjectives are called for.
7. Ratings should be confined to past or present accomplishment.
8. Each question should concern one quality only.
9. A general statement is often the most valuable part of a rating.
10. Unfavourable ratings should be followed up with definite suggestions for improvement.
11. Each rating should bear the signatures of the rater and of the department head, the date, and the name of the institution.

The usual frequency of rating is not more than once every six months and not less than once a year, with periodic cumulative records because these are more apt to be accurate than a single rating. Although there is some disagreement among librarians as to the desirability of discussing ratings with staff employees, this practice is recommended in good personnel procedure. Personnel experts say that friendly, informal discussion between each assistant and his supervisor provides the soundest basis for staff development. In 1943 Miss Marguerite Giezentanner constructed a service rating form for use in college and university libraries. The form lists seven factors on which an assistant is to be rated: (*i*) contract with people, (*ii*) understanding the job, (*iii*) quality of work, (*iv*) knowledge and use of books, (*v*) professional spirit, (*vi*) executive ability, and (*vii*) quantity of work.

Several factors are listed under each of these headings to help the rater make a fair appraisal. An example is given below:

1. *Contact with people*

Factors to consider:

1. Understanding of and interest in different types of people.
2. Friendly and helpful attitude toward students and faculty.
3. Courtesy, tact, poise, tolerance, good deportment.
4. Thoughtfulness of others.
5. Ability to get along with fellow workers.
6. Acceptance of criticism, suggestion.
7. Personal cleanliness; neatness, business-like appearance.
8. Pleasant voice, speech.

Rating: Exceptional---------; Above average----------; Average----

Below average----------; Poor--------

What should this staff member do to make her contacts with people more pleasant and advantageous?

Miss Giezentanner's service rating form has not been tested for reliability or validity. It is the only one specifically designed for college and university library use, however, and it will serve as a guide to college librarians in constructing their own forms until standardized rating scales have been devised for this purpose.

Tenure

The activities of the A.L.A. Board on salaries have contributed significantly to the improvement of most library personnel problems but have not shed much light on the problem of tenure College libraries will find some help in determining principles and practices of tenure in "The statement of principles, 1940, academic freedom and tenure" of the American Association of University Professors. In the absence of any specific library statement, the attempt is made here to suggest certain principles which should receive consideration in the operation of tenure regulations in the college library:

1. The purposes of tenure regulations should be stated. The primary aim would seem to be to retain able assistants and to eliminate the unfit.
2. The probationary period for the more responsible positions should extend beyond one year but should probably not exceed three years.
3. After the expiration of a probationary period library assistants should have permanent or continuous tenure on the same basis as other members of the faculty, and their services should be terminated only for adequate cause.
4. Tenure provisions for staff members below the rank of department heads should be carefully safeguarded. Tenure beyond a year's appointment for faculty members is usually accorded only to those with the rank of associate professor or higher,

but the instructor has more opportunity to advance to these ranks than the professional library assistant has to advance to a library rank where there may be equivalent regulations regarding tenure. There are only a I few top positions in any single library system and the turnover in these positions is quite small. Even if tenure is provided for the higher library ranks by virtue of the fact that they carry the equivalent faculty rank of associate professor or higher, the chances of a professional assistant reaching a top library position are comparatively remote.

In interpreting these principles, the following suggestions are offered as a basis of acceptable library practice:

1. The precise terms and conditions of every appointment should be stated in writing and be in the hands of the institution's officers and the staff member before the appointment is completed.
2. During the probationary period the staff member's work should be carefully studied and every effort should be made to develop his ability. Service ratings should be kept. Transfers from one position to another should be permitted if the staff men shows promise of doing better in another position than the one he entered.
3. After the probationary period, the proposed dismissal of a staff member on account of incompetency or neglect of duty should be preceded by a warning and specific statement in writing of defects. Sufficient time should be allowed for the staff member to seek a position elsewhere.
4. Staff members who do not desire to continue in their positional are responsible for giving at least a month's notice in writing their intention to resign.

Dismissal

The authority to nominate members of the library staff pre supposes the right to recommend their dismissal. Each of these powers is usually vested in the librarian. The major cause of dismissal has to do with factors affecting the efficiency and usefulness of the staff member. Continued incompetency to do the work assigned, continued criticism of and friction with fellow staff members, and violations of college rules and regulations are just cause for dismissal. It frequently happens that a young librarian, in his desire to secure a position, accepts an offer in which he is later unable to render the most efficient service. If the appointment were originally made on a temporary or probationary basis, this person should be dropped from the staff provided his services cannot be used in some other position in the library. In such cases the librarian has a moral obligation to help the staff member secure a new position and it is unfair to regard the separation from the service of the library as a case of dismissal.

REFERENCES

Bingham, W. Van Dyke and Moore, B. V. How to interview. 3d rev. ed New York, Harper, 1941.

Bishop, William Warner. The library's contribution to scholarship. In Kuhlman, A. F., ed. The development of university centers in the south. Nashville, Tenn., Peabody press, 1942, p. 17-32.

Buker, Lucy M. Service rating plans in public libraries. (Unpublished Master's thesis, School of Library Service, Columbia University, 1936).

Estes Rice. Faculty status in the city college libraries. Col. and research lib. 3:43-5, December, 1941.

Fay, Lucy E. The staff manual for the college library. A.L.A. bull. 31: 464-8, August, 1937.

Gapp, Kenneth S. The librarian's task in improving personnel. Col. and research Jib. 1:132-7, March, 1940.

Herbert, Clara W. Personnel administration in public libraries. Chic A.L.A., 1939.

Kraehenbuehl, John O. Lighting the library. Col. and research lib. 3: 231-6, June, 1941.

Maloy, Mrs. Miriam C. Faculty status of college librarians. A.L.A. bull 33:232-3, 302, April, 1939.

McAfee, Mildred H. The college library as seen by a college president Col. and research lib. 2:301-5, September, 1941.

McCrum, Blanche P. An estimate of standards for a college *library,* rev. ed Lexington, Va. Journalism laboratory press, Washington and Lee University, 1937. The staff: qualifications, education, status, p. 43-53.

Parker, R. H. Mechanical aids in college and university libraries. A.L.A. bull. 32:818-19, October 15, 1938.

Probst, J. B. Service ratings. Chicago, Bureau of personnel administration and the civil service assembly of the U.S. and Canada, 1931 (Technical bulletin no. 4).

Randall, William M. and Goodrich, Francis L. D. Principles of college library administration. 2d ed. Chicago, A.L.A. and the University of Chicago press, 1941. The library staff and its functions, p. 109-42.

Reece, Ernest. Programmes for library schools. New York, Columbia University press, 1943.

Richardson, Louise. Developing a college library staff. Col. and rescr lib. 1:322-5, September, 1940.

Timmerman, Hazel B. What vacations and" holidays do librarians allow? A.L.A. bull. 33:63-5, February, 1939.

6

Librarianship Education

Certain of the subjects are proper studies for librarians. This claim rests on what used to be called a philosophy of librarianship. There is no generally accepted 'philosophy' of this kind, and most librarians would accept that the term is not particularly helpful. However, it continues to be used and we should try to discover what is meant. The word 'philosophy' inevitably has many uses, and if we use it in the sense which implies a total systematic philosophy structure or system, existing as a thing in itself, then it is apparent that there can be no philosophy of librarianship. In education the position is the same, since philosophies of education derive from some other foundation or system of beliefs. If, however, we use the term in a different and more limited sense, which involves the pursuit of truth, or the setting up of principles as a guide to action, or the creation of theories which explain reality, then philosophy is necessary and inevitable, even if the word is not used. Everybody displays attitudes of some kind, even if these are not fully conscious, and these are the rudiments of theory, or an embryonic philosophy. The search for an adequate theoretical structure has in recent years became more important in the UK because of developments in library education.

Modern courses in librarianship, particularly when they are conducted at university level, require a theoretical foundation, firstly to provide a coherent pattern of study in each subject area and secondly to link the various studies together. Within the individual subjects considerable advances have been made: there is an adequate theory of classification, for example, and the principles of industrial management and administration can be applied to library organisation.

As was have already referred to the pragmatic British attitude to theory, although this pragmatism is really an embryonic theory in itself. There exists an assumption that many ideas may be perfectly sound, but that practice is something else. Proposals are 'all right in theory, but not in practice". There is a philistine belief that theories are a frivolous luxury which practical men cannot afford. It seems not to occur to those who hold this view that in many areas if the theory cannot correspond with practice, then the theory is wrong, inadequate, incomplete or incorrect. Behind this lies the feeling, perhaps inevitable in what is still to some extent a Christian culture, that there is bound to be a gap between the ideal and the real. This is indeed so, and if we pursue the matter we come up against a conflict between moral principles and scientific theories. This confusion is inherent in the social sciences because they deal with human institutions, human nature and human values. The theory and practice of librarianship are part of the social sciences, and library science is concerned with social processes, but these involve ethical principles and value judgement. It follows that some, probably an increasing proportion, of its practices are amendable to the application of true scientific principles, whereas others are not. We have stressed this problem because it is one more manifestation of the so-called two culture split, which must concern us all. In the sphere of religion and ethics we recognise that there is a gap between our aspirations and what we achieve. It is within this gap that the various kinds of hypocrisy flourish, and it is this area which the novelist primarily explores. But in the scientific realm, if a theory does not correspond to the facts it is false, and should be abandoned. The communist world is caught up in this dilemma, because the communists claim that Marxism is a science, so that when they commit crimes they have to be designated as 'errors'. The real error is, of course, to suggest that social life is wholly amenable to scientific or pseudo-scientific laws.

S.R. Ranganathan

The pioneer work has been done by Ranganathan, and his 'five laws' can be applied to all library studies. Because his approach is deductive and his laws seem simple to the point of absurdity, their value has been regularly underestimated or misunderstood in Anglo-Saxon countries where deductive theories are not usual. It is a fact that almost every aspect of modern librarianship can usefully be studied as part of one or other of these laws, and most deficiencies in library services can be shown to relate to a failure in observing them. From the teaching point of view, provided that the laws are satisfactorily applied to concrete situations (and this is a large proviso), the result can be an immense improvement on the vast jumble of disconnected facts which formerly passed as librarianship.

In spite of this achievement, there remain certain limitations and difficulties which should be noted. In the first place, as Ranganathan has himself admitted, these are not scientific but *moral* laws--even ideals. A moment's thought will make it apparent that in fact 'books are not for all', that many libraries are not 'growing organisms', that the appropriate reader is not found for every book, and so on. In other words, these are professional principles of conduct, or service ideals and the word 'science' is misleading. This inevitably limits the scope and range of the theory. It is also limited by the lack of a social context, although there are obvious sociological implications: for example, 'books are for all' assumes the desirability of total literacy, political democracy, and the emancipation of women. Those who consider, as we have considered in these pages, that socio-logical factors represent a fundamental part of the theory of librarianship, must therefore go beyond the five laws in order to identify or discuss these factors.

The Traditional View: One unsatisfactory element in librarianship has always been that it seem to be inevitably an adjunct of something else. It this is always so, then the limitations of its scope must be recognised. Professor Irwin, if I understand him correctly, has taken this view. For example, he states 'The librarian as such is neither a maker of history nor a maker of literature. He is an intermediary, whose only memorial lies in the books he preserves and the scholars who read them; his fate is to serve as the anonymous channel of recorded tradition. It is noteworthy that the librarians of former ages, if they are remembered at all, are always remembered for something other than librarianship.... If indeed there is one lesson that the history of libraries teaches us, it is that something over and above technical knowledge is needed to make the great librarian: a library cannot live on librarianship alone'. Here, at least at one point, Professor Irwin is stating that librarianship as such consists of 'technical knowledge' and that is all. If this view is correct, then there is little more to be said; that is the end of the matter--with the traditional custodial function of the librarian. I have tried to suggest in earlier chapters of this work that, while it is true that the librarian is an intermediary, he may also be in the modern world something more-- and that as soon as he starts to interpret the literature he is no longer merely a custodian. If this is the lesson that the history of libraries teaches us, then perhaps we should look at history again.

The Secular Missionaries: Many public librarians used in the past to regard themselves as agents in the struggle for popular education and enlightenment. This is the tradition implicit in the writings of L.R. McColvin, and in several official reports on public libraries in the UK, and explicit in Broadfield's book, *Philosophy of Librarianship*.

It reveals the application, or the attempted application, of nineteenth century liberal and 'progressive' ideals. The positive side of this approach was the missionary wish to spread enlightenment and high culture, so that these should no longer remain the privilege of the few. This often took the form of a generous desire to share a personal response to literature. Such an enthusiasm can be found in the writings of Lawrence Clark Powell, the American librarian and library educator.

Admirable though these professional ideals were, they are inadequate today because they do not easily relate to the characteristic of a so-called mass culture. It is noteworthy that modern statements are sometimes positively hostile to this outlook, and younger librarians now often feel that other people's tastes in literature should be left alone--who is to say that a personal response should have a general value? For example, P.H. Ennis in a passage quoted in chapter 13 (p. 241) concerning the cultural educational programme of the early twentieth century refers to a 'peculiar cultural imperialism'. He goes on to claim that this 'imperative' is no longer important, at least in the USA, because of the changed cultural situation. (It may be of some significance that Ennis is a sociologist and not a librarian.) The challenge facing modern cultural workers is not at all to increase the number of people who can appreciate traditional high culture, but rather to work out an appropriate role in a cultural context of an entirely different order. If the positive side of this progressive tradition produced librarians as cultural missionaries, the negative side was the twentieth century struggle for liberal values under attack from the enemies of freedom.

This concept should be preserved as an essential part of any modern view of librarianship, although a concentration on the fight against censorship and tyranny is not enough by itself, at least in societies which are relatively 'open'. Some would regard this liberal tradition as a religious hangover, or, more appropriately perhaps, as a Christian heresy, since it isolates one element in Christianity (the unique value of the individual) and ignores others Arnold Toynbee has described Marxism also as a Christian heresy, which in our context isolates the missionary spreading of the Word according to infallible secular authorities. This is, of course, why the socialist countries have well developed library services. But we cannot adopt there library 'philosophy', because we have taken the view that in closed societies librarianship in our sense cannot exist except as a travesty.

If there still remains a professional requirement to stress the importance of intellectual freedom, then this imperative should be restated in modern terms. For example, even within the realm of the information scientist it can be claimed that efficiency and progress are impossible if information services are not free, and if political or religious dogma obstruct the flow of communication. In the free world the secrecy is not due to direct political control, but arises from strategic considerations, or from the nature of competitive industry. Many have considered that advanced industrial states must eventually permit intellectual freedom in every field and on every level, partly because they cannot otherwise advance, and partly because universal education produces a large number of specialists and professional people who will not in the long run tolerate ideological control. The argument is that modern societies cannot exist without an intelligentsia--and that the information freedoms which become necessary will destroy dictatorships. This analysis is commonly applied to the Soviet Union, but there is not sufficient evidence for any safe predictions to be made. The key question is perhaps nor whether, but *when,* authoritarian controls will break down, since in many fields scientists can continue to operate independently of political processes, and information can flow freely for a long time within restricted and isolated areas, without necessarily affecting as a whole.

The Information Process

Both the practice and the theory of librarianship have become substantially modified by the development of special libraries, and the consequent emphasis on the information role and the techniques of information retrieval. As a result of this imposing new structure, with all its electronic devices, some have considered that it is in this world that the basic elements of a new theory of librarianship must be sought. This approach concentrates on the information process itself, without reference to the wider social and cultural issues which I have considered essential. D.J. Foskett's paper 'The creed of a librarian--no politics, no religion, no morals' can be taken as an excellent example of this attitude. Having stressed the need for a philosophy (by which Foskett means an appropriate professional set of ideals), he then goes on to say that in providing reference service for readers, the librarian can only do so effectively if he possess the quality of imaginative sympathy which will enable him 'to put himself in the reader's shoes', and to ignore his own prejudices, attitudes, opinions and beliefs--hence the title of the paper. This ability is undoubtedly a central professional requirement and it is one which is necessary in other callings, for instance teaching or the priesthood. The individual separates himself as a librarian from himself as a man, and there need be no conflict. Foskett points out that the core of professional purpose depends for its success on library organisation, on systems of classification and indexing and so forth. All this is indeed true and important, but there is a deliberate limitation in the scope of the enquiry, and the key questions remain unanswered.

We are suggesting that the real problem begins where this enquiry stops, and that we should explore the social implications of this particular ideal (which is really a creed for the individual considered as a professional worker, and not as a person who inevitably has social even professional (commitments) beyond the boundaries of the information process. The librarian, as librarian, provides information, but there may well be times when his convictions as a man will oblige him to ask 'What is the information for?'; (information is never an end in itself). And if the answer is that it is to be used for what the librarian as a man regards as totally evil purposes, then this indicates the real professional dilemma. Information has been defined as 'knowledge put to use', but if the librarian is indifferent to the nature of the use, he is not a man but a thing. There is a parallel with the moral responsibilities of the scientist whose research may result, for example, in improved methods of biological warfare. This was the dilemma of German liberal librarians during the Nazi period, and those who co-operated with the regime, for whatever reason, used this same argument that what they did or did not do as librarians had to be separated from their beliefs as men. The implication seems to be that a specialist can and should isolate his functions from other general human considerations. This is why the specialist provokes alarm and distrust, and the librarian should be the last person to submit to this form of intellectual betrayal. As we noted in another paper on professional ideals, the librarian, particularly in special libraries, is not a free agent, and the point we are making here is that a conflict may arise between the aims of an organisation and professional ideals in the sense which includes a commitment to a wider system of values. Ronald Staveley has made his own characteristic contribution to this discussion. In his paper 'Personal viewpoints', he notes that library philosophies rest on some foundation of general beliefs, and then goes on to discuss briefly the implications of certain well known systems of belief, such as humanism, existentialism, plantonism, pragmatism, logical positivism and Marxism.

He notes that a library 'philosophy' might derive inspiration from any of these, but it cannot be said that any general conclusions emerge from his survey, and the impression is left that perhaps we might hop about and collect something valuable from any or all of them. If most of us who reject and closed system of traditional beliefs were honest enough to admit it, it may be that this is what we habitually do, in the hope that the consequent hotch-potch will eventually add up to something coherent.

A 'philosophy' does emerge from Staveley's survey, it is precisely this same concentration on the personal relationship of the librarian and the 'client' and the message in the end is roughly similar to that of Foskett noted above.

The Communicators

Some librarians and some library school programmes have attempted to place theories and problems of communication at the centre of a theory of librarianship. In the considerable literature dealing with this subject, that part of it which concentrates on the communication process, is limited in the same way as is limited in the same way as is the theory of information retrieval. It has also become a specialism in itself, with its own jargon, so that nothing is communicated except to other communicators--and the conclusions reached, if any, have little relevance to librarianship as a whole.

Apart from this literature, however, there does exist a substantial body of work which deals with social communication problems in general, and with the need for social control of the communication media. Raymond Williams has repeatedly called for a 'Communication centre', and for an 'Institute of Communication research'. He has also insisted that communication should not be regarded as a secondary process, but as part of a primary struggle to learn, to educate and to understand. It is possible that the problem of communication does have this special importance, and if this is so, we should ask ourselves whether libraries and librarianship should be regarded as falling within this context. Those who write books about communication problems rarely mention libraries, and it is not difficult to discover why. Libraries are largely dependent on other cultural agencies: they do not originate communications, but transmit them.

Williams refers to the people who generate communication processes as the contributors. He then distinguishes four man kinds of contributor, *ie* the creative artist, the performer, the reporter, the commentator or critic. At first sight the librarian appears to be none of these. He has been referred to as a middleman, but if we examine the communications world we shall find that modern communications are full of middlemen who all have a part to play. The communication systems are networks which depend on the co-operation of a number of people. This is true of radio, the film, the press and television; they are all collective enterprises, and the four types of activity mentioned above are inextricably mixed together. Communication depends on large scale organisation, and libraries are indeed one of those organisations. Modern life is so complex, and the quantity of literature so appalling, that it requires a high degree of library and bibliographical organisation before literature can be effectively used. This has to be done not just in isolated places but on a national scale, and librarians, to use the late Barbara Kyle's words, have a duty 'to preserve knowledge so that none is lost, organise knowledge so that none is wasted, and make knowledge available so that no one need be deprived'. This task is formidable indeed, and it seems no longer appropriate to refer to agencies which successfully perform it as 'anonymous channels'.

The librarian does not write the literature in his library, but it must be organised before it can be read, and the information his library contains cannot be reached if he fails to produce it when required. In so doing he may have to evaluate it and interpret the available sources. To this extent libraries are part of the national communication process, and library studies must include an examination of communication problems in society. In other words, librarianship must adopt those elements in communication studies which are relevant and adapt them for its own use.

Sociology of Knowledge

We noted above that the alleged theoretical failures in Britain may arise because full time education for librarianship on an extensive scale is relatively recent. Yet if we turn to the United States where library education is half a century old we find a similar situation. Many years ago Pierce Butler lamented the poverty of theory in American librarianship: more recently Jesse Shera, in the essays collected in *Libraries and the organisation of knowledge,* linked this weakness with the pragmatic tradition and the American predilection for useful knowledge, and a 'democratic' hostility to philosophy. Shera has attempted to provide a theoretical foundation by insisting that the core of professional studies must be sought in the sphere of epistemology or, she called it (in his earlier work with Margaret Egan *Bibliographic organisation*), social epistemology. This is a substantial contribution and the current preoccupation with the 'fluid' state of the structure of knowledge has increased its importance. For example, Kenneth Boulding in *The Image* (1956) claims that the problem of 'knowledge', or what he calls our 'image' of the world, is of fundamental importance because 'we are in the midst, or perhaps only at the beginning, of a profound reorganisation of the departmental structure of knowledge and of academic life.... There is something abroad which might be called interdisciplinary movement'. Because, *inter alia,* of the *growth* of knowledge he draws the comforting conclusion that we must examine he process of education from the point of view of what is the *minimum* knowledge which must be transmitted. The student has usually operated on the principle of knowing as little as he can get away with.

Shera states that the two fundamental questions for librarians are: (1) What is knowledge?; (2) How is it put to work? In my own case I was influenced by similar considerations in *Bibliography and the Provision of Books,* but the work suffers because it is limited to the second question above, *ie* I was concerned with social processes and the barriers to the free flow of information, without reference to the structure of knowledge itself. It may well be that this limitation came about because the approach was in the first instance bibliographical whereas Shera has always rightly insisted that *classification* studies should provide the basis for bibliographic organisation. This is most important, particularly when one considers the still prevalent tendency to study reference material without an adequate link with the classification techniques which are inherent in information retrieval. At first sight knowledge about knowledge may seem 'academic' in the old fashioned and useless sense, but this theoretical construct should provide a foundation for improved techniques of information retrieval. The practical application is possible, but the results remain within the realm of *method* or technique. The wider social context is missing, and it is this which is essential if we are thinking (as we are here) of aims, purpose or goals. Information retrieval is a means, not an end. The theoretical framework (quite properly) is constructed of concepts, not precepts; ideas not ideals. (In the case of the secular missionaries these missing components *are* present.) It may well be that a true sociology of knowledge should provide this context, but my impression is that as an academic discipline this study has developed very little.

To return to Shera's formula, it seems to me that the subject of our enquiry is not only 'what is knowledge?' and 'how is it put to work?' but also *'for what purpose?'* Without this third element our 'philosophy' cannot be a guide to action, and in a vocational education this is that is required. (Ranganathan would affirm that his 'five laws' provide the answer to the third question, and that in studying the first and the second question we are learning how to obey the laws. He often writes as if they were eternal entities who become distressed when they are not obeyed!) It is perhaps Shera's deliberate exclusion of social values which gives his writing an almost sinister lucidity. For instance, an emphasising the importance of the search for order as a basic psychological need he refers to 'pattern seeking' in the sciences and 'pattern making in the arts as if these were identical activities: the wider cultural implications are not considered.

With regard to education for librarianship, the study of the structure of knowledge can certainly be regarded as part of an essential core. But as Shera himself admits, 'Librarianship is a composite of many disciplines'. It all depends on what one means by a 'core', and whether a 'composite core' is a nonsense thing. One is obliged to conclude that the theoretical foundations of librarianship are weak, not because of the limitations of library education or because of the Anglo-American anti-metaphysical tradition, but because there are certain unresolved and possibly inherent contradictions. Shera says 'one cannot remember Chaos', but one may have to live with it most of the time. Or, to be more precise, we can often construct orderly patterns only by the evasion of too many realities.

Improvement of Librarians

The improvement of the staff member in service quite naturally depends upon other factors than the natural ability of the individual. It depends upon the amount and quality of his training, upon his experience, upon his orientation to the library and the position in which he finds himself, upon his attitude toward his work while employed, and upon the possibility of additional academic and professional training. Because library staffs and salaries in most colleges are small, the opportunities for additional training may be less attractive to the staff member than the opportunities which a progressive library administration finds for stimulating growth with-in the service of the library.

There are a number of administrative plans for developing the ability and usefulness of staff members in service.

Some of these plans are discussed in the following paragraphs.

Orientation of the New Staff Member

This has already been touched upon in the discussion of the selection of library personnel. In any progressive library programme, fan essential feature is the practice of acquainting the new staff member with the policies of the college and of the library, with the general layout and special features of the library, and with the functions in the particular division of the library in which the new staff member will work. An important part of this induction plan is the emphasis which the librarian places upon the educational function of the library. An effort is made to give each newcomer an understanding of the proper approach towards aiding students in a way that will be educationally significant. The librarian also indicates clearly what the new staff member may expect in supervision. He sees to it that the new staff member familiarizes himself with the staff or divisional manual and with other published library instructions and guides. As a rule the new assistant in the college library is chosen for a particular position. But if he fails to make a proper adjustment to this position, an effort is made to place him in work where he will render the most efficient service for the good of the library. Whenever possible, the new employee is given some opportunity for experience in all or most divisions to the library's work, even though this may not last beyond an orientation period. The knowledge of what goes on in each phase of the library programme is indispensable to good service in any one branch.

Staff Manual

A simple method for making known the policies and practice in a large college library is essential for effective service. It is for this reason that many college libraries codify their policies and practices for staff use in what is commonly known as a staff manual. From inquiries sent to two hundred and forty-four college and university libraries, Wilson and Tauber found that forty per cent prepared and used a staff manual. Although their study confirmed what one would expect, namely, that the staff manual is most useful in the large college library where there is a considerable turnover in professional and clerical positions, they discovered that "in many of the smaller libraries, the staffs of which often consist of a single professional worker, such manuals are indispensable media of instruction for a constantly changing body of student workers." They found, also, that the size of the library is not the only factor of importance. Staff manuals were found useful where library practice varied from the standard codes and manuals, where student help was used to a large extent, and where members of the staff were frequently rotated from one position to another in a particular library.

As a device for improving librarians in service, the staff manual has three main functions:

1. It introduces the new staff member to the library's policies and to the specific duties in the division of service in which he will serve. It fixes and promotes thoroughness. Failure to follow library practices carefully and accurately cannot be excused with the statement, "I was not told about it."
2. It assists a staff member to broaden his point of view. It not only introduces him to the work in all departments of the library, but it stresses the

educational objectives of the library and the proper professional attitude necessary to attain these objectives.

3. The preparation of the manual is usually a cooperative affair. In preparation, it affords an opportunity for experienced members of the to systematize and organize their work more effectively, to refine perceives to eliminate duplication of duties, and to determine responsibility.

As an administrative device for improving the service of the library, the staff manual:

1. Promotes efficiency by insuring a proper sequence of work, by securing uniform procedures in routine, and by improving administrative organization.
2. Provides an effective medium for interpreting the library to the administration and the faculty.

Not all librarians agree that staff manuals are important in library management or worth the effort they take to compile. Wilson and Tauber found that some librarians objected to manuals because they tended to "crystallize action and thought," permitting "little freedom of expression of a professional attitude;" others said that manuals were expensive and took too much time to prepare in relation to their worth; and still others felt that there were acceptable institutes which were simple and effective. There can be no question that the compilation of a staff manual is time-consuming, but no substitute will prove quite so satisfactory or efficient. Ordinarily, staff manuals do not prescribe the action of the professional assistant as the instructional phases of his work where individual judgment and responsibility are most important. The essential aim in a staff manual is to eliminate mere personal opinion in routines and in technical detail, to make sure that all elements of library efficiency have been given proper consideration and weight in the formation of a final judgment, and to insure that rules, regulations, and practices are based on a sure foundation of facts and sound educational principles. There will always be opportunity for individual initiative on the part of the staff member if the administration of the library is enlightened and effective.

Staff manuals are generally of two types, the general manual and the departmental manual. The general manual deals with policies and practices in the library as a whole. It is intended to give the new assistant a fundamental background knowledge of the library its policies, internal organization and clientele, and particularly to inform him of his responsibilities and privileges as a member the staff. The departmental manual, which is sometimes combined with the general manual, contains concrete and specific information about the work of the department in question, the relation of the department to other departments, and the way in which the work is carried on in the department. College libraries are more likely in compile general manuals and, in the small libraries, these are particularly designed for student assistant use. Antioch, Kenyo Floor Stone Mather, Wheaton, and Lawrence colleges have typical general manuals; Birmingham-Southern, Bowdoin, and Swarthmore have manuals for student use. 'The nature of information contained in a general manual is illustrated in the following outline, prepared by Miss Lucy E. Fay:

Manuals are not static instruments of managerial instruction; revision will be found necessary and desirable. For this reason, it is best to prepare and publish the manual in some simple, inexpensive manner with provision for revisions. A typescript, loose-leaf form is best for the first edition and one copy should be available for each department of the library's work. In subsequent revisions it is desirable to mimeograph the manual so that copies may be made to other libraries and to library schools.

Staff Meetings

The typical library staff meeting has a two-fold function, namely, to facilitate the general administration of the library and to improve the librarians in service. Unfortunately, as one writer has pointed out, it is used primarily for the discussion of administrative detail and only secondarily has attention been given to the improvement of librarians in service.

The staff meeting provides an opportunity for the exchange of ideas on procedures, services, and problems as they arise. For their reason, it is desirable to hold regular meetings, not less often that once a month, and to arrange a time when all staff members, can be present. In the medium-sized and large college library, it may be possible to use library time for the meeting, arranging the schedule so that only one or two members are absent on regular duty, and providing for a rotation, of work so that all members have an opportunity to attend most of the meetings. In one library the staff meets at a monthly luncheon meeting and follows this with an hour of business or discussion. The officers consist of a chairman and a secretary, and minutes are kept for official purposes as well as to acquaint those who were unable to attend with the plans and decisions agreed upon at the meetings. In the last analysis, of course the time and scheduling of staff meetings is entirely dependent upon the administrative policy of the library and upon the local conditions in each college. Aside from its value in providing an opportunity for a free exchange of ideas on current problems of library administration and routine, the staff meeting furnishes the logical means for introducing new plans and procedures before they go into effect. The good administrator is interested in the promotion of staff discussion of all aspects of a problem, in the development of all points of view so that out of the exchange of ideas and convictions the very best plans will be adopted and perfected.

Such discussions not only provide a balanced consideration of all facts before decisions art made, but promote interest and *esprit de corps.* If the staff meeting is to be truly effective as a means of improving librarians in service, it must concern itself with something more than the work staff members are doing every day and how they are doing it.

Kenneth Gapp stresses the importance of using the staff meeting for a critical approach to librarianship. He points out that librarians have not yet formulated clearly a philosophy of librarianship in terms of educational objectives and corresponding activities. "The discussion with the staff of the main advances in professional research, of the development of techniques, of policy and of educational objectives keeps alive interest in the newer phases of library service." Another writer emphasizes the necessity for familiarity with the literature of particular subjects taught in the college. Miss Ann Messick's account of her experiments at the Colorado State College of Agriculture shows the advantages and difficulties of conducting staff meetings as a seminar for the discussion and report of the literature of subject fields." Mr. Julian Fowler carries her plan a step further and suggests several small staff seminars, instead of one general meeting, with staff members who are taking courses in the college serving as leaders of discussion. In some colleges members of the faculty are invited to speak It the library staff meetings on recent developments in their fields because it is felt that the staff can better fit itself to serve and cooperate with the faculty when it knows the various activities in the teaching departments. Another plan is for the staff to select, by common consent, some topic or subject for study which is department to the colleges and libraries in question. A given problem is studied for the greater part of the semester or year, or until sufficient time has been provided for real knowledge and understanding. The study of the problem is approached from the point of view of both theory and practice. For example, the improvement teaching through library service or the very practical problem of micophotography in the college library are representative topics. Assignments should be made and reports should be given at the meetings.

The Continuing Education of Librarians

Inadequate salaries, a fixed schedule of relatively long hours, and an unwise overloading and distribution of duties are three obstacles to the continuing education of the library staff. There is a fourth Even under the best of conditions, librarianship has a tendency to become routine and stale. There is routine work even in duties which are predominantly professional, and a great deal more of it in work that goes on behind the scenes. There is the ever present danger that the experienced non-progressive staff member, having adjusted himself to these conditions, will see the routines as ends in themselves and will be satisfied so long as his work; moves smoothly. In the good college, there is a continual challenge to the librarian and the staff to make the library an ever growing factor of importance in instruction. The librarian cannot meet this challenge if he permits himself or his staff to become too preoccupied with routine work. The librarian and staff must continue to grow with the college. Unless they are constantly on the alert mentally and imaginatively, they will not be able to develop a type of library service which is effective in teaching.

The college educational programme is undergoing change at all times, and the library must adapt itself to these changes. "Continuing education," therefore, is 2 phrase significant to the librarian and the library staff. It should be emphasized at the outset that it is the librarian's responsibility to encourage the staff to improve itself. If he fails to do this, it is rather certain that only a limited number of people will make the effort.

Informal Methods of Continuing Education: The informal self-education programme of the library staff consists in the main of reading, attendance at every kind of real cultural entertainment, such as lecture and music programmes, and personal and professional meeting Each of these is discussed briefly in the following paragraphs.

The importance of wide reading in professional and educational journals and books requires no special comment. It is probably true that members of the staff do not keep up with their professional literature as well or as broadly as they should. Some devices such as the routing of books and journals to each staff member, the allowance of library time for at least an hour of professional reading a week, and the provision for the discussion of professional literature at staff meetings have been found useful in stimulating professional reading. Staff reading should not, of course, be confined to professional and educational writings. If one is to work in a college, he ought to read widely enough and deeply enough so that he may talk intelligently with faculty members in their own field and gain something from them as well as contribute to them. Mr. Julian S. Fowler and Miss Louise Richardson in separate articles have each voiced the views of many librarians in emphasizing the importance of reading systematically in the literature of subject fields. Dr. Hurt has suggested a useful outline for carrying out such a reading programme and his suggestions, stated briefly, are these: (*i*) secure a topical outline of the subject content of the field; (*ii*) give brief consideration to the principal encyclopaedic works; (*iii*) locate and examine all guides to the literature of the field; (*iv*) prepare a basic list of textbooks and other general works devoted to the entire field and examine some of the outstanding titles; (*v*) make a similar study of the books and monographs devoted to special phases of the subject; (*vi*) give attention to the sources of printed materials, i.e. the learned societies, institutions, agencies, and individuals responsible for the production of the best publications, in the field; (*vii*) become familiar with the periodical literature and serial publications; (*viii*) consider the pamphlets and ephemeral material; (*ix*) make a thorough study of the reference books; (*x*) note the related fields having publications of interest; and (It) learn the trends of research. If a member of the staff is interested in writing and speaking, he should be encouraged to do so even if this entails some release from scheduled desk duties. When a person writes or speaks, he submits h*is* own powers of thinking and reasoning to an examination by others or to a test by those who are presumably competent to judge If *he* encounters criticism, he learns from that: if his work is accepted it gives him incentive and an *invigorating* pleasure in his work as a whole. As a group, librarians are not as much interested in speaking and writing as the members of some other professions and the obligation to speak and write is certainly less than that of the professor. There is very little time after the day's work to do much in the way of preparing papers or speeches. If a staff member has a natural bent for speaking or writing, he should be encouraged; if not, it is unwise that he should be placed in the position where he feels he has to do either because of administrative pressure. There are other opportunities for cultural improvement, more personal and recreative, such as attending the lecture and music programmes sponsored by the college or by organizations in the community. If desk schedules conflict, some changes should be made so that the same people are not repeatedly barred from enjoying these cultural opportunities. Active participation in local, state, and national library meetings and inspection visits to other libraries are encouraged as one of the best means of improving staff performance and stimulating fur study. The mutual discussion of problems which takes place at these meetings enables the staff member to visualize current practice prevents staleness, and provides that continuous knowledge of what is being done, which is so vital to a broad and progressive professional viewpoint.

The meetings encourage staff members to continue, their academic and professional training because, as Miss

McCrum points out, "it is at such meetings that news of grants-in-aid, scholarships, research funds, and national and state projects of benefit to libraries are announced." Membership in learned and educational organizations may be of equal importance, particularly to the librarian, because such bodies afford stimulating contacts and opportunities for the librarian to contribute to the broader group. A more detailed account of the librarian's relations to professional. Visits to other libraries provide opportunities for studying specific problems in actual practice and afford interesting and valuable contacts. In centrast to these off-campus activities, some librarians favour the participation of the staff in departmental and committee meetings of the faculty because of the opportunity it affords to correlate the services of the library with the new demands in instruction and research.

Formal Study on Campus: Continued formal study, in service and during leaves of absence, is an important source of refreshment; reinvigoration. Fowler points out the necessity for "applying to the enrichment of library service, the academic training that is at hand." He suggests a rotation programme of study which would permit selected and qualified members of the staff to pursue advanced courses in fields in which they are interested without curbing the efficiency of library service as a whole. He further proposes that these staff members act as leaders in staff seminar discussions on the subjects they are studying in order that the whole staff may share in the benefits of the current programme. Whether this particular plan will work or not depends on local conditions in each institution and in each library, but it is generally recognized that the plan of encouraging staff members to take courses while in service is one of the methods for keeping the staff intellectually competent. It enables the staff member to remove deficiencies in his own under-graduate training, it broadens his point of view and deepens his knowledge, and he relearns a good many things about assignments the approach of the particular instructor which will enable him to improve library service to instruction.

Mr. Fowler rightly warns any such programme requires careful planning on the part of the librarian in order to distribute both the load and the benefits to different intellectual fields as well as to different departments of the library.

In some colleges provision is made for staff members to take courses up to a definite maximum limit of units or course hours each semester with or without being excused from library duties for attendance at classes. In certain instances there are special inducements in the way of reduced fees for courses. Significant practices in twenty-six state universities are admirably summarized in the University of Washington staff association survey from which the following is quoted:

> While the twenty-six institutions give opportunity for graduate study for credit, only one exempts all fees, while fifteen other levy, under varying conditions, special rates for librarians. Librarians of the Oregon State systems have full faculty standing and consequently have the benefit of greatly reduced fees for courses. . .. Sixteen universities make no charge whatsoever for taking courses without credit, thus permitting students who do not desire advanced degrees to continue to work along lines of special interest. All but six institutions allow unrestricted selection of courses.

Leaves of Absence for Study : Most college libraries grant leave of absence to staff members, though usually without pay, to provide opportunity for advanced study at professional library schools or large universities after service has begun. From an examination of the practices in two hundred and fifty college and university libraries in 1939, Miss Irene Smith found that:

1. Fifteen give their staffs leave with pay for study, in time varying from two weeks to a year.
2. Several grant a similar privilege on half salary.

3. Only two report that the library staff enjoys sabbatical leaves equal to those conferred on the faculty.
4. About sixty allow leaves without pay for study.

A few libraries provide a sabbatical for staff members, after five, ten or fifteen years of service, though rarely is this comparable in either time or compensation to the sabbaticals awarded to the teaching faculty. Nevertheless these sabbaticals, ranging from a week to an extra month of additional vacation, offer an invaluable opportunity for study or travel. The latest figures reported to. At American Library Association on sabbatical leaves for college librarians are summarized.

In summarizing, it is apparent that the inducements, financial and otherwise, are not markedly favourable in present library practice to the encouragement of further study. The person who is possessed of initiative, originality, and an inquiring spirit will take education periods for summer school study and attendance at institutes, but the majority will not attempt to secure additional training under present conditions. Salary schedules are too low to encourage leaves of absence without pay, and too few libraries are sufficiently well-staffed to permit absences from regular duties. On the other hand, the opportunities for educational and professional development are more abundant than they ever were before. In the professional field, to cite but one example, there are the excellent summer institutes held by the Graduate Library School of the University of Chicago. Although fellowships and grants-in-aid for advanced professional study are not as great as in certain other subject fields, they are increasing in number.

Ethical Relations of Librarians

The rapid development of library service and the consequent increase in the library personnel have served to call attention to the duties and obligations of librarians.

Librarians in their working relations are not isolated individuals; they have professional problems in common which can be met most satisfactorily in a professional way. Because of this fact, they have developed a national professional association which has attempted to raise not only the level of professional competency and to improve working conditions for librarians but also to define the duties and obligations of its members toward the library governing authority, toward the community and society, toward the library profession, and toward one other.

The first practical suggestions for a code were made in an ad-dress to the Illinois Library Association in April, 1903 by Miss Mary Plummer. By 1929 the American Library Association had drawn up suggestions for ethical relationships governing the conduct of the librarian in his work and profession, and these were officially adopted in a code in 1938.

Code of Ethics Adopted by the American Library Association

Preamble: 1. The library as an institution exists for the benefit of I given constituency, whether it be the citizens of a community, members of an educational institution, or some larger or more specialized group, those who enter the library profession assume an obligation to maintain ethical standards of behaviour in relation to the governing authority under which they work, to the library constituency, to the library as an institution and to fellow workers on the staff, to other members of the library profession, and to society in general, 2. The term librarian in this code applies to any person who is employed by a library to do work that is recognized to be professional in character according to standards established by the American Library Association. 3. This code sets forth principles of ethical behaviour for the professional librarian. It is not a declaration of prerogatives not a statement of recommended practices in specific situations.

The code applies specifically to all aspects of college library work and to all members of the library staff, a fact which is some-times overlooked by those who think of ethical codes simply is terms of staff relationships to the public at the charging desk. This fact is clearly stated in the code. It emphasizes that librarians can-not act as isolated individuals in their work. The library is interpreted by their actions. They belong to a class which has professional problems which must be met in a professional way.

I. *Relation of the Librarian to the Governing Authority* 4 : The librarian should perform his duties with realization of the fact that final jurisdiction over the administration of the library rest in the officially constituted governing authority. This authority may be vested in a designated individual, or in a group such committee or board. 5. The chief librarian should keep the governing authority informed on professional standards and progressive action. Each librarian should be responsible for carrying out the policies of the governing authority and its appointed executives with a spirit of loyalty to the library. 6. The chief librarian should interpret decisions of the governing authority to the staff, and should act as liaison officer in maintaining friendly relations between staff members and those in authority. 7. Re-commendations to the governing authority for the appointment', of a staff member should be made by the chief librarian solely upon the basis of the candidate's professional and personal qualifications for the position. Continuance in service and promotion should depend upon the quality of performance, following a definite and known policy. Whenever the good of the service requires a change in personnel, timely warning should be given. If desirable adjustment cannot be made, unsatisfactory service should be terminated in accordance with the policy of the library and the rules of tenure. 8. Resolutions, petitions, and requests of a staff organization or group should be submitted through a duly appointed representative to the chief librarian. If a mutually satisfactory solution cannot be reached, the chief librarian, on request of the staff, should transmit the matter to the governing authority. The staff may further request that they be allowed to send a representative to the governing authority, in order to present their opinions in person.

This section of the code establishes the relationship of the collibrarian to the chief administrative officer of the college and to the board of trustees. Certain of the suggestions are more directly applicable to the large college or university library, such as those pertaining to staff resolutions. In general, however, it places the appointment of the staff squarely on a basis of merit and relieves the librarian from pressure to 'make nominations for appointments by interested parties. It should perhaps be mentioned that the librarian and the staff of state colleges are employees of the state and are therefore subject to state laws. The laws of each state have a section devoted to the conduct of public officers, and the regulations therein should be known to the librarian and to members of the library staff.

II. *Relation of the Librarian to his Constituency.* 9 : The chief librarian, aided by staff members in touch with the constituency, should study the present and future needs of the library, and should acquire materials on the basis of those needs. Provision should be made for as wide a range of publications and as varied a representation of viewpoints as is consistent with the policies of the library and with the funds available. 10. It is the librarian's responsibility to make the resources and services of the library known to its potential users. Impartial service should be rendered to all who are entitled to use the library. 11. It is the librarian's obligation to treat as confidential any private information obtained through contact with library patrons. 12. The librarian should try to protect library property and to inculcate in users a sense of their responsibility for its preservation.

This section of the code applies particularly to public lib and in reality lays the foundation for a sound programme of public relations in public library work. The general features of the come however, apply equally well to college libraries, and it cannot be stated too emphatically that "impartial service" is a factor of great importance in effective relationships with students and faculty. It; is probably one of the standards which is most frequently violated intentionally or inadvertently, by college librarians. The impartial enforcement of rules and regulations and the safeguarding of students' privileges as regards new books which may be secured or held out by faculty members comes under this heading. The library staff members are the interpreters of the library to faculty and students, and therefore all users should be given impartial and fair treatment in getting what they need.

III. *Relations of the Librarian within the Library.* 13 : The chief librarian should delegate authority, encourage a sense of responsibility and initiative on the part of staff members, provide for their professional development, and appreciate good work. Staff members should be informed of the duties of their positions and the policies and problems of the library. 14. Loyalty to fellow workers and a spirit of courteous cooperation, whether between individuals or between departments, are essential to effective library service. 15. Criticism of library policies, service, personnel should be offered only to the proper authority for the sole purpose of improvement of the library. 16. Acceptance of position in a library incurs an obligation to remain long enough to repay the library for the expense incident to adjustment. A contract signed or agreement made should be adhered to faithfully until it expires or is dissolved by mutual consent. 17. Resignations should be made long enough before they are to take effect to allow adequate time for the work to be put in shape and a successor appointed. 18. A librarian should never enter into a business dealing on behalf of the library which will result in personal profit. 19. A librarian should never turn the library resources to personal use, to the detriment of services which the library renders to its patrons.

On the subject of the librarian's relation to the staff, nothing more need be said since the principles set forth above are obvious even though at times the practice may be difficult. Consideration for staff members is not only an obvious moral duty, it is also the best way to promote the efficiency of library service. Fewer conflicts will result if members of the staff are kept fully informed regarding events in the college and in the library so far as they contribute to the library's welfare. The fundamental point in staff relations to the librarian and to each other is that the interests of the library should be placed above personal interest. It follows from this that criticism of library policy should be curbed unless it is actuated by a sincere desire to further the library's welfare, that criticism of library practice should be made to the one next higher in authority, that personal criticism of one's library or teaching colleagues should be avoided, and that the provisions of the code as they relate to job responsibility, changes in position, and resignations should be adhered to strictly. The staff member must bear in mind that it is not personal gain but opportunity for service which makes librarianship a profession, and no such service should be considered in the light only of its value as a stepping-stone. Three things which young and new assistants should be particularly careful to avoid are intolerance in expression of opinion, a seeming or real resentment to criticism by superiors, and an unwillingness to share in occasional overtime work or some of the less attractive assignments. Courtesy, impartiality, and self-control are essential in dealing with users of library.

IV. *Relation of the Librarian to his Profession.* 20 : Librarians should recognize librarianship as an educational profession and realize that the growing effectiveness of their service is dependent upon their own development. 21. In view of the importance of ability and personality in library work, a librarian should encourage only those persons with suitable aptitudes to enter the library profession and should discourage the continuance in service of the unfit. 22. Recommendations should be confidential and should be fair to the candidate and the prospective employer by presenting an únbiased statement of strong and weak points. 23. Librarians should have a sincere belief and a critical interest in the library profession. They should endeavour to achieve and maintain adequate salaries and proper working conditions. 24. Formal appraisal of the policies or practices of another library should be given only upon the invitation of that library's governing authority or chief librarian. 25. Librarians, in recognizing the essential unity of their profession, should have membership in .library organizations and should be ready to attend and participate in library meetings and conferences.

The efforts of librarians to secure academic status on

their own campuses and to secure recognition of librarianship as a profession co-equal to that of teaching is evidence enough of the importance of: the standards set forth in this section of the code. On the one hand college librarians have the obligation and the opportunity to recruit the very best students from their own clientele for the library profession. On the other hand, they have, as accepted members of the library profession, the obligation to increase the prestige and the, standing of their profession to the best of their constructive ability They cannot hope to do this without adequate and frequent academic and professional training, participation in the intellectual activities of the college, familiarity with current professional and educational writings, and active membership in professional organizations.

Summing Up

It appears from what we have said above that what is required is a new integration incorporating the various elements we have attempted to isolate--a combination of traditional custodial principles, the missionary approach and the rationale of a personal reference service. All this would need to be seen against the background of modern communication problems. Certain themes are constant, and one of them is the importance of background social and cultural studies for librarianship. We have implied that our professional attitudes inevitably rest on personal interpretations of the nature of modern culture. A key question we have asked is whether the librarian should regard himself mainly as the custodian of traditional high culture, and we have answered it in the negative. To some extent, therefore, this book may be regarded as an apologia for prop culture. The interference is that the librarian should be wholly responsive to the modern predicament, and in this role he cannot afford to become a 'square'.

Another assumption which has been present here is that the librarian should seek to be an intellectual, in the sense that the word is commonly understood in Britain. It might be thought that this is self evident and unworthy of discussion, but many of our colleagues go out of their way to repudiate such a suggestion as though it might contain some attack on their integrity as public and responsible persons. As stated here, this is not simply the traditional plea that the librarian should be a 'bookman', or a scholar, but that he has certain cultural responsibilities.

An uneasy awareness of the differences between science and the arts, and their implications for librarianship. The techniques and professional processes involved in all forms of librarianship are the same. In this specific paper, we can repeat that assertion only with a number of provision. The emphasis of Foskett and Staveley mentioned above (and indeed many others) is surely the right one *as far as it goes.* If, therefore, we regard personal reference service as the key professional activity, the main problem is whether the growth of automation and specialisation in science will result in retrieval processes which are different in kind from those employed in the humanities. It is perhaps too early to answer this question with total confidence, but there are new trends developing which may be more significant than is generally appreciated. It has been claimed that in both fields, because the growth points in modern knowledge develop *between* traditional disciplines, the librarian will become increasingly important as an integrating agent. This implies that in science his role will remain decisive, whatever the machines may do in the retrieval of *facts.* It implies also that in the humanities new types of reference service must be evolved. Already valuable work has been reported in some organisations and institutions. However, this work is certainly not yet typical, and it is significant that it is being done in colleges which are directly educational.

The common element, therefore, in both science and the arts, is that the librarian's role is not simply to supply *information* in response to particularly requests, or to make available material for those who require it, or to fill in gaps, but to *provide the connections.* If those who prefer a more precise statement would ask *'what* connections?', the answer can only be that if we knew what connections are required there would be no need to make them. 'Insights' in the humanities cannot be planned or plotted, and the research scientist does not usually know what he is looking for. It is this which makes the library activity at its highest level worthwhile. Needless to say, there are other types of library work, and these are what they have always been except insofar as the machines are taking over. Having agreed with those who stress personal reference service, we would also wish to add that this element by itself is clearly not enough, if we are thinking in terms of a satisfactory set of ideals. It is surely significant that those librarians who make a positive contribution in the field of reference service are motivated by something more than the wish to do a job well.

It is here that we return to the missionary role, which involves the wider considerations that we have constantly stressed. Why in fact should anyone bother with the higher librarianship? Possibly the answer must be individual, and for some their religious beliefs would be relevant. Our own personal bias probably derives from attitudes which might be called 'existentialist' in a non-philosophical sense. Among these attitudes which are relevant to librarianship is a belief in the importance of total 'awareness', both with regard to the self and the world. Relevant also is a distrust of 'objective' abstractions and an insistence on an appreciation of unique circumstances. Such an understanding recognises that theoretical formulations about life or the 'problem' of living are irrelevant if they ignore subjective or inner realities. This attitude is valuable with regard to the reference role of the librarian, since he must deal with a series of unique information problems, and the subjective realities partly reside in the personality of the reader who requires assistance, and of the librarian who supplies it. The key factor is the personal relationship. Beyond all this, the viewpoint reflected in these papers is humanistic in the broad sense, which means nothing very precise except that it implies some kind of faith that in the long run the growth of human knowledge *may* help to modify the human condition for better rather than for worse. Like all worthwhile beliefs, this must be held without reference to the evidence, and if it is not held it is difficult to see why anyone should want to be a librarian at all. At the same time, even if, we reject view that the librarian, as well as his library network, is merely a kind of pipeline, it is as well that our professional claims should recognise the appropriate limits. Librarianship is not a way of life, and those who attempt to make it so become half, or non, persons. It has often been remarked that official professional statements about library ideals are too far removed from what actually happens in libraries. In the same way the 'idealism' of library schools leaves students unprepared for what they eventually face in work situations.

REFERENCES

Brumbaugh. Aaron J. Accrediting associations and the college library. Col. and research lib. 2:206-10. 276, June, 1941.

Butts. R. F. The college charts its course. New York, McGraw-Hili 1939.

Gerould, J. T. The college library building, its planning and equipment. New York. Scribner, 1932.

Gourley', James E. and Mohrhardt, Foster E. Teachers college libraries. Wil. lib. bull. 14:662-3, May, 1940.

Lester, Robert M. Development of junior college libraries. New York, printed for the information of the Trustees, 1937; *also in* Junior col. jour. 8:3-9, October, 1937. Includes Carnegie standards for junior college libraries.

Little, G. T. School and college libraries. *In* Dewey, Melvil, ed. Papers prepared for the World's library congress held at the Columbian exposition. Washington, Government printing office, 1896, p. 916-33 (U.S. Bureau of education, Report of Commissioner of education for 1892-93).

McEwen, Robert W. The North central association's 1943 survey of college and university libraries. Col. and research lib. 4:253-6, June, 1943.

McGrath, E. J. The evolution of administrative offices in institutions of higher education in the United States from 1860 to 1933. (Unpublished doctor's thesis, University of Chicago, 1936).

Marsh, Clarence Stephen, ed. American universities and colleges. 4th ed. Washington, American council on education, 1941.

Mohrhardt, Foster E., comp. A list of books for junior college libraries. Chicago, A.L.A., 1937.

7

Student Assistants

As per practice, a considerable amount of employment is given to student assistants in university libraries. They perform a lot of routine tasks such as desk duty in the library and in departmental reading rooms, shelving, filing, and typing. When they are carefully selected and well-trained and when they are not so numerous as to overwhelm the library staff with supervisory duties, student assistants can render a useful service to the library while helping themselves financially and educationally.

Traditionally, there have been two contrasting points of view regarding the employment of students in the library. On the one hand, librarians have sentimentalized the role of student employment as an important factor in developing initiative and character. This point of view *sees only* virtue in student help and attributes only favourable and beneficial results to such activity. On the other hand, there are librarians who feel that student employment interferes with the work for which the students principally come to college and that it has decidedly adverse effects on the service of the library. Putting put it blutantly, they strenuously object to being bothered with student help. However one feels on either side of this question, the fact remains their librarians can hardly escape the necessity of employing and training student assistants. In the past, colleges have found it necessary to provide remunerative work of some sort for a substantial number of students who would not be able to attend college without financial assistance up to the outbreak of World War II, this number was increasing each year. There is no reason to believe that the situation will change markedly when conditions are normal again. Under such conditions, therefore, it seems highly improbable that the library would be excepted from the campus departments which usually employ students, even if librarians wanted to eliminate their student help.

Looking at the picture realistically, it would seem best to accept the fact that students are going to be employed and to try to get from the situation the best service possible for the library while attempting to make the student's experience educationally as well as financially profitable. The problems and difficulties presented by the employment of students are very real and common.

One of the chief problems relates to the number of part-time student assistants the library is obliged to employ in order to cover its work schedule. Student help is notoriously inefficient without proper training and careful supervision. The proportion of full-time staff members to part time student assistants is, therefore, a matter of importance in operating a library efficiently. There are at present no standards to determine what this ratio should be; if there were they would probably be of little use. In the last analysis the amount of student help in proportion to full-time staff is a question for each college to answer for itself.

College instruction could probably be carried on if the library staff were reduced to two or three librarians for ordering and cataloguing books and a part-time student staff for policing and handing out books over the loan desks. But if college expects its library to familiarize students with the use books and to provide the kind of educational service that is vocated throughout this book, then the professional staff must large enough and sufficiently free from routines and supervisory duties to give proper attention to readers' needs. The prevailing ratio between full-time staff and student help for a selected group of libraries in colleges of less than one thousand enrolment.

The ratio of student help to fulltime staff is considerably greater in the small than in the large college. When it is considered that student assistants work only a few hours each week and when it is considered that they frequently shift change positions, it seems highly probable that the proportion of student help in the smaller colleges is too large to insure the kind of library service that is educationally effective. All this is a matter of opinion, however, unsupported by evidence of a factual nature which is entirely lacking on this subject in the professional writings. In the absence of such evidence, the sensible opinion of Miss Mildred Camp may be quoted as typical of the opinion of most experienced librarians:

> In these days we are frequently asked how far we may use student assistants with economy ? We can use them to the extent that their work can be adequately supervised and no farther and we cannot use them to such an extent that the trained assistant in charge of their work cannot accomplish her own work. It is better to train students for proficiency in the less technical work than to put them at the more difficult things that require more constant supervision. More time can be saved in this way. It is very poor economy for any library to have too few trained and experienced people to supervize the work of student help. It is a detriment to both the library staff and the public.

Full-Time Clerical Assistants Vs. Student Assistants

There is a widespread feeling among librarians borne out by experience, especially in the smaller collages that can much students help is a determinent efficient libraries service. Dr. Randall states. "Student assistance should not be expected to fill the need for additional full-time staff members." The weightiest practical reason for student help is economy. Brown and Bousfield contend against this argument that, "The time expended on the almost continual training of new student attendants is one factor which should be considered. Another more important consideration is the inability of students to work a sufficient length of time to gain the experience necessary for many library duties which can be performed by clerical assistants of several years' experience." In a study of student employment practices in six well-known college libraries, Miss Helen Brown observed that it had been found desirable to replace some part of student service by full-time clerical assistants. She further stated that "The employment of a clerical worker to replace several student assistants working an equivalent number of hours is a great saving in the cost of staff time for training and supervision."

This statement is true, of course, but it must be recognized that it implies an actual increase in library personnel costs. The problem of most librarians is to convince their college administrators that the staff time thus saved can be utilized for services which are vital to the development of the student and his advancement along the road toward real education. The one type of work in which students are almost universally used in college libraries is loan desk work. There are two principal reasons why this is so. In the first place there are a good many routines in connection with loan desk work which students can perform without much training provided they are carefully supervised. At least one staff member is generally available at the loan desk to give this supervision.

In the second place, loan desk work varies in volume from one part of the day to another, from one day to another, and from one week to another. This variation requires great flexibility in loan desk scheduling if the service is to be furnished efficiently and economically. It is easier to provide this flexibility with a large number of part-time student assistants than it is with one or two full-time clerical assistants. It is also possible to schedule student assistants more easily at irregular hours such as lunch and dinner periods. All libraries in the Brown survey "emphasized the greater leeway of irregular time which an amount of money spent for student service can give over the same amount spent for clerical service."

On the other hand it has been found that clerical assistants produce better results as typists than do student assistants. There is also a surprisingly large amount of detailed routine work in the acquisition and preparation divisions of a library which can be done more efficiently by persons giving full-time service. To do the work satisfactorily in the *first* place requires several weeks and sometimes months of careful training and supervision. If the librarian or department head in charge of this work is obliged to give this training to several student assistants, and perhaps to repeat it frequently because the turnover in student help is generally high, he will be pushed to complete his own work and will have no time for improving or developing the service. Typical examples of duties for which full-time help is preferable to student help include: the typing of catalogue cards, alphabeting and filing in the card catalogue and shelf list, the preparation of book orders after the bibliographical checking has been completed, and the general office work of the librarian.

Selection

In most small college libraries, the staff is composed largely of student help. The quality of service depends much upon the ability of this student staff; therefore, a careful and intelligent selection of student assistants is a matter of great importance.

The main requirement for a student assistant is his ability to do the work assigned. Brown and Bousfield regard this criterion as the sole basis of appointment:

> There is one principle which does not seem to be generally recognized in the appointment of student attendants. The all-important function of a college library is to serve its clientele. Students should be selected to work is the library solely because of their ability to do the work better than other candidates. Considerations such as aid to needy students and the value of preparing students to enter the library profession, are entirely subordinate. The employment of students with these objects in view may result in deterioration of service to many for the benefit of a few.

Although in theory students should be selected solely on the basis of their personal fitness, in practice it is often necessary to give consideration to factors other than ability. The very existence of student employment on the campus is evidence of the necessity of providing needy students with some form of remunerative work. In her study, Miss Brown found that the factor of need was a first consideration in several situations in the appointment of students to library positions. And all librarians, in the colleges she studied reported giving special consideration to students interested in library work as a career. The consideration of need as one factor in selection is not necessarily a handicap to wise selection. It should be remembered that the needy students are often more actively motivated in their studies and work than the average student. Students interested in library work as a career are naturally desirous of doing their work well and of learning as much as they can about library procedures.

The ability to do the work assigned is a rather vague and indefinite criterion of selection. It must be interpreted in terms of definite qualifications. Other qualities mentioned less frequently included: subject knowledge, ability to get along with people, familiarity with the collection, and contact with student life.

If the tabulation below is a fair cross-section of library opinion, the requirements of student employees lie in accuracy, method responsibility, and good health. Accuracy is no doubt stressed because a large amount of student time is spent in such tasks as shelving, charging, and discharging books--duties in which repeated errors would cause great inconvenience to readers and a considerable waste of time. Courtesy is not mentioned in the first ten qualities but it cannot be emphasized too strongly in the selection and training of student assistants. The factor of a student's scholastic promise is not among the requirements most frequently mentioned. Probably a majority of librarians would agree with Mr. McHale that "we have no place in the library for the failing student . . . (but) on the other hand, merely because a student is on the honour roll is no guarantee that he will be a titanic success as a circulation assistant." Somewhat more enlightening is the opinion of Miss Mildred Carnp that "outstanding scholastic attainments do not necessarily mean that the student has the greatest number of qualities desirable in library assistants, such as the capacity for careful, painstaking work, a desire to conform to established regulations, ability to work with other people, and the right attitude toward his work as a library assistant."

Table 2: Qualifications required for student assistant work in order of frequency of mention.

Qualification	*Frequency of Mention*
Accuracy	68
Availability	54
Good health and eyesight	35
Need	28
Ability to type	26
Ability to use card catalogue	21
Neatness	21
Ability to take responsibility	20
Experience	15
Quickness	10

Methods of Selection

Student employment is made possible in college libraries from two principal sources: (*i*) scholarships or grants-in-aid ; and (*ii*) special funds allocated to the library for student service. In a few exceptional instances, student service may be paid from general college funds without a direct assessment against the library budget.

Though there is insufficient evidence in print on which to base an opinion regarding the respective merits of each of the plans mentioned above, there seems to be little doubt that the direct employment of student assistants from library funds provides a degree of flexibility in the management of student help which is not always possible under a scholarship plan. The underlying purpose of scholarships is to provide financial help for students of high scholastic promise. It has already been pointed out that scholarship is not regarded as a first requirement by librarians in the selection of student help. In line with the basic assumption upon which scholarships are awarded, it is also true that there are sometimes special requirements regarding the training and work given to students."

More serious, however, is the situation reported in certain colleges where the librarian does not have the final authority in the selection, appointment, and dismissal of students employed on a scholarship basis. If the librarian is held responsible, for the operation and service of the library, there should be no interference with his authority to select assistants qualified to do the work required of them. In practically all colleges where student assistants are employed and paid from library funds, the selection of help is made from an "eligible" list by the librarian or the staff member in charge of student help.

The "eligible" list is composed of all those students who have shown need of part-time employment in order to attend to remain in college. In a few colleges the selection of student assistants is made by the librarian without reference to an "eligible' list or to any outside authority; and, in others, the selection and assignment of student help to all college departments is made by the college personnel officer.

In the latter case the question of qualifications may be, and often is, subordinated to that of student need. The prevailing practice of selection from an "eligible" list has much to commend it. The personnel department maintaining the list usually has a convenient record of the qualifications and experience of students whose names appear on the list. These records may be consulted by any member of the faculty desiring to employ student assistants. In the second place, the personnel department or officer usually sets the rates of pay for the campus as a whole and thereby eliminates the tendency of some departments to bid against one another for the best student assistants.

While selecting students for work in the library, the librarian or staff member in charge of student help must keep in mind these things: (*i*) the duties of each position to be filled; (*ii*) the character of the work; (*iii*) the amount of time required for doing the work each week and the need for consecutive working time; (*iv*) the minimum qualifications and special qualifications such as lettering ability or pre-service experience; (*v*) the personal qualities that seem desirable; and (*vi*) the physical requirements. A great deal of relevant and useful information on the background, qualifications, school and college record, special skills and interests, and health record of possible candidates may be secured from the dean's office and the registrar's office. The records in the placement bureau or personnel office will be particularly helpful for the light they shed on the student's previous work experience in college. The recommendations of faculty members who are intimately acquainted with the work of the library are often helpful. This is about as far as the busy librarian can go in the initial stages of selecting student help. Attention has been called, however, to the advantages of using intelligence tests in selecting student assistants.

The experience of Iowa State College Library with the National Institute of Industrial Psychology test scores and the American Council on Education Psychological examination scores indicates that such tests provide a reasonably accurate estimate of the student's probable success in college library work. After the preliminary sorting of candidates is made from the records and tests mentioned above, the students who survive the initial weeding-out process should be interviewed or re-interviewed in order that the librarian may choose the best from among them.

If the applicant seems to be personally desirable, it may be possible to determine more about his qualifications at this time by requiring him to take some "simple tests for skills, such as informal tests for typing, lettering, use of the catalogue, and shelving." Examinations are given in some libraries without the student having had any special instruction, or, as in some cases, following instruction offered by the library making the selection. If the library is large and has several departments in which student help is used, the general inter-view with the staff member in charge of student assistants should be followed by an interview with the staff member or members who will directly supervise the student's work after appointment. The final appointment may depend to some extent upon the student's schedule and course of work.

One library has a policy of eliminating candidates, with exceptions, who have extra heavy oratory schedules unless they are free for scheduling at irregular periods such as at meal hours at the loan desk. Another college establishes a weekly minimum of hours below which no student is permitted to work. A third gives preference to freshmen and sophomores because after they are trained the library has the possibility of benefiting from their service for a longer period.

Training and Supervision

The employment of student assistants is not completed until: they are properly introduced to the work of the library as a whole and trained in their particular positions. The best training comes from actual doing under careful supervision but it is obviously necessary to give new students some special instruction in their particular duties at the outset. Where there are a considerable number student assistants, this instruction is generally given to all students at one time or to several groups.

The method of giving the instruction varies but follows in general some such pattern as follows:

1. A meeting of all new student assistants is scheduled at the opening of college at which time the librarian or staff supervisor of student help explains in detail the nature and responsibility of student work. Attention is given to such matters as these: the importance of accuracy, method, punctuality, and courtesy in loan desk work; the rules and regulations of the library; the need for strict impartiality in serving student readers; the rules regarding substitutes when students are unable to work their scheduled time; the limits to which students are permitted to go in helping readers; and the proper care and handling of library books and equipment.
2. Students are shown the location of various reading rooms and are given simple instructions in the use of the catalogue and the classification system. The students may then be given a manual with instructions that they will be given a brief test on the information contained in the manual when they return for practice work.
3. After students have been given general instruction in the use of the library and certain simple practice problems to acquaint them with library procedure,

they are then usually introduced to the work of the particular departments in which they will serve. The supervisor of each department will introduce the students to the routines that will be expected of them.

In fact, complete training of the student assistant in the preliminary instruction period is impossible. It is necessary to follow up this preliminary instruction with careful supervision and guidance because most students are relatively unfamiliar with library practices and the materials with which they work. Such instruction is provided through individual guidance, manuals and departmental instruction sheets, and student staff meetings. The student staff meetings are particularly valuable for giving general working directions and explaining new policies in loan desk work. The frequency with which meetings will be held will depend somewhat on the adequacy of the supervisory staff responsible for service to readers. If there are a number of full-time professional staff members in loan desk work it may be possible to reduce the number of student staff meetings to the minimum required to take care of the general routine and the announcements of changes in practices and routines. Aside from giving general directions and correcting faults which have shown up in the daily work, these meetings are valuable in promoting interest and morale. As an additional aid to supervision and instruction, most libraries attempt by one means or another to measure the accomplishment of student assistants in service.

This is done largely on the basis of personal opinion and comparison, but a few libraries use special rating forms to evaluate student services. Mount Holyoke College Library, for example, uses an employee rating scale designed to guide the supervisor in grading the student assistant on such factors as the following: output--quantity and quality, accuracy, organization, cooperativeness, disposition, dependableness, persistence, vitality, initiative, tact, poise, ability to learn, power of analysis, ability to meet people, supervisory ability, and personal appearance.

Working Hours and Remuneration

Most librarians feel that the number of consecutive hours and the total number of hours per week a student assistant can work have a great deal to do with the value of his services to the library. Brown and Bousfield are of the opinion that "better results will obtained if no student is employed for less than 15 hours per week." In the light of data revealed in the Brown study of six eastern college libraries, this figure is higher than the student working hours which obtain in these libraries. Miss Brown discovered that "the median number of hours worked weekly by student assistants in the selected group of college libraries ranges from 5.03 to 10 hours." " More attention should be given to discovering, be experimentation, the real facts regarding the minimum number of hours a student can work each week and still render effective service.

It may possibly develop that the number of hours is not as significant as differences in the ability of students and in the types of work to be done. In regard to the wages of student assistants, the evidence seems to show that in most colleges there is a fixed wage rate.' By adhering rigidly to a fixed wage, it is difficult to give superior students compensation for special merit or for work of a more responsible nature. Moreover, there is little incentive on the part of the student assistant for improvement in the discharge of his duties.

When it is desirable to reward a student for superior service where the wage rate is fixed, the only alternatives to increased wage compensation are a change in position to one of higher responsibility, such as from page to senior student assistant at the loan desk, or a change from one position to another particularly suited to the academic work and interests of the student. Such devices as these rarely mean a great deal to the student unless his work happens to be in a large college library where there is considerable range in the variety and types of work open to him. In colleges where students are employed on a graduated wage scale, first consideration is given to the type of work done and to the student's proficiency in doing the work assigned. Although the practice is condemned by some libraries, some consideration may well be given to length of service in libraries where the opportunity, for a variety of work is not open to students. About the only incentive to good service here is the increase in salary.

REFERENCES

Brown, Helen M. Conditions contributing to the efficient service of student assistants in a selected group of college libraries. *Col. and research lib.* 5:44-52, December, 1943.

Camp, Mildred. Student assistants in the college library. Lib. jour. 59: 923-5, December 1, 1934.

Downey, Mary E. Work of student assistants in college libraries. *Lib. jour.* 57:417-70, May 1, 1932.

McHale, Cecil J. An experiment in hiring student part-time assistants. *Libraries* 31:379-82, October, 1931.

Oberheim, Grace M. *Predicting success of student assistants in college library work.* (Unpublished Master's thesis, School of Library Service, Columbia University, 1939).

Randall, William M. *The College Library.* Chicago, University of Chicago press, 1932.

8

Teaching Services

There is a growing penchant to the part of college administrators and faculties to look upon the library in connection with the entire curriculum as definitely instructional. This trend not merely reflects modifications in old forms of service but includes variations in vitally important functions of the library. The forces and influences which have helped to make college libraries a true instrument in teaching.

Concept of the Library in Education

The first step in discussing this topic is to understand what is meant by the teaching service of the college library. The discussion of actual practices in the body of this chapter may, then, be seen in clearer perspective. Dr. Louis R. Wilson has admirably summarized the conditions under which a college library becomes it essential part of the teaching programme:

> Books are considered as means of extending experience and as aids to thinking rather than solely as sources of information. The library is of as a functional unit of the school or of society rather than as a place or as a collection of books. Library materials are conceived of as materials of instruction and not merely as books or periodicals, and they include many new aids to learning such as pamphlets, maps, globes, pictures, slides, film and sound recordings. The function of the librarian has likewise been differently conceived. The librarian, who formerly was frequently

> though of as a technician or administrator concerned primarily with library house keeping, is more frequently considered a member of the staff responsive to the interests of the administrator, teacher, pupil, or other colleague or patron, and qualified to participate fully in the planning and accomplishment of the educational purposes of the school and of the community.

Evidence that librarians are not alone in thinking of the library as an important factor in teaching is to be seen in the increasing frequency with which administrators, college faculties, and librarians have come together to discuss the common problem of how the library and its services may be most effectively used to strengthen the educational programme of the college. In 1937 college presidents and college librarians met together at the New York meeting of the American Library Association to discuss each other's responsibilities in making the library "an educational instrument as far beyond the best college library existing today as that best library is beyond its prototype of a half century ago." The study of the place of the library in instruction has recently become a matter of increasing interest and concern to the Association of American Colleges and other educational associations; studies on the use of the library and its place in instruction have been sponsored by these associations. As late as 1942, the Southern Association of Colleges and Secondary Schools sponsored a work conference to discuss problems confronting higher education in the southern region and the library was a major topic of emphasis. About one hundred and fifty persons attended the conference, which included presidents, deans, instructors, and librarians from all types of colleges and universities in the region. At these conferences and in the statements of educators and outstanding librarians, two major points were repeatedly stressed: (*i*) librarians should be primarily concerned with organising their books and services to provide the most efficient kind of collection for "teaching with books," and (*ii*) the use of the library as an effective teaching instrument depends as much upon faculty promotion and cooperation as it does upon the librarian's efforts to integrate the library's services with the various educational processes.

Direct and Indirect Teaching Services

All library services properly conducted and administered contribute to teaching. When a librarian assembles material for student use, directs a student to the best source of information on a subject, or instructs the student in the use of materials which will help him to help himself, he is not "merely a service officer without any independent intellectual function of significance, but one with definite and positive duties in the field of instruction." Quite naturally, there are certain types of library service which contribute more directly than others to teaching. The following example will serve to illustrate this point. At a certain college the reference librarian gives two or three classes in library instruction to student in English just prior to the time these students are required to writer their English research paper. This library instruction may properly be regarded as a direct teaching service even though it may be given quite independently of the machinery of hours and credits. In this same institution the reference librarian prepares annually a list of topics on which the library has recently acquired a substantial amount of new material. This list is turned over to the members of the English department, before student research papers are signed, for any use the faculty may wish to make of it. This service may properly be regarded as an indirect teaching service since it well furnish the topics upon which certain research papers are signed. The one service is connected directly with instruction be cause it involves the act of teaching; the other is connected indirect with instruction because it consists in making accessible information which may improve the quality of instruction and facilitate the student's search for library information.

Indirect Teaching Services

No attempt will be made here to discuss the basic services connected with preparing and assembling books for use since these are treated independently in several chapters of this book. Nor is it possible within the confines of a single chapter to enumerate *all* the services which libraries have and are developing, beyond their basic services, to facilitate the teaching function. Rather, the purpose here will be to describe trends and to note innovating practices which may later develop into trends.

Faculty-Library Cooperation

As has already been noted above, an increasing emphasis is being placed on the coordination of faculty and library effort in the common goal of instruction. Dr. B. Lamar Johnson of Stephens College more recently Dr. Harvie Branscomb of Duke University have made this the major thesis of two important books which have provoked thought and discussion in library and faculty groups throughout the country. Few disagree with their basic premise, though a good many librarians are confused and skeptical regarding methods proposed for accomplishing this closer coordination in a common goal.

The general principle underlying faculty-library cooperation is the simple one that the library can function effectively only as a part of the whole instructional unit. The faculty work under a distinct handicap when the library staff is not aware of the teaching methods and objectives in the different departments and the college in a whole. On the other hand, the library is limited in the services on render to teaching without an alert faculty which appreciates and uses these services. For the best service each is dependent upon the other for intelligent understanding and full cooperation. It is because of this mutual dependence that many college librarians now regard the coordination of library and teaching effort as their main They are working toward it, principally in two ways: (*i*) by organizing their services to meet needs suggested by a deliberate study of college and curricular objectives, and (*ii*) by formulating plans of library development through self-surveys conducted joint with the administration and faculty. In some instances the surveys have employed specialists from the outside, and it is no accident that their published reports stress the importance of close integration of the library with the administrative and educational policies and practices of the institution. In preparing the groundwork for the self-survey, the techniques recommended by Miss Blanche P. McCrum in the Washington and Lee survey have proved exceedingly helpful. Dr. E.W. McDiarmid's study of survey methods and procedures is important for the information which it brings together on measurements, appraisal units, and tests. A practical and comprehensive plan for surveying and developing the book collection with faculty aid has been worked out and applied at Mount Holyoke College by Miss Flora B. Ludington. In order that the self-survey should have values which carry beyond that of getting the faculty and college officers to take stood of their responsibilities in the library programme, it must be supported by a continuing programme of library interpretation. "It is not the responsibility of the librarian to tell the instructor how to conduct his classes any more than it is the function of the instructor for to tell the librarian how to run the library." But, with instruction as the main goal, the instructor should be far better informed of library practices and policies than he now is in order to cooperate fully with the library. The steady increase in the output of college library publications--new book lists, student and faculty handbook and book bulletins--is evidence of the growing importance of having regular channel of communication to the faculty.

Selectivity and Cooperation in Book Selection

Changes in methods of teaching and curriculum have added to the importance of the library book collection as instrument of true teaching and have, accordingly, increased the responsibility of the library and teaching staffs in the selection of library materials.

In *Teaching with books,* Dr. Branscomb presents convincing evidence to support the view that colleges have thought too much in terms of quantity and not enough in terms of quality in developing their libraries. The data he presents show that the total number of titles used by undergraduates in any one of five typical colleges falls in the vicinity of ten thousand volumes. Even taking into consideration the differences in the individual requirements of the institutions studied, a library of twenty-five thousand books would have served the needs of undergraduates in all of the five colleges combined. From this and other recent evidence there seems to be widespread if not general agreement that a respectable college library can provide effectively for teaching with books' with a much smaller collection than was hitherto thought possible, provided the collection is carefully selected and systematically weeded. A live and useful book collection can be developed and maintained only if there is cooperation between the members of the library teaching staffs. Specific recommendations for promoting cooperation in the development of an efficient, compact collection are set forth in the report of the workshop committee of the Southern Association:

1. Library funds should he allotted to each department according to its needs, and, to encourage the participation of all members, no single person should dominate selection.
2. Subject sections of the reference collection should be developed by the librarian with the assistance of departments concerned.
3. Books for general reading should he selected co-operatively by the faculty and the staff and, whenever possible, with students' aid.
4. Curriculum committees should not admit **new**

courses in fields in which library resources are inadequate.

5. The librarian should be responsible for the proper development of the whole collection, should make available to the faculty helpful bibliographical tools, and should systematically check holdings against authoritative lists.
6. The librarian should notify the faculty member of the arrival of books he has requested or in which he is particularly interested, publish classified mimeographed lists of new acquisitions, and place new titles on proper display before stacking them.

Attention is also being given to the formulation of a well considered programme of book-buying -- one which has a reasonable expectation of being followed throughout a number of years. That such a plan should be laid down in detail in print for all to read and study is perhaps not necessary on every campus, but the kind of library at which the college is aiming, the purposes for which book funds are intended, and the practices regarding the purchase of duplicates and research materials should be as clearly understood by the faculty and administration as by the librarian. Recent studies have tended to show that too many libraries do not have such a programme, and that the procedures for selecting books are decidedly ineffective.

Library Materials

There was a time when the Master of Arts chanted, *Timeo virus unius libri,* by which he meant to express his fear of debating with the man who had thoroughly in hand the material in one text. Today there are only a few fields in which the teacher may repeat this saw without being criticized. The modern professor believes that students are best educated by using many books. A good teacher awakens a student's interest in a subject, the student goes to the library with a list of suggested readings or topics, and it is highly important that he should be able to find authoritative books on the subject in which he is developing an interest. It follows, as a necessary corollary, that he must also have direct and easy access to books. Direct access to books is, in the opinion of most teachers and librarians, one of the most important factors in forming and moulding the student mind. The case has never been better stated than by Dr. Branscomb in his chapter entitled *Making hooks accessible.* After stating the practical reasons for favouring direct access to books, he concludes:

> Most readers, however, will feel that the major reason for the open self practice ... is that books on locked or closed shelves are dumb and meaningless--so many physical objects to be stored and kept in order. Displayed to possible readers, the collection becomes alive with suggestion. The problem of education is to a large extent one of creating an environment which is intellectually stimulating. The library is a cultural and educational influence of great potential power. To remove the books from sight is a step to be deplored on educational and moral grounds. Long Plato remarked that the "pursuit of wisdom is not, as fools suppose, as musical as Apollo's lyre," but not all undergraduates have made this discovery. There probably is no better way to bring about this discovery, which each one must make for himself, than by displaying in their infinite variety the volumes which the college has chosen for its book collection.

The open stack principle, so wisely championed by Dr. Branscomb, loses some of its significance, however, as the book collection grows in size. Thirty-nine of the fifty college libraries whose statistics are tabulated in the latest listing of the American Library Association have more than fifty thousand volumes and fourteen of these have more than one hundred thousand volumes. For the occasional student, no library is too large or complicated in its arrangement; but for the typical undergraduate, the stack collection of a library in excess of fifty thousand volumes is likely to prove confusing and may even prove a damper on the intellectual interests kindled by the professor. Librarians have attempted to meet this problem in several ways, the most important of which are: (*i*) training students in the arrangement and location of books in the library; (*ii*) frequent and systematic discarding of books which are no longer of value; and (*iii*) bringing out the "active" collection by segregating "little-used" material in a restricted section of the stack. Efficiency cannot be claimed for a collection in which only one out of every two or three volumes will ever be used in teaching. Recent studies have tended to show that the rate of obsolescence in the book collection is much greater than is commonly thought.

The measures mentioned above have been connected directly with making the book collection of the main library more efficient and accessible for student use. A number of other activities affecting the accessibility of books have added to the significance of college library service. One of these may now be mentioned. In a number of junior colleges and in the more progressive smaller colleges, the librarian has sometimes set up classroom libraries. At Stephens College, where the classroom library has been particularly successful, the library staff in 1937-38 reported sending more than two thousand volumes to fourteen different classrooms used by thirty different instructors. These books were placed on open shelves in the classroom and were available for student use or borrowing' at any time a class was not using the room.

As classroom libraries have been developed at Stephens College and other smaller colleges, they have become an important means of making it possible for students and teachers to work together with books.

Broader Concept of Library Materials

With the continuing development of new and improved methods of reproduction (slides, pictures, phonograph records, and the like the range of materials which the college is utilizing in the instruction of students is rapidly increasing. Some idea of the range and extent of these new learning materials may be gained by examining the following list of aids: museum objects, models, silent motion picture, still pictures, stereographs, flat pictures, opaque projections, glass slides, film strips, posters, cartoons, maps, charts, graphs, diagrams, phonograph records, radio transcriptions, sound motion film, and other visual materials with sound accompaniment.

For the most part the handling and use of these materials in instruction have seen performed by the several teaching departments of the college. The art department has cared for pictures, prints, photographs, and he like; the science departments have handled their own slides and films; the music department has provided phonograph records for instructional and "general listening" purposes. College administrators and teachers have felt this arrangement has been satisfactory while recognizing that it involved some duplication in materials and expense.

With the introduction and use of some of the more complicated radio-visual materials such as radio transcriptions and film, the idea of a central agency for handling all audio-visual materials has been freely discussed. The library has sometimes been 'mentioned as the logical agency for this work though college librarians have been slow in realizing that these newer materials fall into the some category of learning materials as books and other reading materials. Library schools, moreover, have only recently provided training in the administration of audio-visual aids. Nevertheless, there is a growing feeling among college librarians that they will be missing an opportunity to render a useful service to instruction if they do not take the initiative in providing for their users at least some of the more commonly used audio-visual materials. Although it is not possible at this time to point to .any one four-year college where the library is undertaking a full programme of audio-visual service, the following libraries are handling one or more types of such materials as part of their regular service, and most or them have contributed reports of their experience to the professional journals: Adams State College, Antioch, Blackburn, Carleton, Teaching College (Columbia University), Dickinson, Georgia Teachers College, Hamilton, Lawrence, Rockford, Skidmore, Smith, Stephens Union, Vassar, Washington State College, Wellesley, and Williams. In the Peabody Demonstration School of George Peabody College Nashville; a library-centered audio-visual educational programme has been successfully developed since 1938. Although carried on at the elementary and high school level, this programme offers a number of points of interest to the college librarian who is considering the servicing of audio-visual aids.

Several principles have been developed in the administration of the programme:

1. Audio-visual materials (but not equipment) may be purchased of the library book fund. Expenses incidental to borrowing or renting films and other needed materials are also charged to the book fund.
2. The library assumes no responsibility for the production of materials. Although our faculty include candid camera fans, motion picture amateurs, and sound recording enthusiasts, the library does not find it practicable to furnish these persons with equipment or supplies. . . . The librarian is nowhere expected to sponsor book production; no more should he undertake the production of audio-visual materials.
3. In modern setup the librarian assumes no responsibility for supervision which is a function of the audio-visual consultant. In most institutions at least one faculty member can be found who will be able to assist in an informal initial programme of teacher training and guidance. In some cases

the librarian might prove to be the person best qualified for this service also.

Counseling and Informal Guidance

The college library demonstrates instructional practices not alone in the excellence of its book collection, not alone in the provision for direct access to books and the newer types of learning media, and not alone in the provision of an atmosphere favourable to study and reading, but also in the individual guidance and instruction it gives to students at the time they are using library materials One writer has stated this point forcibly in these words:

> After all, the student is the individual we are trying to serve. Here as in no other phase of our work we must consider ourselves as teachers Out meeting with the student is the moment at which all our efforts have been aimed--our book buying, our cooperation with faculty, our administration and organization. It is the point at which we bring about the union of the class and the library, the student and the written records of his subject. It is the point at which learning takes place. The importance of this student contact cannot be exaggerated. It is the final test of our library programme for our ultimate success depends upon how effectively we do our work of teaching the use of books and libraries.

The points at which such contacts are most commonly made in the college library are the circulation and reference desks. In addition to the assistance given to students in pointing out where and how information is to be found in books, however, there are now being developed in some libraries interesting programmes of informal instruction. The nature of these programmes is summarized briefly in the following:

1. In certain libraries there are special staff assistants who serve as advisers to students. At Teachers College, Columbia University, for example, there are three library staff members assigned to work directly with students in their use of the library.

These assistants are known as "consultants," and they give special attention to aiding students in the preparation of term papers, theses, and bibliography. An important phase of the instruction is the participation of the consultants in class meetings at the time the individual student is preparing to meet an assignment involving considerable library use.

2. The assistance which students need most when they first come to college "centers at the card catalogue." In some of the larger college and university libraries, a special reference assistant has maintained an information desk near the card catalogue during certain hours of the day and evening. A study based on the results of five year's service at the information desk of the University of Illinois library not only demonstrates the educational usefulness of such service but reveals these interesting data on the nature of the questions asked: forty-eight per cent of the questions concerned general matters of location and rules, thirty per cent involved instruction in the use of the card catalogue, and twenty-one per cent were of a subject nature, involving instruction in the use of the catalogue and of general reference books. The smaller staffed college library may not always be able to maintain an information assistant at regular library hours, but a member of the staff can be assigned, with beneficial results, to such work at the beginning of each semester and period of major term paper assignments.

3. In a few libraries the members of the faculty have been encouraged to spend free reading periods in the library where they can read is their own fields and work with students who are studying it the library. This particular programme of faculty-library cooperation has been promoted most widely

in the smaller colleges with forward looking programmes of college instruction. But it is also true of one of the larger colleges and of colleges with a more standard type of curriculum. The college programme at the University of Chicago calls for all freshmen and sophomores to take certain basic survey courses requiring heavy use of the library, and faculty advisers are located in the college library to aid the students in their work. The faculty distribute their office hours for conferences with students so that at least one instructor is available at all hours during the day. When a student has some difficulty in his reading, he is then at library to consult his instructor without delay. The professor in talking with the student has only to step into the reading room to get books which he may need to refer to in the course of the conference." A similar plan in one field is carried out at Wesleyan.

4. The variety and kinds of individualized reference and readers' advisory service offered to students are well known. Some of these have already been mentioned in the preceding chapter and others art discussed in the chapter which follows on the encouragement of student reading. Perhaps less well-known are the services which some of the smaller libraries in progressive colleges are now offering in the college guidance programme. Three types of activity will illustrate the nature of their contribution to the educational programme : (*i*) many libraries are developing special collections of career literature displaying and publicizing books' and pamphlets as part of the college vocational programme; (*ii*) some librarians are participating in orientation and counseling programmes, as for example in one college where the librarian is in charge of the library and of counsiling and (*iii*)

some libraries are making case history studied of student reading for use in the college guidance programme. In one institution these records are made available to the student's major professor or faculty adviser, to the dean of men and dean of women for use in academic and vocational guidance, to the college physician the psychologist, the instructor, and to counselors who have suppervision of the student dormitories and extracurricular activities..

Improvement of Physical Facilities

While the training, imagination, and understanding of the library staff are of prime importance, the effectiveness of the library in teaching will be increased immeasurably if conditions for the comfort of the reader are made favourably for the use of books and study. This implies a convenient arrangement of books and reading space, direct access to books, and a reasonable amount of seclusion for serious study where the student will not be continuously interpreted every time a person enters a reading room or charges a book from the circulation desk. At Wellesley College the main reading room has recently been remodeled on the alcove system in order to introduce some suggestion of the secluded quiet of the English college. At Rockford College (III) four divisional reading rooms, following the general plan of the curriculum, house all reference and circulation materials in the humanities, social sciences, arts, and sciences. More attention has been given in recent years to the selection of comfortable chairs and to scientifically designed tables for improved reading purposes. Modernized lighting systems are receiving increased attention, but stack lighting still remains largely satisfactory. Air conditioning, at least to the extent of proper humidification, is being provided in new and remodelled buildings. Because many library reference and periodical rooms are crowded with students using their own study books, librarians are giving some attention to the provision of separate reading rooms for this purpose. The increasing tendency to introduce graduate teaching methods on the undergraduate level is reflected in the provision of special reading facilities in the way of carrels, seminars, and conference rooms grouped in such a manner as to provide convenient contacts among teachers, students, and books. In these, and in many other ways, libraries are working to secure conditions which are conducive to effective study.

Improvement of Instruction

Studies in reading and in the use of the library are now appearing with increasing frequency. They range from informal studies of reading with reading in a particular library to detailed, scientific reading investigations conducted under the auspices of a graduate library school. They promise a future influence on the relationship of library service to instruction which is bound to increase the educational effectiveness of the library. The nature and implications of such studies as have already been made are summarized briefly in the following review: (*i*) they have furnished the faculty a measuring stick by which to determine the effectiveness of their parallel reading methods by providing factual information about the quantity and quality of student reading, (ii) they have revealed weaknesses it library administration and physical facilities, inaccuracies and carelessness in faculty assignments, and student inability to use library indexes and tools effectively, (*iii*) they have aided in the discovery of student reading interests and have served as the basis for developing a library-faculty programme to encourage free reading, (*iv*) they have thrown light on the significance of reading for scholarship and have revealed the extent of library use as the student progresses toward academic maturity, (*v*) they have thrown light on the effectiveness of varying methods of instruction for promoting reading and library use, and (*vi*) they have furnished a basis for evaluating the quality of the book collection and for improving the programme of book acquisitions.

Direct Teaching Services

It seems reasonable to assume that if students are to get the best out of their college education, they must be able to read efficiently and to locate material in the library pertinent to their class problems. There are a large number of other abilities which most college students must be trained to use effectively, but these two art fundamental to all others.

Improvement of Student Reading Ability

It has been estimated at various times that approximately twenty per cent of college entering classes are in need of remedial work in reading and that, if they do not receive it, their studies will suffer to a marked degree. Because of this awareness on the part of the colleges, many experimental courses in remedial reading have been set up. Some of these have been frankly experimental and entered on with open skepticism; some have been established as an integral part of the freshman curriculum and have been known as courses in study methods or in corrective reading. In other institutions the work has been done haphazardly by those members of the faculty who were interested enough to work with individual students in need of help. The situation may be summed up by saying that "the majority of colleges are aware of the reading problem and that a few of them are doing something systematic about it. In view of these conditions and in view of the library's close relation to all matters pertaining to reading, it is, logical to inquire as to what part the librarian will have in the programme for improving student reading ability. Whatever his potential contribution, the college librarian has not played a prominent part in systematic remedial reading programmes to date. A survey of remedial reading programmes in a large number of colleges and universities, conducted by the University of Minnesota in 1942, placed the responsibility for the work in one hundred and eighty-nine institutions as follows:

Administrators	23
Psychologists	45
Instructors in education	63
English instructors	50
Speech instructors	3
Librarians	2
Research workers	1
French instructors	1
History instructors	1

Thus it can be seen that the responsibility for this work is centred largely in the administration and the departments of education, psychology, and English. There are two major things standing in the way of a library-sponsored remedial reading programme: (*i*) there is not enough known about the specific reading skills necessary in each of the content areas, and (*ii*) librarians do not possess a sufficient knowledge of all aspects of reading, including the methodology of reading instruction, to make a real contribution. Miss Mildred Hawksworth Lowell has set forth a number of strong reasons why librarians should take the lead in this matter, but such development as she envisages takes place slowly and librarians will first have to prepare themselves "in the physiological, sociological, analytical, and educational areas of reading." Until such time as this takes place, it is the duty of the libraries to familiarize himself with the current literature of remedial reading and to cooperate to the best of his ability in working with those who have charge of these programmes.

Instruction in the Use of the Library

Most college librarians and teachers will agree that an

extraordinarily large number of students seem to have no method what ever in the use of the library when they first come to college such students enter the college library for the first time without conception of the way in which to charge out a book--much so with any understanding of the use of particular reference sets and library indexes. Either they glance over the shelves in a perfect aimless way or ask the reference librarian to do their work for them. If the student body is large, it is practically impossible even the most efficient and best informed reference librarian minister to all their heterogenous wants.

It would, therefore, set to be a matter of common sense that students should be some instruction in how to manipulate the machinery of library efficiently and quickly. On this point there seems to be general agreement, among librarians, but on the manner and method of giving instruction there are wide differences of opinion. There are who feel that the introduction to the library during Freshing Orientation week is most important. Others believe that a required course in the early months of the freshman year is the best method. And there are those who believe that instruction can best be handled in connection with class work at the time the students are most likely to be using library materials intensively. Some librarians combine different methods and, in addition, offer specialized bibliographical instruction to upperclass students in different fields. Fach of these plans or methods is described briefly in the remainder of this chapter.

Orientation of Freshman Week. Library instruction during Orientation week gives the student a friendly introduction to the library in a general over-all view of library services. There are those who feel that such instruction has very little value even under the best of conditions because the student has not yet felt any real need for using the library and because his attention is far too much taken up with the multitude of new impressions that greet him upon his entrance to college. Where instruction has been successfully given during Orientation week, it has usually been carried out by means of lectures and group visits or tours of the library. At one college the librarian gives a general lecture highlighting the divisions and contents of the library as an introduction to the tours. These tours follow the next day, in groups of twenty-five students or less, at which time the students observe and take notes on the procedures for locating and finding books and on the main points of use of major reference works and magazine indexes. A broader view is gained at in another college where the librarian attempts to introduce student to teaching and study methods employed at the college. This lecture is followed by group tours in which the more important steps. In finding information and obtaining books are emphasized counters, exhibits, and replicas of card indexes are commonly used in connection with the instruction during the library visits. In some libraries the tours are followed by a short test and students are started to call for the results of this test later, at which time they are given individual instruction if the need is indicated. If the library is large, it is valuable to have a library handbook for distribution during the tours or at the time of the lecture. The programme as a whole should be developed in full cooperation with the faculty in charge of Orientation week. In most instances students are advised rather than required to attend the library lecture and tours during Orientation week.

The usefulness of this instruction depends in part, therefore, on the number of students reached. Some evidence on this point is afforded in the following examples. At Oregon State College, where Freshman week precedes the general registration of all students, the freshmen are scheduled for a brief talk by the librarian, after which groups are taken through the library building by members of the library staff. Of the 1,393 students enrolled as freshmen during the first two registration days of the fall term of 1942, approximately eight hundred took part in the library tours. The visits were scheduled in groups of twenty to forty students and one hour of instruction was given to each group. A mimeographed guide to the library showing the arrangement and content of materials on each floor of the building, together with outline plans and a schedule of library hours, was distributed at the time of the tours. Prior to Freshman week at the Woman's College of the University of North Carolina in the fall term of 1943, the chairman of the Freshman class sent a mimeographed letter to each new student recommending attendance at the library tours and stating the schedule for these tours during Freshman week. Approximately six hundred new students were enrolled this term of whom more than four hundred were counted in attendance at the library tours. The student library handbook was distributed at the end of each tour, which lasted for approximately an hour. In both institutions the library staff felt that the tours were worth while but that the effectiveness of the instruction could have been improved by scheduling smaller more numerous groups another year.

Instruction of New Students in the Use of the Library. Dr. Peyton Hurt found the graduate students at standford and the University of California was unable to use the card catalogue and magazine indexes effectively and that they lacked any knowledge of the important bibliographical sources in their special fields. Out of one hundred and eighty-nine students, primarily graduates, at Teachers College, Columbia University, who took a test on magazine indexes, only twenty-nine had ever heard of the *Education index;* only twelve had ever used the *International index;* and although the majority of them had used the *Readers' guide,* they were not clear as to its scope. Miss Lulu Reed, analyzing the results of a valid and scientific test on student competence to use the library which was given to all levels of undergraduate students, found that: (*i*) students had not acquired specific and detailed knowledge of reference tools, such as dictionaries and encyclopaedias, (*ii*) students had not learned to associate types of questions with types of books most likely to answer those questions, (*iii*) students had not learned to associate topics with general fields of knowledge and consequently were not able to benefit, to a maximum degree, by labels indicating divisions of the classification scheme, (*iv*) students had not learned to use parts of books effectively and lacked adequate knowledge of bibliographical features such as footnotes, bibliographies, and indexes, (*v*) student interpretation of specimen entries in the *Readers' guide, New York Times index,* and document indexes revealed inability to understand and locate information by means of these tools, (*vi*) students were not able to evaluate sources of information readily, and (*vii*) students did not understand the functions of various library departments.

Many institutions are seeking in various ways to remedy the deficiencies revealed by these tests. Current practice in library instruction, however, still lags far behind what has been shown in to be necessary if students are to use the library effectively in their college work. Indeed, only a limited number of colleges making a systematic and worthwhile effort to provide such instruction. In all too many instances, the instruction is still largely experimental after years of effort with first one method and then another, and it is often too brief to be of real value. This is due in part to the fact that too few college libraries are sufficiently well staffed to give instruction to large entering classes, but even more often to the fact that very few college teachers are informed regarding the need of instruction or are sufficiently interested to work with the library staff in doing something about it. More than one informed and able librarian has stated that the solution to library instruction must begin with the stimulation and guidance of the faculty in the library-teaching method. Instructors in junior colleges and teachers colleges give more evidence of understanding the importance of the library in the teaching programme and show a greater willingness to cooperate with the library staff in developing student ability to use library facilities than those in colleges of the liberal arts. With respect to the subject content and method of library instruction for freshmen and sophomores, current methods are usually of three types: (*i*) a required course in which all new students participate with or without credit, (*ii*) an elective course open freshmen and sophomores with or without credit, and (*iii*) a series of lectures and exercises given in connection with class work in subject courses at a time when the students are most likely to be library materials intensively. Very few colleges offer a required course in library use. In the few institutions that do, the classes meet once or twice a week for periods ranging from three to weeks. In some colleges a limited amount of credit is offered in one or two colleges the course is given by the librarian and library staff. In one college it is given by a lib school staff, little or no special time being set apart for preparation for the class meetings. When standard text books on library instruction are use the material has to be adapted to conform to local and as a consequence, most library prepare their or text. Attempts at correlation with subject courses have not always proved successful, but two typical examples of how this is accomplished are suggested in the following statements:

> When the library science instructor requires a student to prepare a bibliography, she suggests that such bibliography be related directly to a subject field in which the student, in any of his academic courses, has been called upon to prepare a term paper. This is but one illustration of our fixed policy of attempting to make the library science assignments such that they will facilitate a student's progress in his other courses.

> A textbook was written after conference with instructors who were asked to list the skills that they wanted their students to have in the use of the library; type of lessons they would suggest to give the student more pleasure in the use of the library; whether or not they would expect

> term papers, research topics or other forms of independent use of the library and in what fields these would most likely fall. Questions at the reference and circulation desks were checked for two years with the idea that we would provide for as many answers as we could in this course to take care of the general needs of all students.

The usual method of lecture and discussion for presenting material in required library courses is sometimes supplemented by the use of visual aid charts, sample sets of Library of Congress cards, and her forms of visual aids, though the information dealing with their value and effectiveness is extremely meagre.

Strictly speaking, there are few if any elective courses in library freshmen only. When elective courses are offered--approximately the same number of libraries offer elective as do required courses they are open to all students though one or two institutions make a special effort to secure freshmen and sophomores. The classes meet more frequently than in the required courses, usually include a laboratory period once a week in which students work out practical problems, and run from fifteen weeks to the full year fall college credit is given for the courses. Classes are relatively small and instruction *is* given by one person, the librarian, or the assistant librarian, or the reference librarian. A greater use is made of special devices in teaching, such as visual aids and syllabi, and more emphasis is placed on the bibliography of special fields than in required courses. The chief weakness of elective courses is that they teach too few students, but this is offset in part by the fact that in practically all cases the libraries offer additional instruction for freshmen either during Orientation week or through class lectures in subject courses. The chief merit of elective courses, as they are now given, is their more substantial content and more varied method of presentation. Classes are small and the library instructor has sufficient time to do the job well. There is no evidence, however, to show that the class work in elective courses is being more thoroughly integrated with academic work than in required courses.

Certain basic information and skills determine the subject ton-tent of both required and elective courses. The major topics generally include the following: (*i*) the card catalogue and its use, *(ii)* periodical indexes and their use in locating information in magazines, (*iii*) the major reference books which the student is likely to use at his particular level, and (4) the application of this knowledge to the preparation of a bibliography in good form. To these four major topics there is sometimes added: (*i*) a general introduction to the arrangement of books in the college library, (*ii*) information relative to the parts of a book, (*iii*) instruction in note-taking, (i*v*) something concerning the value and use of government documents, and (5) methods for surveying the literature of a specific field.

The most prevalent type of instruction is that which is offered in connection with existing courses in the curriculum. Most commonly the instruction is given in the English courses because students have to write term papers in these courses and all freshmen are required to take them. The instruction, consisting chiefly of one or two lecture periods, is given in the early part of the fall term or is timed to precede the assignment of a term or research paper. Where there are many sections of English, the instruction naturally extends over a considerable period of time, and the effectiveness of timing the 4 library lecture with the research paper is lost unless the time assigned for the paper is staggered in the various sections. The actual instruction is given by the library staff, a member of the English department, or by both. The lecture method predominates as favoured method of instruction although there is evidence of increasing use being made of slides, film, and ether visual aids.

Summarizing the three methods of instruction--required, elective, and coordinated courses--it is evident from the foregoing that the trend is toward making such instruction an integral part of the assignments in the subject courses. If the faculty is sympathetically aware of its responsibility in this direction, the library instruction programme will provide the basic information and skills which students need in using the library effectively. The advantages of the coordinated type of approach are evident. It offers a structure for an organized programme of library instruction which is all too frequently lacking and it justifies a degree of faculty planning and participation.

The student learns to manipulate the machinery of the library card catalogue, book guides, indexes to periodicals, encyclopaedias, and other reference books at the time he most needs to use the library's resources. Library instruction is, therefore, not an end in itself, but a means to an immediate gain in using the library efficiently. The weakness in the method is that the faculty are often too little informed about the need for library instruction and their responsibilities in this direction, and, therefore, the instruction provided is sometimes more or less a makeshift. There are encouraging instances, however, where faculty are taking their responsibilities seriously and these will undoubtedly have their effect on the development of library instruction work elsewhere. At Smith College, where library instruction is given by the English faculty in the English classes, the training is motivated by the fact that each freshman 8 required to write a research paper as part of her English course. The instruction is, therefore, closely correlated with an immediate, need. Before the student embarks on finding material on her chosen topic, she is required to perform a "library exercise" involving the use of about two dozen reference books, periodical indexes. Mother Library materials. The instructors in some of the sections it accessible in the library when their students are doing the work on their "library exercise." Assignments are staggered in the van-section's in order that the students will have a reasonable opportunity to use the library materials without too much difficulty.

At Teachers College, Columbia University, the library instruction is closely coordinated with the student's work through the library consultant programme, previously mentioned. The programme here is primarily for graduate students, but the method is equally applicable to undergraduates. The most important phase of the instruction is offered as a regular part of the course *Orientation in educational research* in the Department of Educational Research. The associate librarian lectures on methods of surveying the literature of a specific field including the bibliographies of theses and research studies, bibliographic form, annotations, and book reports. The lectures are supplemented by discussions and problem assignments In addition, at the request of the instructor in charge, the library offers instruction to classes. These vary from nursing education English, and guidance to children's literature. Four members of; the staff take part in this instruction, three of them library consultants, and one in charge of the school library laboratory which houses the children's books.

At Swarthmore College the reference librarian gives lectures classes in English composition. The library groups receiving this instruction are divided according to the students' major subjects for example, premedical, engineering, political science, economics, etc. The library lecture is given after the term papers are assigned and is based on the sources which will produce material for these papers. Because of this plan, no two lectures are ever the same and the instruction is fitted to the individual student's need. In library instruction, which is given in connection with subject courses, it is worth noting that the faculty contribution is much greater than in any other method of instruction. In several *instances* the English *faculty* give the major part of the instruction.

At Oregon State College, the library instruction is a regular part of the English courses and is given throughout the year--with special emphasis in the third term when heavy library use is anticipated--by members of the faculty. The library staff does a large amount of incidental directing and explaining when students are doing their research papers. The subject matter of the lectures on library use given by the members of the English department includes: an understanding of the plan of the card catalogue and the ability to use it, the use of periodical indexes, the use of bulletins the use of general reference books, the making of bibliographies, finding material, taking notes, forms and methods of scholarly documentation, constructing outlines, writing the research paper; the use of various reference books on biography, mythology, *etc.,* and the location and use of sources of material in the library. Whether instruction in library use can be given most effectively by the library staff or classroom teacher is a question which can be answered only in terms of particular situations, but there can be little doubt that faculty participation in instruction which is an integral part of course assignments is the ideal solution to the library instruction problem.

Instruction of Upperclass Students in the Use of the Library : Few colleges provide the bibliographical training necessary to equip upperclass students for independent library investigation in their major fields of concentration or for later graduate research. The failure to provide such training is perhaps less serious in the instance of the graduate because he has his faculty adviser to direct his research work and most university graduate departments in the arts and sciences offer an introductory course in bibliography and research methods in their fields. With all evidence pointing to an increasing use of graduate teaching methods on the undergraduate level, there is a real need for bibliographical instruction for students whose special field of concentration requires extensive use of library materials.

A description of current practice in library instruction for the advanced levels of undergraduate work is further complicated by the seeming confusion which exists regarding the meaning of the term "bibliographic instruction." In some institutions it is apparently interpreted as training in historical bibliography and in others it is applied to instruction in the literature of various subject fields. In so far as it is possible to present a picture on the basis of the information supplied by the few institutions where some form of systematic instruction is given, the work seems to follow these patterns:

1. At the request of instructors, lectures are given to upperclass students in general and special bibliographical tools. At Swarthmore College the reference librarian gives one lecture at the beginning of each term to junior and senior "honours" students in the departments of English and economics and to others who request it. The reference librarian at Pomona College gives three lectures the second semester to junior and senior "honours" students who are studying in the field of government. A comprehensive, mimeographed bibliographical guide to the literature of government is provided for the students who attend the lectures. Juniors and seniors at Mills College receive some bibliographical instruction through two lectures which are given as a part of the courses in history and child development.

2. Instruction is provided by means of an elective course dealing with general bibliographical aids in finding library materials and the correct method of preparing a bibliography. Rockford College offers such a course for upperclassmen entitled *Library method; and reference books.* For some time the assistant librarian at Vassar College has offered a one-semester elective for sophomores, juniors and seniors in bibliography. Union College (Schenectady)

recently announced a bibliographic course for the pre-graduate student. Only seniors who are planning to take graduate work and who are on the Dean's "honour" roll list are entitled to admission. According to the outline of the course, about a third of the semester course is given over to instruction in such common library tools as the catalogue, periodical indexes, general bibliographies, footnotes, and proper bibliographic form. In the remaining time, students are divided into two groups, arts and science, for training in subject bibliography on the college level, and for instruction in carrying out, under close supervision, some problem in bibliographic research. On the graduate level in colleges, the librarian of Claremont Colleges offers a seminar in *Bibliography and methods of bibliographical research* to graduate students; the associate librarian of Teachers College Columbia University, offers a similar semester course to experienced undergraduates and graduates. In some instances, courses are given by members of the faculty and may be required. At Oregon State College, for example, the departments of chemistry, entomology and horticulture give courses to upperclass students and graduates in the history and literature of their special fields. It is probable that faculty members in many other institutions include study in the literature of their subjects without specifically mentioning it in the scheduled description of their courses.

3. In most colleges, the reference librarian or some member of the staff gives individual help to upperclassmen and graduates who need bibliographical instruction in the preparation of term papers, seminar reports, and theses. Mills College requires that all theses presented for the M.A. degree must first be passed upon for form by

the reference librarian. The method used to reach the students is to require attendance at two lectures by all who are writing theses. Bibliographical sources are discussed at one lecture; the form for footnotes and bibliography is emphasized at the other.

Conclusion

The role of the library as an active agency in the teaching programme has been emphasized throughout this chapter. The desire to relate the library to the curriculum and to the needs and interests of the faculty and students has prompted many experiments in mutual cooperation, in the relating of library books and journals and non-book material to all college teaching activities, and in the improvement of physical facilities to provide for the comfort of the reader. Emphasis has been laid on the importance of the open stack principle; library and reading studies to determine library efficiency teaching effectiveness, and student reading ability and interest and special library guidance and counseling services. Although the need for training in library usage has been definitely established, the existing programmes for furnishing this instruction leave much to be desired, particularly at the upper levels. If the library is to be regarded as an important instrument for implementing instruction, steps must be taken to improve the ability of students to read intelligently and to locate and use materials in the library for dealing with the problems relating to their class work. All new students should be given a friendly introduction to the library and to the library staff by means of a general lecture and group tours during Orientation or Freshman week; such general information as they may be given at this time should be supplimented by a readable handbook setting forth the procedures for getting books and for finding information in the library Later on, after the student comes to feel the need for using the library through class assignments, the librarian and library staff should be operate with the departments of English, history, and other heavy reading departments in giving more specific instruction in library materials. Experience has shown that the use of standardizes library tests prior to giving this instruction offers a convenient, effective method of determining what students need instruction most and in what areas they need the most instruction; that attention should be given to the growing importance of visual methods of teaching in giving this instruction; and that closer cooperation and integration of library instruction with the regular teaching pro-gram is highly desirable. Upperclassmen, who plan to do graduate work or whose field of concentration requires intensive use of the college library, should receive in an elective course or by explanation in existing courses some instruction in the more important general bibliographies, in the subject bibliography of their special fields and in the method of bibliographic form. Finally, all graduate students in colleges which offer graduate work should have training and practice in bibliography and research methods. They may well in addition, if they have not already had such instruction, be given training in the use of the card catalogue, periodical indexes, and in the general reference and bibliographical tools commonly found it college libraries.

REFERENCES

Boucher, Chauncey S., The Chicago plan. Chicago, University of Chicago press, 1935.

Brown, C. H. and Bousfield, H.G., Circulation work in college and university libraries. Chicago, A.L.A., 1933. Tests and studies of library service, p. 121-30.

Coney, Donald, and others, A survey of the Indiana University library. Chicago, A.L.A., 1940, (mimeographed).

Danton, J. Periam, College librarian looks at the college president; Snavely, Guy E. College president looks at the college librarian. Association of American colleges bull. 23:344-56, November, 1937.

Eurich, A.C., Amount of reading and study among college students. Sch. and soc. 37:102-4, January 21, 1933.

Davidson, John S., The use of books in a college library. Col. and research lib. 4:294-7, September, 1943.

Gaskill, H. V., and others, Analytical study of the use of a college library Lib. quar. 4:564-87, October, 1934.

Gosnell, Charles F. (review of), List of books for college libraries, 1931-38. Lib. jour. 65:531-2, June 15, 1940.

Hirsch, Felix E., The use of the book collection in the teaching programme of a progressive college. Col. and research lib. 2:48-54 December, 1940.

Hoole, W. Stanley, Reading of Birmingham-Southern college students. Peabody jour, of educ. 14:151-7, November. 1935.

Ireland, N. O., A vocational guidance experiment in a college library. Lib. jour. 63:17-19, January 1, 1938.

Johnson, B. Lamar, Vitalizing a college library. Chicago, A.L.A., 1939. Library and instruction, 8-39.

Lancaster, Mrs. C.M., Library experiment with reading records. Junior col. jour. 12:27-30, September, 1941.

Ludington, Flora B., Evaluating the adequacy of the book collection. Col. and research lib. 1:305-13, September, 1940.

Ludington, Flora B., Teaching function of the library. Junior col. jour. 6:69-73, November, 1935.

McCrum, Blanche P.A, College library makes its own survey plan. A.L.A. bull. 31:947-52, December, 1937.

McDiarmid, E.W., Conditions affecting use of the college library. Lib. quar. 5:59-77, January, 1935.

McDiarmid, E.W., The library survey. Chicago, A.L.A., 1940.

Shane, M. Lanning. Audio-visual aids and the library. Col. and research lib. 1:143-6, March, 1940.

Smith, G. Donald, The librarian and the student. Col. and research lib. 2:119-23, March, 1941.

Stewart, Nathaniel, Case history approach for college student reading. Wil. lib. bull. 17:220-5, November, 1942.

Thompson, R. L. and Nicholson, J.B., Significant influences on general circulation in a small college library. Lib. quar. 11:142-85, April, 1941.

Van Pattan, Nathan, Buying policies of college and university libraries, Col. and research lib. 1:64-71, December, 1939.

9

Library Service Interpretation

The foremost objective of the college library, is to make its service contribute as effectively as possible to the educational programme of the college. In so doing, it performs certain functions: (1) it provides study and reference materials required for supplementing classroom instruction; (2) it provides technical and specialized study materials needed to keep the faculty abreast of their fields; (3) it provides, as far as possible, research materials needed by members of the faculty; (4) it encourages students to use books independently and attempts to develop in students sound habits of reading; (5) it participates in such programmes of post-collegiate education for alumni as are sponsored by the college; (6) it provides study materials needed by extension and correspondence students in colleges where such instruction is offered; and (7) it cooperates with other libraries in strengthening the total resources in the region of which the college is a part.

Notably is of the greatest importance that--through a clear interpretation of these functions and the activities which are performed in carrying them out--the administration, faculty, students, and others concerned with the welfare of the college should be thoroughly informed as to what the library is and what it does. The success of the college library in carrying out its functions is dependent upon the confidence and respect of those it serves. Progress can be made only as the record of library achievement is made known. The main objective of library interpretation, therefore, is to assist in making the library an integral and real part of the educational programme of the college.

Organization for Interpretation

Library interpretation in most colleges is often a very haphazard affair. This is only natural since a great deal of publicity must of necessity depend on the opportunity to prepare a news article, make a talk, or arrange an exhibit. On the other hand, if the results are to serve a useful purpose, there should be a clearly defined programme of interpretation and one person to guide and plan its development. The more systematic and definitely pointed the interpretation plan is, the more effective it will be and more easily managed. This is not to say that interpretation should be the work of only one person. A simple but effective organization will utilize the skills and cooperation of all members of the staff because above all other persons they are the active agents of interpretation. In the small college library, the librarian will direct the work and plan the organization, largely utilizing student help for carrying out the routines. In the large college library, the work of planning and directing publicity may well be delegated as a part-time activity to a member of the staff working under the direct supervision of the librarian. It is necessary, of course, for this person to be released sufficiently from other duties to give real attention and time to planning publicity. Such a person would assemble information for local newspaper and student reporters or for the college news bureau, prepare and write the copy for book bulletins, make arrangements with the person in charge of library departments for exhibits and for faculty participation in planning exhibits, arrange for competent student help to make posters and signs, and perform other duties related to interpretation work.

Unless some one person gives thought to planning and directing the interpretation work there is real danger that it will become a routine affair, unrelated in any real way to the functions which the library is attempting to perform. Also, there is likely to be duplication of effort and a great lack of coordination. The approach to library interpretation is twofold: (1) through personal contact between librarians and the individuals and groups they serve, and (2) through the planned distribution of information about the library. The former is often spoken of as "public relations" and the latter as "publicity." Public relations involves relationships with (1) campus groups: the college administrative officers, boards and advisory committees, the faculty council, department, heads, teachers, faculty committees, and students; and (2) off-campus groups: the alumni and Friends of the library groups; members of the college community; professional, accrediting, and educational councils and associations, and foundations. Publicity includes the following media of interpretation: the annual report, handbooks, the college catalog, book bulletins and booklists, local and student newspapers, bulletin boards and posters, exhibits and book displays, and the radio. Progressive college libraries are trying to use most of these various types of publicity media. The college catalog and annual report have always been used though not always recognized as an avenue of interpretation. College libraries have always had displays and exhibits, but here again these media have often been so routine in nature and hit-or-miss in planning.

Library Relationships on Campus

Developing an adequate programme of library service is not alone the responsibility of the library. As has been repeatedly pointed out in this book, good library service is a cooperative undertaking the combined effort of the administration, faculty, library staff, and students. Upon their knowledge of the aims and methods of the library rest their judgment and willingness to cooperate. The relationships of the library to the various campus groups have been discussed in detail in different parts of this book, but it may be well to summarize some of these relationships here in order to show their importance in interpretation. Certain functions in interpretation, such as determining objectives, establishing the proper relationships with administrative authorities, and preparing official reports, are the responsibility of the librarian. On the other hand, the members of the library staff are the persons who come in contact most frequently with the users of the library, and they must have all the facts on policies, methods, and services. These data are provided partly through staff meetings, bulletins, and booklists but largely through individual conferences between heads of departments and the librarian. It is not enough, however, to have the facts. The attitude of the staff member towards those he helps is even more important. Upon his tact and patience in working with students and upon-his competency and friendliness in contacts with faculty will depend much of the success of the library and its interpretation programme.

Administrative Officers

In an important chapter in *Teaching with books* Dr. Branscomb points out very clearly that little can be accomplished by the librarian without the support and cooperation of the college president. A majority of librarians are directly responsible to the president. He approves the budget and staff appointments even though the final authority in these matters rests with the board of trustees. In developing the policies of the library, he is consulted at every step.

The librarian's annual report is directed to the president and through the president the major needs of the library are transmitted to the board of trustees. Thus, in most colleges the development of library service is in the last analysis determined by the librarian working closely with the president.

If there are differences of opinion or lack of mutual respect, they must be ironed out or they will inevitably lead to a weakening of library service. It is equally important, states Dr. Branscomb, that the college president should see to it that in the organization of the college "the librarian is not separated from but rather is brought into vital relationship to, the educational pro-gram."

In most colleges this will mean that the president will have to be given a clearer picture of the range and importance of library service in the educational programme than he now possesses. In a few colleges the librarian is directly responsible to the dean, but in all colleges he has close relationships with the business manager and his assistants. These relationships vary in different colleges but in general involve the placement of library orders, the payment of bills, the checking of library balances, the determination of insurance inventories, the employment of the clerical staff, and the review of the budget. Satisfactory relationships here are based on common sense and good business administration. The business manager expects the library to be well organized and managed. He will not object to the librarian's taking a strong stand on library needs and support, but he expects him to temper his requests to the known financial ability of the college, to combine the ideal with the practical, and to effect both a balanced library programme and a balanced financial programme. On the other hand, the librarian has a right to expect full cooperation from the business manager in the arrangements for checking library balances, in safeguarding the library's interests where special funds are involved, in taking a broad educational view and not a penny-saving attitude toward library support, and in assisting the library to meet unusual and unexpected financial obligations which may arise after the approved budget is in operation. Other important administrative relationships include those with the dean of men and the dean of women in matters of student cooperation and discipline, the personnel officer in the employment of student help, and with other officers in such matters as student counseling.

Administrative Board or Advisory Council

In most colleges there is an administrative board or advisory council which acts as the planning (executive) committee of the faculty and serves in an advisory capacity to the college president. The board considers matters affecting the library--such as personnel, finances, and curriculum policy. It would seem desirable, therefore, that the college librarian should be given a place on the board or advisory council. The library, of all departments on the campus, can least afford to be self-contained. Universities have quite generally recognized the importance of this relationship and have in their statutes or by-laws made provision for the librarian as an *ex-officio* member of the board. But in colleges, the librarian is seldom represented on the board or advisory council. This is unfortunate since this is one of the important committees on which the librarian might serve, both for his contribution and the increased effectiveness of the library's service which would result. His function on such a board would be to keep library services abreast of new developments and to hold library interests before the group. Without such representation, the librarian is at a disadvantage in making the library a more effective instrument of instruction than it has been heretofore.

Faculty

The importance of this relationship requires little comment. Without the cooperation of the faculty, the librarian can do little to coordinate library services with instruction. Without adequate library support, college instruction is handicapped and faculty research is blocked. Library, laboratory, and classroom must be so planned as to reinforce the teaching process in every possible way. The improvement of library service should therefore be, to a far greater extent than is at present the case, a matter of faculty-library cooperation. In most colleges where the librarian is a member of the faculty with professorial rank, he is automatically a member of the faculty council and has the right to vote. The faculty council determines the policies and methods concerning admission, teaching, counseling, and examination. Membership and attendance by the librarian and members of the staff in the council meetings will afford many opportunities for learning at first hand about matters which have an important bearing on library service. Much of the work of the council is done through committees. Where these committees are concerned with educational policy and curriculum changes, it would seem to be the part of wisdom that any administration seeking to improve the conditions of college work would see to it that the librarian and the staff members who hold responsible positions are represented on these committees.

To relegate the librarians to the status of an administrative assistant or a clerk is equivalent to dwarfing much of the driving force which contributes to the success of a college. In the highest and best type of library service, the librarian is more likely to be a liaison instructor between classroom and library rather than a mere clerk handing out books. Although it is unfortunately true that little is done to bring the judgment and experience of the librarian and the members of the library staff to bear on the determination of policies formulated in faculty committees, it is true that the library has other opportunities to establish close relationships with the faculty. The librarian works closely and intimately with department heads in the preparation of the book budget and in the determination of budget allocations for books. Through the faculty library committee, there is opportunity to discuss and formulate policies which affect jointly the work of the teaching staff and the library.

The staff, in its contact with faculty, furnishes information of first importance in teaching and research.

These cooperative relationships are all important in developing a genuinely educational type of library service, and they afford an opportunity to stress the joint responsibility of the library staff and the ; faculty in this enterprise.

Students

Service to students by the librarians in cooperation with the faculty is the main task of the library. Library relationships with students are conducted mainly through: (1) services at the loan and reference desks and personal conference; (2) talks, group tours, and instruction in the use of the library and bibliography; (3) publicity in the form of printed literature, displays, and exhibits; and (4) the student library committee. The nature of the first two relationships has already been discussed in detail in previous chapters. Publicity is discussed later in this chapter. The student library committee, a fairly recent phenomenon in college library administration, is discussed briefly at this point. Not more than a half-dozen colleges have student library committees and few of these are mentioned in the professional writings. Yet close student-library relationships are necessary to an understanding of the conditions of student use of the library and to the development of constructive measures of any sort for improving library service.

The student library committee, in the light of its stated functions, may properly be regarded as one device for encouraging friendly associations. These functions are usually given as follows: (1) to establish a cooperative spirit between the students and the library staff in order to aid the library in meeting curricular and extra-curricular student library needs; (2) to encourage students to participate in the recommendation of book purchases for the library; (3) to help the librarian interpret the objectives, policies, rules and regulations of the library to the student body; (4) to promote general and recreational reading and to increase student appreciation of good literature; (5) to forestall criticism of the library by keeping the librarian posted on student library needs; and (6) to help relate the work of the library to instruction. The stimulation of student reading in books of a general and recreational character is emphasized by all committees now functioning. Membership on student library committees ranges from five to eight persons. The committee is commonly appointed by the student government association in consultation with the librarian.

Miss Ruby Dare, describing the student committee of the Greenville College library emphasizes the importance of selecting students who have "an interest in literature evidenced by considerable general extra-course reading; a sufficiently attractive personality to be able to lead students; ability to carry responsibility; reliability; and a ready enthusiasm for serving on such a committee. Consideration is sometimes given to class, residence hall, and student library staff representation on the student library committee. The members of the committee ordinarily elect their own chairman. Meetings are usually irregular, with the librarian always in attendance. The duties and work of the student library committees naturally vary according to the special needs of each library. Activities in which such committees have successfully promoted the aims of the library at Rockford, Wellesley, Scripps, Mills, Greenville, and Penn. State include the following: (1) the preparation of book reviews for the student newspaper; (2) aid in the planning and arrangement of library exhibits in and outside the library building; (3) assistance in the selection of books of particular interest to students; (4) planning a programme to encourage students to build their own personal libraries while in college; (5) supervision of residence hall libraries; and (6) assistance in making surveys of student opinion and the use of library resources. This last activity would seem to be one of great potential usefulness to both students and the library. The library stands to gain understanding, otherwise inaccessible, of the conditions of student use of the library, and to benefit in the development of any changes that are made by the sense of general confidence which such cooperation tends to develop. The students gain whatever values may come from friendly associations with the librarians, by the improvements in library service they are able to suggest, and by a broader understanding of the purposes and uses of the library. The librarian plays an important role in the formation of the committee, in attendance at its meetings, and in guiding its work. In all these activities he remains in the background as much as possible. His function is advisory, suggesting problems to be considered, discussing possible solutions, and sharing with the committee his special knowledge of library work.

His personality, ability to talk easily with students, sense of humour, and tactfulness and patience in dealing with suggestions and complaints will have a great deal to do with the success of the student advisory committee on the library, library relations off campus The chief values of cooperation between the library and various campus groups have already been suggested. An attempt is now made in the following pages to define the range of relationships beyond campus boundaries in which cooperation is applicable and desirable. Such relationships are second only in importance to those on campus in a broad view of interpretation because they stimulate personal and professional growth, afford new opportunities for useful educational service, establish contacts which may be helpful in the development and support of the library, and help to interpret the distinctive contribution which college libraries can make to society.

Alumni and to Friends of the Library Groups

Interpretation to alumni may take two forms: (1) lending and reference services, and (2) publicity designed to encourage gifts. The opportunity to provide an educational service to alumni through the distribution of reading lists, the lending of books for scholarly or technical work, and the uses of the reference facilities of the library have already been touched upon in an earlier chapter; There will be a great diversity in the requests received by the college library for information and book loans. Some of them will be answerable by a book lean or a collection of pamphlet material about a particular subject. Others will necessitate a letter in which the specific information is given with reference to sources which may be borrowed by the alumnus from the college library or from some other library.

Still others will lead to conferences between the reference librarian and members of the faculty and will result in the sending of a systematic course of reading to meet the alumnus's particular need. Publicity for gifts may take the form of direct appeals to individual alumni for special purchases or the publication of lists of deside-rata in the alumni magazine. As a prelude to either, it is important to build up good relationships by keeping the alumni informed of library progress and development. In addition to articles in the alumni journal, the librarian should take every opportunity to know the alumni and to meet them at reunions. When a person has been out of college for twenty years he has forgotten all about the library. A regular column of library notes in the alumni magazine and an occasional picture of some interesting phase of library work will help to build up interest and goodwill. Some colleges have found that an organization of Friends working steadily and intelligently toward definite goals has added much to the value and usefulness of the library. In actual practice, these Friends of the library groups are composed largely of alumni. The initiative in suggesting the idea of the Friends organization may well be taken by the librarian. He knows what such organizations have contributed to libraries in other institutions, what has been written about them, and what methods have been used in establishing and keeping them going. Beyond this initial stimulation, the librarian's relationship to the Friends organization is largely a subordinate one. Unless there is some one person among the alumni or college friends who has the interest, understanding, and energy to take an active part in creating enthusiasm and membership for the organization, the results are not likely to prove lasting or worth while. If the Friends organization is simply the librarian's show and if the group relies on him to keep it going and alive, its value is largely lost. Although the librarian remains in the background in the actual development of the Friends organization, he has an important contribution to make as an adviser to its promoters and leaders. At the time of establishment, the Friends organization should be given a "frank and full statement of what the library now is, what it is doing, what it desires to become, and how its friends can aid in its progress toward that goal." After the group is established, the librarian is the logical person to furnish the information about gifts that are needed to build up the collections and services. Unless this relationship exists, there is the possible danger that the Friends organization may prove an embarrassment to the library by leading to gifts of rare and special collections which are not pertinent to curriculum needs and which result in a heavy administrative expenditure from an already over-taxed budget.

College Community

In both service and interpretation, it is important that the college librarian take into account the community in which the college is located. Some libraries, such as Oberlin, maintain full public library service for residents of the community. In most colleges, provision is made for townspeople to use the library as a reference center and to borrow books of a scholarly or research nature if they are not in use by the faculty and students. State supported colleges have a greater obligation not only to citizens of the local community but to residents of the entire state. Regardless of the nature or extent of library service to the community residents, the library cannot afford to overlook these persons in its interpretation programme. News of the college is published in local newspapers which are often read throughout the state.

Associations and Foundations

In addition to the necessity of maintaining close relationships with alumni, friends, citizens of the local community, and the general public, librarians are under professional obligation to participate in the work of their national and state library associations. Moreover, since libraries are an integral part of colleges, librarians are naturally concerned with the interests and activities of educational associations and philanthropic foundations. These organizations have had a tremendous influence on the whole educational field and have contributed directly to the growth and development of libraries in institutions of higher education. It is important, therefore, that college librarians should identify themselves as closely as possible with the aims of these organizations by attendance at some of their meetings, contributions to convention programmes, and by wide reading in their published reports and proceedings. The value and significance of these outside relationships may be more readily understood by the newcomer to the library profession by a review of the purposes and work of the more important of these organizations. This review follows in the briefest and most general terms.

American Library Association. Founded in 1876, the American Library Association is the oldest and largest library association in the world. Of its many objectives and accomplishments, three are of particular concern to college librarians: (1) to raise standards and promulgate ideals of library service; (2) to assist libraries to operate with the utmost economy and efficiency; and (3) to improve the status of librarians by working to advance salary standards, by maintaining an effective placement and personnel service, and by increasing professional knowledge through original research. The Association conducts and disseminates important educational research studies, furnishes comprehensive book selection and bibliographical services, and fosters a programme of sound educational interpretation. The programmes of the Association deal with important current educational problems.

Association of College and Reference Libraries. Of the five major divisions of the American Library Association., the one most closely identified with college library interests is the Association of College and Reference Libraries. Established as a division under its new name in 1940, though having a continuous existence as a section of the Association since 1889, the A.C.R.L., as it is popularly known, aims "to bring together in an annual meeting college and university librarians and staff members, librarians and staff members of reference libraries, as well as the reference librarians of public libraries, for the discussion of their common problems and the problems peculiar to academic and scholarly work." Through its section committees, and professional journal, *College and research libraries,* it has stimulated experimentation and research for the improvement of college library service and it has helped to integrate the efforts of college, university, and reference librarians with those of kindred groups such as educational and research agencies.

Other National Library Societies. The American Library Association maintains close relationships with six affiliated national societies and nine other national library societies. Although membership is limited to libraries concerned with the collection and service of research materials, librarians in larger colleges are concerned with the work and publications of the Association of Research Libraries. In recent years this Association has made available at a price that most large college libraries can afford a valuable research and catalog tool in the *Catalog of books represented by Library of Congress printed cards* and has continued to sponsor the important annual list of *Doctoral dissertations accepted by American universities.* College libraries hold institutional memberships in the Music-Library Association and college librarians have contributed to such valuable technical tools as the *Code for cataloging music* and the *Subject headings for the literature of music from the Library of Congress subject headings.* Through its treatment of technical problems in special fields, particularly those relating to the subject and content of college and university departmental libraries, the Special Libraries Association has furnished valuable aids and tools for the college library. In the pages of its official bulletin, *Special Libraries,* college librarians are finding practical and useful information on the handling of special collections, audio-visual materials, and ephemeral or fugitive materials.

Close relationships exist between college librarians and the Bibliographical Society of America, which has as its purpose the promotion of bibliographical research and publication. College librarians have served as officers of the Society and as members of its various committees. The semi-annual meetings of the Society have considered bibliographical matters of direct interest to college librarians, such as the problem of bibliographical instruction in colleges. The Society has sponsored and published research in which college librarians have participated and benefited, such as *Incunabula in American libraries* and *American newspapers, 1821-1936; a union list of files available in the United States and Canada.*

State and Local Library Associations. State, regional, and local library associations have contributed to college libraries primarily through strengthening the American Library Association and through annual or biennial meetings which have enabled librarians and staff members to come together for informal discussions of common problems. Moreover, they have challenged, perhaps not so much as they should, college librarians to cultivate a broader view of their profession than is possible by restricting themselves merely to campus problems. State associations have introduced and interested college librarians in such problems as state aid for public libraries, regional libraries, and reading studies. College librarians, on the other hand, have contributed to public and school members of the state association by discovering and promulgating opportunities for cooperation through the loan of books, the promotion of library exchanges, and the publication and dissemination of bibliographical works and studies. State, regional, and local associations sometimes have publicity committees, publish bulletins, and in other ways influence the attitude of the public towards libraries, including those of the colleges.

Accrediting Associations. The work of the North Central Association and the Southern Association of Colleges and Secondary Schools has been particularly beneficial to college librarians. The basis of accreditment, as previously indicated, is no longer limited to quantitative measurements but is to be found in the adequacy of the book and periodical collection for the academic programme of the particular institution and in the use of these materials by students and faculty. College librarians have played an increasingly active part in the development of the criteria of measurement for the associations. In 1935 Dr. Douglas Waples and his colleagues at the University of Chicago Graduate Library School developed more exact measures for the evaluation of the part the library plays in the achievement of educational objectives. In June, 1942, the North Central Association again appointed committees, on which college librarians were prominently represented, for revising forms and checklists. In 1940 the Southern Association invited college and university librarians to assist in redefining its standards for college, teachers college, and junior college libraries; and in 1942 the Southern Association sponsored a work conference on problems of higher education in which the library was a major topic of discussion and in which libraries were invited to participate.

From this brief review, one is perhaps justified in concluding that at no time has the accreditation movement established closer relations with college librarians or shown greater effectiveness in evaluation than it is manifesting right now. More and more, it is plain, accrediting associations are taking college librarians into their confidence with reference to the actual evalution of library service. The importance of this relationship lies in the increased opportunity it gives librarians to make their services more truly effective in the educational programme.

Learned Societies, Councils, and Educational Associations. College librarians, taking their cue from their university colleagues, are increasingly recognizing the importance of the relationship of the library to learned societies, councils, and educational associations. The councils and associations, on the other hand, are taking a more active interest in recent years than ever before in problems directly and indirectly related to libraries. The four major councils are the National Research Council, the Social Science Research Council, the American Council of Learned Societies, and the American Council of Education. Their constituent members include among other associations: the Association of American Colleges, the American Association of Teachers Colleges, and the American Association of Junior Colleges. The constituent associations maintain approved lists of colleges and establish criteria for accrediting which take into account the adequacy of the library. The four major councils have three major purposes: (1) to be of service to the government; (2) to promote research; and (3) to serve as a coordinating function between the constituent agencies. Unquestionably, the exercise of the last two functions has some bearing on the problems of college libraries. An illustration of this fact is to be seen in the activity of the Social Science Research Council in the promotion of a nationwide movement to collect and preserve source materials in each state. This activity has been coordinated with the work of various committees of the American Library Association and has resulted, among other things, in the publication of a study of the methods and equipment for reproducing research materials by photographic processes.

The importance of educational associations to college libraries lies in the fact that these associations would appear to have comprehended more fully the strategic role of the library in education than many of the administrators and faculty members of individual colleges have. Through the meetings, projects, standards, and publications of these associations, college librarians are finding an increasing opportunity to interpret the educational function of their libraries to college administrators and to faculties. The Association of American Colleges has frequently stressed the fact that the college library should be coordinated more effectively with the educational and recreational programmes of the college. That point of view was taken in its Library Project of 1937. The purpose of this project was to study the library from the standpoint of its educational effectiveness. The study was undertaken by Dr. Harvie Branscomb and culminated in the publication of *Teaching with books,* which, as the title suggests, has as much to do with the improvement of teaching as with library procedures for coordinating the work of the library with instruction.

In 1957 Dr. William Warner Bishop, writing in the bulletin of the Association of American Colleges, pointed out the same general truth, namely, that "success in college teaching in the next few decades will more and more depend upon success in making the college library a true teaching instrument." In the task of making the library a more vital factor in teaching and in broadening the responsibility for bringing this about, it is apparent that college librarians will benefit tremendously by close relationships with learned societies and educational associations. Hence it behooves college librarians to become acquainted with the purposes of these societies and associations, study their programmes and reports, and establish a friendly basis for cooperative action.

Foundations. The contribution of the endowed foundations to the growth and effectiveness of college library services has been mentioned at several points in this book. It is apparent that these foundations--particularly Carnegie and Rockefeller, and the General Education Board--have played no small part in the development of the college library. The purposes of these foundations in supporting college libraries are similar to those reported above. Summarizing the Carnegie Corporation gifts of over four million dollars for academic libraries. Mr. Robert Lester, secretary of the Corporation, states:

> ... It is believed that as the years go by, the usefulness of books will become more and more impressed on the consciousness of the academic community, and that the wide-awake professors, librarians, and presidents--and there are many of this kind who drive students to books--will so adapt college teaching that students will be eager to draw upon what President Wilkins has termed, "the transforming riches of the library."

Foundation money for libraries has gone into buildings and equipment, library endowments, librarianship endowment, the purchase of books, library surveys, bibliographical research, bibliographical publications, and cooperative projects. Inasmuch as these foundations, more than any other outside agencies, have contributed directly to the support of library service and to the improvement of book collections and facilities, it is of the utmost importance that college librarians be familiar with their policies of philanthropy.

Publicity: The Media of Interpretation

Up to this point an attempt has been made to show the importance of close and cordial relationships between the library and certain groups and organizations which use its services or contribute to its growth and development. The remainder of this chapter will be devoted to a description of the media which are commonly used to interpret the services of the library to these groups. These media were listed at the beginning of the chapter but may be mentioned here again for the sake of clarity and emphasis: Annual reports; Handbooks; College catalog; The newspaper; Bulletin boards and displays; Book bulletins and booklists; Exhibits and book displays; and Radio

Annual Reports

Annual reports such as those most commonly issued--emphasizing the number of new accessions, volumes in the library, and circulation use--are not a positive force in the interpretative programme of the college library. Their effectiveness as a medium of publicity is further restricted because many librarians are preparing reports for too limited a circle of readers. "No longer can the report be regarded as for the eye of the president alone. It is a document that should be read by faculty and governing bodies and by every member of the staff." Studies dealing with annual reports such as those by Professor Fay in 1934 and Professor Russell in 1936 have been helpful in acquainting librarians not only with present practices, but more particularly with deficiencies in reporting and suggestions for improvement.

Professor Russell's questionnaire on college library reports was directed to the librarians of 500 colleges of the liberal arts type. The most significant revelations of his findings were: that fully one-half of the librarians in American colleges either never make a report of any kind or are uninterested in reporting procedures; that there is a tendency for the stronger and better colleges to be more attentive than the weaker colleges to the matter of library reporting; that annual reports are usually not intended for any readers except those directly connected with the college in some official capacity; and that about half the colleges give no publicity whatever to the library report.

Purposes of the Report. There can be no reasonable quarrel with the usefulness of the annual report of the librarian to the college and to the administration. The single necessity of an annual accounting for funds expended in relation to services rendered would be sufficient if no other considerations were involved. To this purpose, however, must be added others of less obvious but genuinely practical importance: (1) the report enables the librarian and the library staff to comprehend the course of events by study of all departmental reports and thereby to discover means for the improvement of service; (2) it serves as a practical device for keeping members of the board of trustees and faculty posted on library purposes and achievements; (3) it may serve to interest alumni and friends of the library in making donations to meet special library needs; (4) it is a valuable document for investigation and research in graduate library schools; (5) it provides a history of the college library and a record of its contribution to instruction; and (6) it may be considered, in the opinion of Professor Fay, a valuable primary source material for historical and social science classes, when and if the reports of college librarians "progress toward greater unity in form, arrangement, content, and availability."

Ideally speaking, the preparation of the annual report should be an all-year task. A file of clippings and notes will certainly prove useful when it comes to the actual writing of the report, but few librarians have the patience or time to keep such a record. If the library issues a mimeographed booklist of accessions, the notes prepared for the monthly cover sheet will serve as a reminder of outstanding events, salient figures, and important gifts. The successful report is interesting and graphic.

Contents of the Report. In analyzing the contents of reports submitted in connection with his study, Professor Russell selected twenty-five reports which he considered superior to all the remainder. It would seem probable, therefore, that an analysis of the items treated in these reports would suggest the contents of a satisfactory report.

The use of a topical outline, is a help and time-saver in assembling and organizing the material for the annual report. The final form of the report, of course, will vary according to the points which the librarian wishes to emphasize. Some librarians put a great deal of care and energy into making the report as complete as possible. Others write a brief summary of the chief events and incorporate summary digests of the staff reports. Still others prefer to concentrate on one particular phase of library activity each year and to build the whole report about this topic. Such a plan has been followed very effectively in recent years by the librarian of Wellesley College. Good writing, careful organization, and individuality are equally essential to all of them, however.

Form of the Report. In presenting the information contained in the report a conscious effort should be made to avoid technical expressions and to express the pertinent ideas so that they will be readily grasped by one unfamiliar with library procedures. Graphs and tables are frequently used effectively. A typewritten copy is the final form in which most college library reports appear, but it is obviously impossible to reproduce sufficient copies economically in this form if the report is to go to a large number of people. Professor Russell noted in his study that a growing "number of the colleges either mimeograph or print the library report and are thus able to provide enough copies to supply many interested readers."

If the annual report is to qualify as a valuable medium of publicity, it should be sent to the president of the college and to other administrative officers, the members of the board of trustees, the faculty library committee, the faculty, the library staff, and a select group of alumni, friends, and students. In addition, an effort should be made to give it wider public notice through a brief summary in the newspapers and alumni magazine. Libraries which issue book bulletins frequently publish the highlights of the librarian's annual report in one issue each year. In some colleges a summary of the librarian's report is published in the president's annual report. In colleges where this is done, there would still be need for a complete mimeographed or printed report for circulation to the faculty, to library schools, and to friends of the library.

Handbooks

Each year more and more college libraries are offering their students and faculty some sort of guide to library resources and services. The guides now in print are notable for their variety in scope and their ingenuity in form and presentation No two publications have quite the same format, content, or tone since each one naturally reflects the attitudes and needs of a particular institution.

Library Handbook for Students. A library handbook for students may have permanent values The information it contains may be used by students throughout their undegraduate years as well as after college. "To learn to use the William and Mary College Library," writes the author of the guile of this library is with adaptations) to learn how to use almost any non-technical American library and to provide oneself with one of the most important tools for remaining an educated man or women." Permanency, therefore, is an advantage which handbook have over certain other forms of printed library publicity. The library handbook for students is also important for its instructional value and its timeliness. A student writing a paper on "Literary culture in colonial Virginia" will need to use the general periodical indexes as well as book In high school or during Fresh-man week he has probably heard about but the Reader's guide but at the time he had no occasion to use it has since forgotten that it exists. A good handbook will explain the general periodical indexes and associate their use with writing themes on current topic Later, a suggestion from the teacher or the librarian may send the student back to his handbook at the "psychological time This same quality of timeliness applies to all of the usual types of information found in the handbook-- from the discussion of reference books to the schedule of library hours. The library handbook has direct publicity value. In many if not in most colleges, the handbook is about the only printed matter which the library can afford to publish. If it is well designed and printed, if it is interesting and informative, and if it is distributed at a time when its pertinence to college studies is readily apparent to the student, the handbook not only contributes to the prestige of the library but it also provides a very real link to instruction. Library handbooks for students differ according to their approach (the purpose for which they were written) and the individual differences in college library organization. Yet it is possible from an examination of a large number of such handbooks to reconstruct a "type" or at least to point out features which are common to all. A typical handbook is printed and bound in a stiff paper cover. The word "handbook" is used in the title. The average handbook costs 2½ cents a copy, measures 4-3.4 by 7-3/4 inches, and fills 22 pages. Other favourite sizes are 4 x 6 inches and 6 x 9 inches. The contents usually includes these topics:

- Purpose of the handbook
- Hours
- Staff
- General information about the book collection and the building
- How to borrow books--steps traced from filling out a call slip to returning the book
- Reserve books
- Card catalog
- Classification
- Reference books
- Reference room -- arrangement of books, personal services
- Periodical indexes
- Periodical room -- arrangement of periodicals, current and back files
- Browsing room
- Library rules and regulations
- Floor plans
- Index

The contents of the larger and more comprehensive handbooks, such as Wesleyan's *Library Handbook,* may give additional information under such headings as "The use of books--their parts and make-up," "Personal book buying," "Facilities for graduate study," "Access to stacks," "Government documents," "How to compile a bibliography," "Local libraries," "Books and reading," and "History of the library."

Handbooks are frequently distributed from the various loan desks in the library. Obviously, then, there must be something about the cover, the title, or the printing and design on the cover to catch the student's eye. New York University combines a clever cartoon with a good title-- *The guide;* Antioch offers the house and lot-- *This is your library;* Vassar appeals by the artistic quality of an original print reproduced on the cover; the Woman's College of the University of North Carolina depends on a combination of fine printing, simple design, and a catch title--*Help yourself.*

A handbook is intended primarily as an instructional leaflet. No amount of "window dressing" will make a good handbook if the text is badly arranged or poorly written. The first thing, therefore, is to maintain the interest kindled by an exciting cover and to present the material in such a way that the student will get the maximum: benefit from reading it. It is a marked characteristic of the best library handbooks that they introduce the student to the main services of the library by function or department. To illustrate with one specific example: under the heading, "How to find books easily," the Williams College *Library handbook* introduces the card catalog as the logical starting point in investigation, interprets its use by means of sample cards and brief notes, tells what a call slip is and how it should be filled out, directs the student to the stack and the particular section indicated by the call number, tells how the book may be charged when found, and repeats briefly the rules and period of loan. The word "function" is used to describe this method, not simply because it groups material on processes which logically follow one another, but also because it suggests a method of investigation which is an important part of library instruction. The same approach should be used throughout the handbook. An effort should be made to link specific library aids with the student's class problems. The description of periodical indexes offers an opportunity to associate these tools with the preparation of source themes. The index may also serve as a device for making the association of library aids with class problems more vivid and understandable.

The style of the handbook should be simple, friendly, and clear. Illustrations, charts, and diagrams of all sorts are helpful in explaining library aids and guides. A large number of the smaller college libraries, and a few of the larger, mimeograph their handbodks. A printed handbook is superior to any reproduced by the newer printing substitutes, and it need cost very little more if careful attention is paid to the method of printing and revision. From the angle of economy, such items as library hours, library staff, and rules may be printed on the inside of the cover, front and back, because these are the items most frequently revised. A new cover for a new edition is desirable in any event and this suggestion will free the text of numerous corrections.

Library Handbook for Faculty. The preparation of a college library handbook is made difficult by the necessity for keeping in mind a variety of readers--the tyro and the sure-footed, the indifferent student and the serious student, the bewildered freshman and the experienced faculty member. Most libraries attempt to strike a happy medium and to present the essential information for all types of readers in a single handbook. A few libraries have given considerable thought to this problem and attempt to meet the needs of different readers by separate handbooks or by a special arrangement of material.

Pennsylvania State College and the Woman's College of the University of North Carolina issue two handbooks, one for undergraduates and one for graduate students and faculty members. Some duplication of the material in the student library handbook is inevitable but there are distinct advantages to having two handbooks. A handbook for the faculty serves two purposes. It is an administrative device for keeping the faculty informed of library methods, staff personnel, hours of service, and like details. As such, it serves a useful reference purpose. In the second place, it promotes library-faculty cooperation and library effectiveness in teaching. This second and more important purpose is not accomplished unless the handbook contains information on such matters as these: a clear statement of book policy defining faculty responsibility as participants in book selection; the necessity for some organization within the teaching department to insure systematic checking and ordering of library materials; the special collections and special materials (films, records, etc.) available in the library for supplementing modern methods of teaching; the policy of the library in regard to helping students with reference services; the responsibility of the faculty in making assignments to library material; and the facilities of the library for the promotion of research. Frequent revision is perhaps not as essential as in a student handbook, but a thorough indexing greatly facilitates its use.

College Catalog

The college catalog is sent to all prospective students applying for admission to a particular college and to other institutions of higher learning. This would seem to stamp it as an important medium for interpreting library services, but actually it has not been used for this purpose by librarians except to record the more obvious facts of size and to inform students about hours, regulations, and directions for finding materials in particular departments or rooms in the library. Specific deficiencies noted by Miss

Florence King in her extensive study of the library in the college catalog included the following:

1. The library is given a relatively small space in the college catalog in proportion to the importance of its instructional function.
2. The catalog is indexed inadequately for the purpose of making available all information about the library and library personnel.
3. The importance of the library is obscured in the catalog by the unfortunate position of descriptive information which tends to emphasize its architectural rather than its instructional character.
4. In respect to matters of administration, organization, and service to readers, the library does not receive the attention it deserves in order to present sufficient, significant, and effective information for either the student or the professional group.

A consideration of the purposes of the college catalog will help to show its value as a medium of interpretation for the college library. In the first place, it is intended to acquaint prospective students and their parents with an accurate statement of what the college offers in the way of a sound education. Therefore, it should include a statement of the place of the library in the college programme and of its book and periodical resources for serving instruction. Direct teaching services such as library talks and group tours during Freshman week, instruction in the use of the library, and printed handbooks and guides should be mentioned. The assistance given to students at the reference and readers' advisory desks should be stressed. Special materials of value to teaching--such as slides, pictures, maps, and pamphlets--should also be mentioned. Since the catalog is intended primarily for student reading, the description of library resources and services should be direct and simple in language. As a reference tool on the campus, the catalog is in constant use by teachers and students. It should contain a brief summary of library rules and regulations and specify the hours of library service during the regular session, summer session, and vacation periods. All important information pertaining to the library should be fully indexed, particularly when this information appears in two or three different places in the catalog. Library facilities close by and available to faculty and students should be mentioned in terms of their special usefulness to these groups. The library staff should be listed as a group and those with academic ranking should also be listed in their proper place with the teaching faculty.

Student Newspaper. The student newspaper provide? an outlet for library interpretation through news articles, feature stories, book columns, and student editorials. The aim is to make the students aware of the value of the library in their education and to stimulate them to use its resources. News articles are best handled through interviews with student reporters. If the librarian makes arrangements for a regular interviewing period at the beginning of the year, it will improve the chances of having a continuous appearance of library news in the student newspaper. The following types of stories have appeared frequently as news stories in student papers: remodelling and other physical changes in the library building, staff activities (personnel changes, staff member appearing on radio programme, etc.), rare book exhibits, book displays in special fields, new rules and regulations, student library prize awards, recent accessions to the magazines, important magazine articles of the month, recent books, browsing room talks and music concerts, special collections, gifts, and special facilities for student study.

Obviously the list is almost limitless and could be extended in each college, depending on the current happenings and the resources of the library. Feature stories which interpret library services or special resources are even more important than news stories. In every college library there are pamphlet collections, bibliographical tools, government documents, and special services which are not used so much as they should be because students do not know about them or do not understand their usefulness. Articles about these materials or services are more likely to be accepted as feature stories for the student newspaper than for the city newspapers, particularly if a member of the library staff prepares the material and "puts into the story an interest that the editor might have neither time nor inclination to find." Feature stories have appeared in student newspapers on the resources and services of the library as a whole, on special collections in the library, on the kinds of questions received and answered at the reference desk, on the card catalog and special catalogs and indexes, and on student reading interests as shown through the circulation records. The same kind of interpretation is made possible through a regular library column in the student newspaper, although the emphasis in the column is usually on new books or books about a particular subject. Such columns have appeared under the title of *Look'n 'em over, From the library, Bits about books, The bookshelf,* and *A Word to the wise.* Student editorials about the library have pointed to the need for additional space, to student honour in borrowing and in handling library books, and to the educational opportunities to be found in using the library.

Local Newspapers. Events in the college library which possess news possibilities to local and state papers are rather limited unless the library receives numerous gifts and possesses collections of unique or special regional interest. If the college is large enough to have a separate news bureau division, the library news should be prepared in rough form for the person in charge of this office. If this person is made to realize the aims and objectives of the library, and if he is given an insight into the nature and importance of library materials and services, he will probably do his best to see that library news is presented even though it may not have the "spot news" value of the "Betty Coed" type of story,

If the publicity releases originate with the library, such as in colleges where there is no news bureau or person designated to send out college news, certain techniques of modern news-writing must be complied with before the articles are to be considered for publication. These principles are summarized by Miss Marie D. Loizeaux in her *Publicity Primer:*

1. Typewrite all copy.
2. Use paper about 8'/2 x 11 inches.
3. Write on one side of the paper only.
4. Double or triple space.
5. Place the name of the library in the upper left hand corner of page one, together with the name of the person sending the story, position, release date.
6. Copy should start one third or halfway down the first page; do not caption or title a story.
7. Number all pages after the first.
8. There should be no hyphenation at the end of lines and no dividing of paragraphs from one page to another.
9. The first paragraph must answer the questions, who? when? where? why? and what?
10. The copy should be written with accuracy, brevity, and clearness,
11. The end of the story should be indicated by an "end mark."
12. The word "more" should be written on the bottom of the page to indicate that copy is unfinished and is to be continued on the next page.

Besides the techniques involved, the story itself is the chief concern of the news editor. Miss Loizeaux stresses the importance of "making the story interesting" and of "writing with the non-user of the library in mind." College library stories--at least those which are significant from the point of view of library interpretation--are rarely of the light, human-interest type. Their chances of being accepted for printing are determined in large part by their significance and the appeal of the lead, or opening sentence in the first paragraph. With the increasing emphasis placed on news photographs, it is probable that the library story would receive more favourable attention on the part of newspaper editors if it were accompanied by photographs. The point is usually made that pictures should feature people rather than objects and that close-ups of a reader using library tools is better than a large group picture.

Bulletin Boards and Posters

Bulletin boards and posters offer many possibilities for interpreting library services. They may be used to stimulate interest in selected books on a particular subject; to call attention to special resources and services; to present short, graphic summaries of important national and local news; and to announce programmes and lectures. Posters not only guide and instruct but have cultural values also. A striking poster may satisfy a student's aesthetic instinct as completely as a beautiful piece of sculpture or a finely printed book.

In planning bulletin boards, it has been found useful to keep an informal file of ideas for bulletin board use--titles that appeal, slogans, notes on special days, authors, and events, pictures, book jackets, and pictorial or outline maps. An effort is made to tie national, educational, literary, scientific, and seasonal events with the use of library materials. Local news clippings are most important --radio programmes, newspaper and magazine clippings about persons and things of local interest, etc. The lesser-known materials which form the background of reference service are often emphasized, such as pamphlets, government documents, bibliographies, and special collections. Attention is called to services as well as to materials. All too often students and faculty are not aware of the help they can get through the reference and readers' advisory services of the library.

Bulletin board displays will not command attention unless some care is given to their arrangement and design. An experienced librarian publicist emphasizes these details in bulletin board arrangement:

1. Neatness, simplicity, and visibility are essential.
2. Few displays should be shown simultaneously in one room.
3. Long lists of explanations on the board will not be read.
4. When the subject is changed, the form of the display should be changed, or else the colour scheme, or both.
5. Pictures, jackets, captions--all should emphasize one idea.
6. Captions and slogans should be brief and arresting, unhackneyed, confined to a single idea, yet expressed with clearness and force.
7. A few book jackets, neatly trimmed, and well displayed, are more effective than a great many shown at one time.
8. Illustrations should excite interest and be to the point, be large enough to be visible at a distance, simple in design, and with no unnecessary detail.
9. Letters and lettering should be neat, simple, carefully spaced, and well-proportioned to the size of board or poster.

10. Background materials may contribute colour, but should be less intense than the rest of the display; can be varied, but must be planned to harmonize with the materials exhibited, and the room in which used.

11. Arrangement of material on the bulletin board may be
    (a) bysymmetric, with formal balance--i.e. with a reversed pattern to the right and left of a vertical center line.
    (b) informal, with occult balance, using a "beam scale" arrangement in which symmetry is gained through balance by size, weight, and/or colour,
    (c) dynamically balanced, so that material is arranged to bring about a forceful line movement of the eye, properly stopped at points of interest at beginning or end.

The poster collection may be supplemented by clippings from magazines and by purchase or gift from educational and commercial firms which make and distribute posters. *Leads No. 7* from the American Library Association, gives specific sources for posters and display materials. The sources of maps listed therein may be supplemented by the excellent bibliography of pictorial maps compiled by Miss Betty Brown. Educational and library posters may be obtained from the National Association of Book Publishers, Metropolitan Life Insurance Co., National Child Welfare Association, National Safety Council, the H. W. Wilson Co., and other associations and publishers. Most of the home furnishing and picture magazines contain excellent poster material in their cover, text, and advertising pages. Textbooks from the field of visual education contain sources of posters and charts. Certain colleges publish lists of posters of particular interest for display in connection with subject materials. Display material sources are listed in articles and pamphlets and in practically every issue of the library journals.

Book Bulletins and Booklists

College library publications of this type may be divided into four groups according to their format, contents, and purpose: (1) book bulletins, (2) mimeographed lists of new accessions, (3) booklists, and (4) Friends of the library bulletins.

Book Bulletins. Printed periodical book bulletins in college libraries are rare. The reason, of course, is obvious. A successful bulletin is expensive and takes times to edit. A monthly of any size and distinction will scarcely cost less than five hundred dollars a year, and two of the best quarterlies now published cost, on an average, seventy-five dollars an issue for publication costs alone. In terms of hardheaded investment, it is unlikely that the library will receive in the early years of a bulletin publication an equivalent in cash or book gifts. Library bulletins are primarily a means for increasing the usefulness of a library. Only indirectly may they help to build up goodwill and support. It is not uncommon, for example, for the editor of a book bulletin to mention special books which the library cannot afford to purchase from its regular budget. And not-infrequently one reads in a later issue the acknowledgment of a gift of some of these items from a reader and friend of the library. The library bulletin increases the usefulness of the library by calling attention to new books received by the library and by interpreting library services to students and faculty and alumni. The library way of doing things and its resources are frequently unknown and a little mysterious to many of its readers. The book bulletin offers an opportunity to clear up these mysteries; to explain the work of the catalog, the order, and the circulation departments; to label and interpret such intangible services as personal guidance in reading and using the library; to describe exhibits and special collections; and to call attention to materials and services which are of little use because nobody knows about them. Although it is not widely removed from the current pattern of printed bulletins, Dartmouth's *Library bulletin* has assets which make it a worthy model for study. It came out first in 1931 and has been the inspiration of many other bulletins since then. Its appearance is pleasing and it never fails to make the most commonplace incidents in library work interesting and amusing.

Distinction and beauty are contributed through the choice of a rich quality of paper and fine typography. In the main, however, its excellence stems directly from the variety, interest, and graceful literary style of its contents. This is accomplished in two ways. First, in approaching every aspect of the work of the library--from rare books down to the most mechanical operation in library routine--the editor of the bulletin thinks primarily in terms of his readers. Second, the style of writing is direct, pleasant, and witty. There is nothing official or impersonal about it. Some of the types of material qualifying for admission to its pages include:

1. Special collections
   Americana
   Italian dialect collection
   Nineteenth- and twentieth-century Spanish plays
   Art library
   Medical library
   Map collection
   Music resources
   Pamphlet collection
   Order department
2. Explanation of library policies and rules
   Open-stack policy

Lists of desiderata
Acknowledgment of gifts
Notable purchases indicating lines of interest
Friends of the library

4. The work of departments
   Interesting summaries of the functions and procedures in
   Catalog department
   Periodicals
   Reserves
   Bindery

Reclassification problems
Faculty return of books
Book selection
Fines

3. Publicity and interpretation
Notice of exhibits
Excerpts from the librarian's annual reports

6. Booklists
Recent accessions -- selected and briefly annotated
Occasional articles about books on a special subject
New periodicals

7. Archival material
Reprints of interesting and

Treasure room
Tower room (recreational reading)

5. Special services
Inter-library loan
Photostats and film
Research services
often humorous letters and documents from the college archives

8. Fillers
Amusing incidents to service
Bookish notes

With less skillful editing, this material might be very dull. Fortunately, the editor of the *Library bulletin* has a facile pen and a rare gift for communicating his sense of high adventure in librarian-ship and books. His handling of Dartmouth's archival lore and culture for brief fillers gives a special flavour to the bulletin. One's curiosity is piqued by titles such as these--"Books behind bars," "$3,000 unwanted" (fines), "Top soil" (this for a discussion of the grimy edges of catalog cards), "To him that hath" (polite reminder to the faculty to get books back within a reasonable time), and "Diversions in Baker street." Articles are signed with the writer's initials, and faculty contributions are frequently included.

One chief difference between Dartmouth's *Library bulletin* and the printed and mimeographed bulletins of other college libraries is the emphasis which the latter place on book notes. Wesleyan's *About books,* issued quarterly and paid for by the Friends of the library, carries regularly two or three pages of book notes about a "few more or less significant books" and occasional articles about books on timely topics or reprints of important booklists which have appeared elsewhere. Pennsylvania State College's *Headlight devotes* ten of its twelve pages, as a general rule, to short notices of new books and, like *About books,* carries short bibliographies on special subjects. The book notes in the *Headlight* are written by the faculty and members of the library staff and are signed in full or with initials. Colby Junior College's superbly captioned and neatly printed pocket digest, the *Book pedlar,* carries several pages of book comment and library news written to meet the needs and tastes of younger students. *Library jottings* of St. Vincent College (Pa.) is an example of what the very small college can do in a mimeographed bulletin. In concise form it records the library news, changes in library regulations, new books, and general book news.

Special emphasis is placed on the format of the book bulletin to the end that it will not only appear attractive to the reader but also reflect credit on the library whose name it bears. Three college library book bulletins add variety by using a different-colour paper stock for the covers of successive issues. Their type is large enough for comfortable reading and in proportion to the size of the page. A six by nine inch page appears to be a favourite size, and six of the book bulletins run to about twelve pages a copy. Local printing costs, the size of the bulletin, the use of illustrations, and the quality of the paper stock influence publishing expenses. Therefore it is impossible to estimate accurately the cost of a "typical" bulletin.

Book bulletins are distributed on the campus to administrative officers, faculty, and selected groups of students by local mail or from the main library loan desks and the departmental libraries. By outside mail they are sent to trustees, alumni, friends of the library, editors of library periodicals, library schools, and other libraries.

Mimeographed Lists of Recent Accessions. Mimeographed booklists far outnumber all other forms of library publications for general distribution. Some of the best of these have qualities in common with the book bulletins just described, although their main purpose is to record the new acquisitions. The actual publication cost is small. One library estimates the cost of its monthly booklist (300 copies per issue) at approximately $2.45 for stencils and paper, but this does not include labour costs.

In planning a mimeographed booklist to keep the faculty informed of new additions, the librarian can take the entire stock of current additions for material or he can make a selection. In the large college library it may not be either desirable or justifiable to issue a complete serial list of current accessions; but, since the demand for this information comes from the faculty who want to know what books are being added in their own and related fields, it would seem desirable to aim at completeness whenever possible. If selection is essential because of the bulk of current accessions, then it is better to eliminate certain classes of material which are less likely to be of use to the larger group than to attempt a haphazard selection of titles from the accessions of each month. One library omits foreign language, fiction, juvenile, and professional library books from its listing. The format and arrangement of the mimeographed lists of accessions are as varied as their titles. Most libraries follow the classification scheme of their libraries, giving suitable captions for each class and arranging titles alphabetically under class. Another plan is to classify the books by subject and to arrange the subjects alphabetically throughout the list. In most cases the information for each title consists of the call number, author, title, and date of publication. For the mimeographed list of accessions, as for the book bulletin, a distinctive title is of considerable importance. Some titles used for the lists include: *Stray library leaves, On the shelf, Library book list, Library leaves, Scout, New books, Recent accessions,* and *Monthly record.* Variety and appearance are enhanced by changing the colour of the cover sheet in consecutive issues and by using a printed masthead for the title on the cover sheet.

While the demand for the mimeographed list of current accessions comes mainly from the faculty, the thing that keeps the publication alive is the librarian's ambition to have a regular channel of communication with the faculty. Few librarians overlook the opportunity to use the introductory pages of each number for presenting interesting and informative notes about staff activities, exhibits, gifts, and new services.

The issuance of a mimeographed weekly, monthly, or quarterly list of accessions is the most interesting, and probably the least hazardous, adventure in publishing on which a college library can embark. The factors which insure success are regularity and continuity in issuance, an arrangement of subjects and titles which will facilitate its use by the faculty, and a page or two of introductory comment with enough of human inspiration, information, and humour to make the list not only a useful tool but interesting and readable. Copies are usually sent to all members of the faculty and administration and are sometimes sent to outside friends of the library. Copies are also posted in the dormitories and in departmental libraries and are available for consultation in the main library by students. Mailing lists are revised frequently to make sure that the list is being sent only to those who really want it and make use of it.

Booklists. In addition to book bulletins and mimeographed lists of accessions, some libraries print or mimeograph booklists. Most libraries are either too small, or insufficiently wedded to print to make the former a practicable proposition. Fewer still are the college libraries that have reported their experience with booklists. For purposes of illustration one has to turn to the university library field. For a number of years now the University of Washington library has been experimenting with booklists in an effort to stimulate student reading beyond their class assignments. Subjects are chosen with the interests of students uppermost in mind: *Poetry, Learning to listen,* and *Your private library.* Current discussion prompted: *Consumer help thyself* and *Why democracy?* Purely literary interest suggested: *Some foreign novels in translation* and *Historical novels.* Many were prepared in response to faculty and student requests: *Elizabethan scene, Americas to the South, Map of America,* and *Canada.* All books are read by the compiler of the list and the book notes are original. A distinctive feature of the lists are the illustrated covers. They are designed by staff members or student artists. For the most part they are original, although a few are adapted from pictures or are copies. The lists are printed on a sheet four by eight inches and the illustration appears on the front cover. This size is convenient for display and for mailing. Approximately eight to ten lists have been issued annually. The expense of publication is kept low by reproducing the illustrations and text by the lithograph process. Booklists can be mimeographed or typewritten if only a few copies are needed for posting on library bulletin boards. Titles should be listed with sufficient bibliographical detail to enable the reader to secure the book quickly from the stacks or shelves and should be accompanied by brief, readable annotations. Copies are distributed through book displays in the library, by professors in classes, at the loan desks, and through the mail to selected libraries and to individuals who request them.

Friends of the library bulletins. The final group of library publications to be mentioned at this point is the Friends of the library bulletins. There are many of these published on behalf of university libraries, few in the interest of college libraries. Several of the library book bulletins, previously mentioned, are distributed to Friends regardless of whether the Friends organization contributes directly to the sponsorship of the bulletin. The necessity for a separate Friends bulletin will depend largely on the interest and generosity of the Friends. An excellent example of an attractive and very successful bulletin sponsored by an active Friends group is *Books for the Knox College Library,* a periodical issued from time to time by the Friends of the Knox College Library to give its members news about the needs and acquisitions of the library. In place of a periodical publication, some college libraries issue an occasional brochure commemorating gifts of Friends or calling attention to needs whether or not there is any formal organization of a group or association by that name.

Book Displays and Exhibits

Book displays are generally intended to call attention to books for immediate circulation, to encourage browsing, and to help the reader in his selection of books. Exhibits have a more specific aim. They are intended to tell a logical story. The books, pamphlets, objects, or other materials used in the exhibit are not available for immediate circulation. The exhibit "must be preserved as a *whole* during the period of the exhibition. A single theme must be stressed throughout so that the student comes away with a tangible idea, easily remembered. Whether the book display consists of one book or a group of books, it should catch the eye and stand out from the surrounding objects in the room.

The various parts of the display, such as the poster or book legend, should help to carry out the idea of the display. Colour, compelling slogans, and skillful arrangement of the books have a great deal to do with the way in which a "display is able to circulate books. The practice of placing several book displays in various parts of the library where many readers pass or come to study is important. A single book placed on a stand in a prominent place on the loan desk will often circulate immediately if a brief note or caption suggests its timeliness and particular interest. Many college librarians have found it worth while to prepare subject displays for use outside the library in college buildings where institutes or some special programmes are being held.

Basically independent reading is encouraged by providing a continuous flow of new books attractively and invitingly arranged to catch the student's eye. One library has its *Under the clock* collection of popular titles; another its *Week-end shelf* which is filled with selections from the new acquisitions. These display centers may well become a permanent part of the library display routine in order that students will form the habit of selecting a book for leisure reading. Some college libraries give their students an opportunity to see all the new books. They put all their new acquisitions on display for a week where students and faculty may look them over and leave reservations for those books they would like to read. This plan has the advantage of letting students see all the new books, an opportunity they would not have if the books were sent directly to the faculty members who ordered them. It is the function of education to lead students to discriminate between the better and the worse, to arrive at a higher standard. Book displays can contribute to this aim by calling attention to older standards works, primary sources, and the more important monthlies and quarterlies which students all too frequently neglect for the digest magazine or the pictorial weekly. If the book display is built around a *subject,* readers are less likely to be concerned whether the books are new or old. Little-known but useful books from the Reference room collection should be brought out and displayed. The success of public libraries in luring readers from the novel or play to history and science through movie tie-ups should not be overlooked by the college librarian.

Most book displays will naturally be developed in connection with the student's class work, but supplementary suggestions may be secured from reading lists, library book bulletins, and library annual reports. In a study of exhibit practices in a large number of college libraries, Miss Agnes Reagan found that exhibits were most commonly prepared to serve these purposes:

1. To publicize little-known or rare library materials.
2. To stimulate reading for information and recreation.
3. To promote interest in a specific subject field or group of subject fields.
4. To call attention to a particular anniversary or special occasion.
5. To promote the work of an individual teacher, or to promote interest in a specific course or group of related courses.
6. To encourage donations by honouring benefactors and by calling attention to valuable gifts to the library.
7. To encourage hobbies.
8. To further the work of student organizations.
9. To publicize research and any other activities of the faculty.

Librarians gave first place to exhibits about particular countries and localities. Such exhibits aimed to cover the history, culture, geography, social life, and customs of the countries represented and two-thirds of the exhibits dealt with North American countries. Other subjects, listed in descending order of frequency in the Reagan study, included the following: current events, graphic arts, literary and author anniversary exhibits book arts, college history, special types of materials such as rare books and little-known resources of the library, and collective and individual biography. Most of the following types of exhibits were reported less frequently but were found in more than one college: exhibits on the Negro, religion, drama, Greek and Latin classics, holidays, science, vocations, arts and crafts, photography, architecture, education, geography, home economics, Indians, music, and physical education.

Miss Reagan found very little evidence of a systematic effort to make exhibits an integral part of college courses. When exhibits were related to academic subjects, they were restricted to one or two subject fields and were systematically promoted in only two or three libraries. While there is little doubt that most college libraries could improve the educational importance of their exhibits by attempting to relate them to curricular purposes, it should not be overlooked that there are strong practical objections to such a plan. In the first place there are other opportunities in the library programme where it is perhaps more important to seek faculty cooperation than in the preparation of exhibits. In the second place it is practically impossible to get around to all departments in such a programme. As a result, the relating of exhibits to the course of a few teaching departments is likely to exaggerate the importance of those particular courses which lend themselves to visual display, and correspondingly to diminish interest in others which may be of equal importance in a student's education. There is also the factor of self-advertisement, seized upon by certain teachers who are always on the alert to any means of making their work stand out. Finally, the primary objective of exhibits should be to stimulate the student mind to broad social and cultural interests. Education is not confined to courses but extends to every phase of student life. Exhibits should emphasize the obvious fact that there are more ways of becoming educated than by merely taking courses. Exhibits should stimulate student initiative, breadth of view, and intellectual curiosity.

The evidence revealed in Miss Reagan's study shows that for the most part the better college libraries are planning exhibits which are accomplishing these very purposes. It is not necessary to be an expert in visual techniques to produce exhibits which are educationally and recreationally effective. Certain definite principles, however, must be observed:

1. Every exhibit should have an objective, that is, a main idea which is to be dramatized. This idea should be the center of interest. Since the story or idea visualized in an exhibit is told, for the most part, on walls or in cases, it is necessary to plan and arrange the exhibit in such a way that the student will know at once where to begin observing, how to progress, and where to end.
2. The design must appeal to the eye. A single object skillfully placed or a balanced arrangement of several objects is far better than a crowded exhibit. Details are important.
3. The method of presentation should be adapted to the purpose of the exhibit and to the group to be reached. Miss Reagan states that: "Materials vary widely and range from books and pictures on the one hand to puppets and playing cards on the other. Illustrated textual materials, pictures, posters, maps, manuscripts, and periodicals have been exhibited most frequently in college libraries." If the object of the exhibit and the materials used can be related to courses which the student is taking or to events which are currently prominent, the exhibit will make a more vital appeal.
4. In any visual presentation colour plays an important role. Through the use of colour contrasts and Background, the important highlights in the exhibit may be put in advantageous position so that it is impossible to avoid them. Illuminations, "props," and exhibit equipment are also important in making the exhibit effective.

For the most part libraries draw upon their own resources and upon loans from members of the faculty and the local community for the materials for exhibits. A number of exhibits are available for loan from art associations and museums, the government, publishers, and societies. *Leads*

No. 7, from the American Library Association, gives specific sources for rented and borrowed exhibits. Many additional ideas and materials for exhibits may be obtained from *Library literature,* college library annual reports, library book bulletins, and professional library journals.

Radio

Little significance is attached by most college librarians to the possibility of relating the radio to college library objectives and library interpretation. Few librarians participate in radio Broadcasts although many college faculties put on radio programmes of some sort. Those college librarians who are concerned with the possible uses of radio in library work have two main approaches: (1) providing radio programme guides and supplementary reading services, and (2) participation in radio broadcasts. For the library to experiment in either direction requires the part time of a member of the staff who has faith in the value of the project, enthusiasm for its advancement and development, and some knowledge of recent scientific studies of the effects of radio on reading.

Programme Guides and Services. As a basis for determining procedures in developing broadcast guides and supplementary reading services, a study was made of the listening habits of approximately one hundred students in a particular college. On the basis of this study and from information obtained from other colleges, it would appear that libraries might usefully render these kinds of radio service to student and faculty listeners:

1. Serious talks, though not as popular as music, news, and drama, have a relatively high ranking for their value to students in college courses and have a considerable reading "pull." Therefore, they need to be more publicized. They appear at more irregular times on the air than certain music programmes in which students show most interest, and they are more apt to be overlooked unless

attention is called to them. In its simplest form this entails setting aside prominent bulletin board space in the library for posting advance notices of programmes. Eye-arresting captions on bright-coloured poster paper should call attention to the announcements. It also means selecting programmes for the bulletin board from the various bulletins and announcements of broadcasting companies.

2. On national radio programmes there are symphonic and opera programmes, news reports, talks, and book programmes which lead to a certain amount of follow-up reading. Students reported having followed up such radio programmes with library reading in current news journals, popular science journals, specific plays and books mentioned in the broadcast, stories of operas, composers' lives, music appreciation books and librettos. Books, pamphlets, and librettos may be displayed in a case beneath the radio bulletin board and tied up with the programme announcements above. A great deal of reading matter directly pertinent to the programmes may be obtained free from programme sponsors or the broadcasting companies. Reprints of important lectures and talks are often available free of charge or for a very small cost. These should be displayed, singly or in quantity, along with such books and journal articles as are put on display.
3. Several colleges report library tie-ups with student-faculty listening groups, particularly in connection with radio programmes designed to stimulate discussion and debate. A very good example of this sort of cooperation was reported in print by the Syracuse School of Citizenship Library in connection with the *Town Meeting of the Air* broadcasts.

4. The college radio programme will provide similar programmes to encourage study as well as reading, programmes such as music appreciation lectures and music broadcasts, interpretation of events back of the news, travel talks, adaptations from great dramas, poetry readings, and popular knowledge talks. The library has a special responsibility to call attention to these programmes and most departments will readily cooperate in supplying photographs of speakers, programme announcements, and even copies of scripts. There is opportunity here also for aid to faculty broadcasters and script writers. Several libraries report that they furnish information for members of the faculty and the student body for talks on the college programme series.

Participation in Radio Broadcasting. Direct participation in the radio broadcast on a scale to amount to anything has been confined largely to state college libraries. The library of Iowa State College, for example, has worked closely with the extension staff of the college in using the radio to encourage reading and to promote the extension of library facilities throughout the state. In 1938 the librarian in charge of extension service reported: "Now the library time on the air has increased so that one full time person is employed for broadcasting under the supervision of the librarian with several assistants spending part time on radio work. The college library is now on the air twelve times a week, the periods varying from five to thirty minutes. The programmes include book reviews, travel, public affairs, short stories . . . and a book which is read serially six days a week." It is not uncommon for college librarians to be called upon to participate in a faculty programme broadcast regularly over municipally owned stations. Book reviews are most common, although book panels, author talks, and prose and poetry readings have been given. Michigan State College reports reviews and readings from alumni publications. Contributions in the faculty broadcasts are made by the librarians of Chico State College, Mills College, and Oklahoma A. and M. College. A few college libraries report having weekly sustaining programmes of fifteen-minute and half-hour periods. The staff of the Oregon State College library has used the radio to interpret the services of the various departments of the library. General talks about the library and its services to the college and to the community are sometimes given by other librarians.

REFERENCES

Bowman, E.L., Outlines of the radio series given by Oregon State College library. PNLA quar. 4: 107, April, 1940.

Brown, B.J., Picture maps. Will. lib. bull. 11: 385-9, February, 1937.

Caverhill, Beverley, A survey of the periodical publications of college and university libraries. PNLA quar. 6: 131-7, April, 1942.

Cundiff, Ruby E., Here are slogans. Wil. Jib. bull. 12: 577-8, May, 1938.

Fay, Lucy E., College library reports. Lib. jour. 59: 189-92, March 1, 1934.

Focke, Helen M., and others. Library bulletin boards. Cleveland. Cleveland Public Library, n.d. (mimeographed.)

Garrison, Gretchen, Display materials. Wil. lib. bull. 14: 326-7, December, 1939.

Ginger, Ruth, Integration in library extension. (Unpublished paper delivered at the A.L.A. Agricultural libraries section at Kansas City, Mo., June 1938.)

Johns, Helen, University library booklists. *In* Crow's Nest, ed. by Guy R. Lyle. Wil. lib. bull. 15: 842-3, June, 1941.

Kelly, Matilde. Display materials. Chicago, A.L.A. Public relations division, 1940. (mimeographed.)

King, Florence L., How is the library presented in the college catalog? Lib. quar. 8: 77-92, January, 1938.

Lazarsfeld, P.F., Radio and the printed page. New York, Duell, 1940.

Loizeaux, Marie D., Publicity primer. 2d rev. ed. New York, H. W. Wilson co., 1939.

Noyes, R.W., Town meeting of the air at Syracuse University. Wil. lib. bull. 13: 100-1, October, 1938.

Reagan, Agnes, College library exhibits: a bibliographical approach. Col. and research lib. 5: 53-61, December, 1943.

Reagan, Agnes, A study of college library exhibit policy and practice. (Unpublished M.S. thesis, University of Illinois Library School, 1943.)

Roberts, Ina, Slogans that circulate books. Cleveland, [The author], 1936.

Russell, John D., and others. The college library report. A.L.A. bull. 30: 216-20, April, 1936.

Walter, F.K., The library's own printing. Chicago, A.L.A., 1934.

Glossary of Terms

Abstract: An abstract is a short summary describing the main idea or content of a work such as an article, book, or dissertation.

Annotation: Unlike an abstract, which is an objective description or summary of a work, an annotation is a critical or subjective evaluation of a piece of work, usually included in a bibliography or citation.

Archives: A special collection or collections that house the records of organizations, governments, universities, etc. An archive can also contain collections of the personal papers of an individual or family, photographs, pamphlets, newspaper clippings, etc. Archives usually house materials of an historic nature. See also *University Archives.*

Article: Sometimes referred to as a paper, an article is a brief composition on a subject, usually appearing in a magazine or journal.

Audio-Visual Materials: Audio-visual materials convey information mainly via sound and image instead of by text. An example of audio-visual material on the Library Gateway is *Louis Agassiz Fuertes Ornithological Artwork.*

Authentication: The process of identifying an individual by a computer, usually based on a username and password. Cornell uses *SideCar* and *CUWebLogin* to authenticate members of the Cornell community.

Barcode Number: The 14-digit number appearing beneath the barcode found inside the front or back cover of a book. Barcode numbers for Cornell library books begin with the numbers "3 1924" and are used to charge, discharge, and renew books on the online computer system.

Bear Access: A suite of network service applications designed to provide services specific to the needs of the Cornell community, such as CoursEnroll, Faculty Advisor, and the online timecard system (COLTS II), as well as general Internet services such as electronic mail and browsers for navigating the World Wide Web. The CU Library Catalog and Library Gateway are available through Bear Access.

Bibliography: A bibliography is a list of citations that appear at the end of a paper, article, chapter or book. There are also books entirely made up of bibliographies. These are usually compilations of *citations* on a particular subject or by a particular author.

Book Return: A place to return books borrowed from the library. The book return is a box located outside the library, near the door of the library, or near the circulation desk.

Boolean Operator or Boolean Logic: Boolean operators, otherwise known as logical operators, are used to construct complex searches in a database. They help make a search more accurate. There are 3 logical operators: AND, OR and NOT.

Borrow Direct: A rapid book request and delivery system. It enables Cornell faculty, staff, and students to search the combined library catalogs of Brown, Columbia, Cornell, Dartmouth, University of Pennsylvania, Princeton, and Yale a collection of over 40 million volumes and directly request expedited delivery of circulating items.

Browser: Software programme used to view web pages. Browsers like Microsoft's Internet Explorer (MSIE) or Netscape allow you to click on a link to another document, and get information from a different computer where that resource is stored.

Call Number: A call number is a combination of letters and numbers that is given to each item held in the library. The letters and numbers assigned to the work describe its subject matter and serves as its address on the shelf. Cornell uses the *Library of Congress Classification* system to assign its call numbers.

Card Catalog: A card file listing books, journals, and other materials arranged alphabetically by author, title, and subject. Since April 1988, cards have not been added to Cornell's card catalog. Records are now added to the online catalog instead. See *CU Library Catalog* for more information on the catalogs at Cornell.

Catalog: A catalog is a compilation of records describing the contents of a particular collection or group of collections. For example, the *CU Library Catalog* has records for most of the items held by Cornell Library and the *OCLC WorldCat* catalog lists the holdings of books, journals, and other materials held by OCLC member libraries all over the world. A catalog can also be a list of items published by a certain body. The *GPO Monthly Catalog* contains records of reports, studies, fact sheets, maps, handbooks, conference proceedings, etc. issued by all U.S. federal government agencies and the U.S. Congress. The library also often owns publisher's catalogs and product catalogs that list items available or for sale. For example, Books in Print lists books currently published in the United States along with their prices.

CD-ROM: A thin disk (Compact Disk Read Only Memory) that holds thousands of pages of information. In the library, some journal indexes and other reference sources are available on CD-ROM. They may be quickly and conveniently searched at a computer workstation.

Charge: To record the loan of a book or other item from the circulating collection of a library to a borrower. In order to charge, or check-out, materials the user must present a Cornell identification card to a staff person at the circulation desk along with the materials to be charged out. Patrons may also use the *self-check stations* at Olin and the Hotel School to charge out items from those libraries.

Charged: If a library item is checked-out, the online catalog will indicate that the status of the item is Charged, or not available. In such cases, users may request a *hold* or recall on the item. Another option, if the item is a book, is *Borrow Direct*.

CIDC: The Cornell Institute for Digital Collections (CIDC) is a cross-disciplinary team established to explore the use of emerging technologies for providing greater access to cultural and scientific collections. Digital imaging has enabled CIDC to make many of Cornell University's rare and fragile collections available on the World Wide Web. Partnerships with academic institutions, museums, corporations, and libraries, national and international, have permitted CIDC to create digital collections from around the world. For more information see the *CIDC* web site in the CU Library Web Sites section of the Library Gateway.

Circulation Desk: The circulation desk is the place to charge (check out), return, or renew books. Circulation staff can also help patrons locate items that cannot be found. Items requested through interlibrary loan and Borrow Direct are delivered to circulation desks and patrons can pick them up from these locations. Course reserve items are also available at circulation desks. Overdue fines are paid at this desk, too.

CISER: The Cornell Institute for Social and Economic Research (CISER) is a cross-disciplinary organization founded in 1981 to enhance the environment for social science research at Cornell University. Its membership includes more than 400 social science faculty who are dispersed administratively, organizationally, and geographically in nine colleges. CISER provides research services to faculty members and encourages collaborative research among Cornell's social scientists. CISER's research support services include assistance in preparing proposals, a data archive, computing consulting support, and computing systems support. In addition, CISER helps investigators identify colleagues with similar research interests, issues publications supporting social science research, and organizes seminars and workshops. For more information see the *CISER* web site in the CU Library Web Sites section of the Library Gateway.

Copyright: Copyright is a form of protection provided by the laws of the United States (title 17, U.S. Code) to the authors of "original works of authorship," including literary, dramatic, musical, artistic, and certain other intellectual works. For more information about copyright, see the *United States Copyright Office* web site - which includes *definitions*, *frequently asked questions*, and *basic information* about copyright.

Course Reserves: In academic libraries, course reserves are library items given a shorter loan period (one-hour, three-hours, overnight, 3-day, etc.) for a limited period of time (usually one term or semester) at the request of the instructor, to ensure that all the students enrolled in a course have an opportunity to use them. These materials are usually kept together in a particular area of the library, such as a graduate reading room or behind the circulation desk. Each library has its own reserve system; however, many reserve items may also be accessed through the CU Library Catalog as Electronic Course Reserves (or e-Reserves). See the *Electronic Reserves* help page for more information.

CRL: The Center for Research Libraries (*CRL*) is an international not-for-profit consortium of colleges, universities, and libraries that provides access to a variety of scholarly research resources, including newspapers, serials, archival materials in microform, microform sets, and foreign government publications in many subject areas. The *CRL catalog* is available in the Library Gateway. CRL resources are available to Cornell researchers through interlibrary loan.

Cross-Reference: Directions that lead you from one subject or name to another in a catalog or index.

CUL: The Cornell University Library (CUL) is one of the largest academic research libraries in the United States. Composed of nineteen libraries, CUL holds over seven million printed volumes, subscribes to more than 65,000 journals, and is networked to over 40,000 electronic databases. Please see *About the Library* and *Libraries/Departments* on the Library Gateway for information on collections, organization, policies, and services.

CU Library Catalog: An online catalog that contains records for materials in the Cornell University Library collection including the holdings of all 17 libraries on the Ithaca campus, in addition to those of the Geneva Experiment Station and the CISER Data Archive. The catalog contains records for books, computer files (including CD-ROM's and networked resources), government documents, journal titles, manuscripts and archives, maps, microforms, musical scores, serials, sound recordings, and visual materials. Some library records (especially for materials in the humanities and social sciences dating from before 1973) are not yet in the online catalog, but are available in the Olin Library Card Catalog, which is located in the lower level of Olin Library. Records for the *Cornell Medical Library* can be found in a separate catalog called *Tri-Cat*.

CUWebLogin: CUWebLogin allows you to access restricted library resources in the Library Catalog and Find Articles/Find Databases/Find e-Journas without needing SideCar. It does this by allowing you to log in to a web form, and then passing your authentication information back to the web server in a *cookie*. For more information about how CUWebLogin works, see the help page for CUWebLogin.

Database: A database is an organized collection of computer records. The most common type of Library Gateway database consists of records describing articles in periodicals, otherwise known as a *periodical index*. By entering search terms related to a topic, patrons are able to retrieve information about articles of interest from the database. Sometimes all the information needed is in a database record and sometimes further searching is necessary. When searching a periodical index (or database), citations offer such information as the title and author of an article, as well as the title of the journal in which the article appears. In order to locate the journal and read the article, a search of the CU

Library Catalog is necessary. See *Finding articles*.

Due Date: A date stamped in the front or back of a book (or other library item) that indicates when the item must be returned to the library. Fines are charged for items not returned by the due date. Patrons can extend a due date by requesting a *renewal*. On occasion, patrons may have to return an item before the due date because the item has been *recalled*.

Electronic Journal: *A publication, often scholarly, that is made accessible in a computerized format and distributed over the Internet. An electronic journal or e-journal may have a traditional paper counterpart or historical antecedent. For example, the journal* American Literature *can be found in both paper and electronic versions at Cornell. The electronic versions are available through the Library Gateway, and the holdings for the paper copies can be found in the CU Library Catalog.*

ETC: The Electronic Text Center (ETC), located on the first floor of Olin Library, provides access to scholarly electronic text and multimedia documents from a set of dedicated workstations in the library and from the Center's Web site. For more information about the ETC and the resources available there, see the *ETC* web site.

Field: When looking at a *citation* from an *index* or *database*, each piece of information is a field. For example, many citations are made up of an author field, a title field, a publisher field and a date field. What fields are called and what is in them can vary from database to database.

Full text database: A full text database is a resource that provides access to the complete text of an item. In a full text periodical resource, both the bibliographic descriptions and the articles themselves will be available. An example of this type of resource is ProQuest Direct.

Greatest Hits List: A listing of hypertext links that represents the most frequently used resources in the Library Gateway. The *Greatest Hits* list can be accessed from the Find Databases page.

Hold: When a book or other item is currently on loan, the library permits another borrower to place a "hold" on it by contacting the circulation desk. The patron who has the item checked out will not be permitted to renew it, and the person placing the "hold" will be entitled to check it out after it has been returned. The CU Library online catalog includes a feature that allows the user to place an item on hold without staff assistance. This service is available through the Requests link at the top of any online catalog record.

Holdings: The total stock of materials, print and nonprint, owned by a library, usually listed in the catalog. Synonymous with library collection. Also refers to the copies, volumes, issues, or parts of a title owned by a library, indicated in a holdings note in a catalog record. For example, Cornell may subscribe to a journal, but certain volumes may be missing; or Cornells subscription to a journal may have begun in 1975 but the journal dates back to 1950; etc.

HTML: Hypertext Markup Language (HTML) is programming language used in the creation of Web pages.

Hypertext: Transparent linkage of textual documents to other related documents on the World Wide Web.

Index: An index is a guide to the contents of a file, document, or a group of documents. An index is used to point to the contents of something. For example, there are indexes in the backs of books that describe and point to the contents of those books. There are also very large indexes that describe the contents of journals and provide enough information to locate an article in a journal. Indexes are usually arranged by subject, author, or keyword. They can come in both paper and electronic form.

Intellectual property: Intellectual property refers to creations of the mind: inventions, literary and artistic works, and symbols, names, images, and designs used in commerce. Intellectual property is divided into two categories: Industrial property, which includes inventions (patents), trademarks, industrial designs, and geographic indications of source; and Copyright, which includes literary and artistic works such as novels, poems and plays, films, musical works, drawings, paintings, photographs and sculptures, and architectural designs. More information is available from the *World Intellectual Property Organization*.

Interlibrary Loan: Interlibrary loan is a form of resource sharing among libraries nation- and world-wide. When a book or other item needed by a Cornell user is checked out, unavailable for some other reason, or not owned by the library, a patron may request that it be borrowed from another library by submitting an interlibrary loan request form. Interlibrary loan requests can be initiated at any reference desk on campus or by using the *Interlibrary Loan form* that can be found in the Services section of the Library Gateway. CUL participates in a number of cooperative agreements with other research libraries, consortia, and networks (e.g., the Research Libraries Group, the Association of Research Libraries, and the South Central Research Library Council). Cornell is a partner in the Center for Research Libraries, a nonprofit corporation located in Chicago that is operated by scholarly and research institutions to strengthen resources and enhance access. Cornell students, faculty, and staff members can borrow any of the center's holdings through interlibrary loan.

Internet: A worldwide network of computers that can be accessed via the campus computer network. The Internet allows local computer users to find and use information resources on computers of other academic institutions, research institutes, private companies, and government agencies.

In Transit: If an item has been returned to the library, but has not been re-shelved in its call number location, the catalog will indicate the items status as In Transit. If patrons need In Transit items immediately, they may inquire at the circulation desk.

ISBN: International Standard Book Number. A unique 10-digit code assigned to a specific edition of a book before it is published.

ISSN: International Standard Serial Number. A unique 8-digit code assigned to the specific title of a serial.

Journal: Although the terms periodical, journal, serial, and magazine have slightly different definitions, they are often used interchangeably. They are published on a regular basis (weekly, monthly, annually, etc.) and contain articles written by various authors. A journal contains peer-reviewed articles written by scholars while a magazine contains more popular articles often written by journalists. The terms periodical and serial are more generic and refer to all types of these materials.

Keyword Searching: Most online catalogs and bibliographic databases include an option that allows the user to search by keyword(s). In this type of search, users enter a significant word or words that describe the research topic, and the catalog or database retrieves all records where the search terms appear whether they appear in the title field, abstract field, subject heading field, contents field, notes field, etc.

Library Annex: The Library Annex is a storage facility for lesser-used materials from the collections of CUL. Materials held in the Annex can be delivered to any of the libraries on campus or used in the Annex reading room. *Annex requests* can be made through the online catalog, through the link Annex Requests available under the *Circulation Services* section of the Library Gateway, or at any circulation desk on campus.

Library of Congress Classification: A classification system developed by the Library of Congress (LC) that is used to organize the collections of many academic and research libraries, including Cornell. This alpha-numeric system arranges materials by subject. Each subject or class is represented by a series of letters and numbers, which are used to create an LC *call number*. To see the main classes in the LC system, go to *Library of Congress Classification.* For a more detailed outline of the LC system, go to *Library of Congress Classification Outline*.

Library of Congress Subject Headings (LCSH): The multi-volume set Library of Congress Subject Headings is an alphabetic guide to and list of the official subject headings used for searching in the CU Library Catalog. These sets can be found in most libraries on campus in the reference area or at locations near the public workstations.

Loan Period: The amount of time a patron may borrow a book or other item from the library. The time varies depending on the type of material borrowed and the status of the borrower.

Magazine: Although the terms periodical, journal, serial, and magazine have slightly different definitions, they are often used interchangeably. They are published on a regular basis (weekly, monthly, annually, etc.) and contain articles written by various authors. A journal contains peer-reviewed articles written by scholars while a magazine contains more popular articles often written by journalists. The terms periodical and serial are more generic and refer to all types of these materials.

Manuscripts: Documents or written compositions, such as letters or diaries, which have not been printed. Often, an author's written (or typed) original "copy" as distinguished from a printed or published version of the same material. Cornell's primary collections of manuscripts are located in the *Rare Books & Manuscripts Collections* in Kroch Library.

Media: Films, tapes, and other audio-visual materials that require the use of special listening or viewing equipment.

Microforms: A term used to describe documents that have been photographed or filmed. Microforms require the use of special reader machines. Common formats for microforms are microfilm, microfiche, and microcard.

Not Charged: If a library item is not checked-out, the online catalog will indicate that the status of the item is Not Charged. This means that the item is available in its call number location in the library.

Numeric Data: Numeric data files are those with significant numeric content, either statistical, coded, or graphically displayed. An example of numeric data found on the Library Gateway is the *FAOSTAT Statistics Database*.

OCLC WorldCat: This database is an online catalog of the holdings of books, journals, and other materials held by thousands of OCLC member libraries. (OCLC is Online Computer Library Center.) Cornell researchers can identify and locate materials in other libraries and collections using WorldCat, and request these materials through interlibrary loan.

Online Catalog: An electronic or digitized version of a library's *card catalog*. The Cornell University Library's online catalog is called the *CU Library Catalog*. It is the database that contains records that refer to the many materials held by Cornell University Library.

Patron Info: A link available through the library catalog that allows Cornell patrons to view their library account information charged items, pending requests, and fines or fees owed. Accessing Patron Info requires the user to enter their Cornell ID number and last name. Patron Info is also accessible via the link View your account or renew a book on the *Library Gateway*.

Periodical: Although the terms periodical, journal, serial, and magazine have slightly different definitions, they are often used interchangeably. They are published on a regular basis (weekly, monthly, annually, etc.) and contain articles written by various authors. A journal contains peer-reviewed articles written by scholars while a magazine contains more popular articles often written by journalists. The terms periodical and serial are more generic and refer to all types of these materials.

Rare Books: Books that are valued for the significance of their contents, their scarcity, their imprint or date of publication, their physical characteristics or condition, or their associations (signed or annotated by a famous author, for instance). Cornell's primary collections of rare books are are located in the

Rare Books & Manuscripts Collections in Kroch Library.

Recall: *A request made by the library to one of its patrons to return a borrowed item* before *its due date. Any item may be recalled at any time for Course Reserve or after two weeks if requested by another Cornell patron. This service is available through the Requests link at the top of any online catalog record.*

Record: A collection of related data fields organized and accessible as a single entity. Examples of data fields are author, title, publisher, abstract, call number, etc. In a periodical index, which is a collection of article citations, each citation is a record. In the CU Library Catalog, each reference retrieved per title is also a record.

Reference Collection: Books not meant to be read cover-to-cover, such as dictionaries, handbooks, and encyclopedias, shelved together in a special section of the library called the reference area. Reference books may not be checked out because they are needed by librarians to answer questions at the reference desk. Their location and circulation status is usually indicated by the symbol "R" or "Ref" preceding the call number in the catalog record and on the spine label.

Reference Desk: When a person has a question about how to find specific information or how to use library services and resources, assistance can be obtained from a reference librarian at the reference desk. Professional librarians and reference assistants staff reference desks to assist patrons with their questions.

Reference librarian: Reference librarians are specialists in the field of information retrieval. Generally they have a Masters degree in library science, and may have other graduate degrees as well. Reference librarians work in public services answering questions posed by library patrons at the reference desk, by telephone, via e-mail, or through an online chat session. They also provide instruction on the use of library resources and information technology.

Renewal: An extension of the loan period for charged library materials. Renewals may be handled in person at the circulation desk, by phone, or through the link "View your account or renew a book" on the Library Gateway.

RLIN (Eureka): The Research Libraries Information Network (RLIN), is an information management and retrieval system used by hundreds of comprehensive research libraries, archival repositories, museums, academic, public, law, technical, and corporate libraries to build an international database of bibliographic information. The RLIN database indexes books, journals, and other materials held by full-member Research Library Group (RLG) libraries. Cornell researchers can identify and locate materials in other research libraries and collections using RLIN, and order these materials through interlibrary loan. As a member of RLG, records for many of the Cornell University Library's holdings will show up in this database. RLIN is available through the catalog and Find Databases.

Self-Check Station: Bar-code reading machines for patrons to check out materials themselves, rather than checking materials out at the circulation desk. Self-check stations are available at Olin and Hotel School libraries. A Cornell ID card is required to use self-check. A receipt is printed indicating when the materials are due back at the library.

Serial: Although the terms periodical, journal, serial, and magazine have slightly different definitions, they are often used interchangeably. They are published on a regular basis (weekly, monthly, annually, etc.) and contain articles written by various authors. A journal contains peer-reviewed articles written by scholars while a magazine contains more popular articles often written by journalists. The terms periodical and serial are more generic and refer to all types of these materials.

Spatial Data: Spatial data is data pertaining to the location and spatial dimensions of geographical entities. Examples of spatial data files can be found within the *Cornell University Geospatial Information Repository (CUGIR)*, accessible through the Library Gateway.

Stacks: Stacks or stack area refer to the space in a library where the majority of library materials are shelved. Often the stacks are made up of multiple floors and contain many rows of shelving units.

Subject Headings: Words or phrases assigned to books and articles which are used to index these items by topic. The Cornell University Library uses *Library of Congress subject headings*.

Telnet: On the Library Gateway., Telnet is an application that is sometimes used to access electronic databases. It is often thought of as access to databases in strictly textual format as opposed to access via the Web, which may provide images, search boxes, and "point and click" technology. Some people prefer using a database via Telnet when available since it can be faster and allow for more complex searching, but it is really a matter of personal preference. You will need to have a Telnet application on your computer in order to use the Telnet databases on the Library Gateway. Different databases and different computers require different kinds of Telnet. There are only two kinds of Telnet: TN3270 for communicating with an IBM mainframe and VT100 for connecting to most other kinds of computers. To learn about downloading and configuring Telnet, go to *Telnet and the Gateway*.

Truncation: Truncation is a symbol put at the end or in the middle of a word in order to catch all variant endings or spellings of that word when searching a database. For example, if conducting research on computers, entering comput? as a search term would yield records with the terms computer, computers, computing, computerized, etc. The truncation symbol is placed at the point in the word where various endings can begin to occur. Databases use various symbols, such as $, #, +, *, !, and ?, to represent truncation. Some databases truncate automatically. Some databases allow for truncation symbols in the middle of the word in order to pick up variant spellings. For instance, entering behavi?r would retrieve behavior and behaviour. The Help or Search Tips links for each database will indicate which symbol to use for truncation, if any.

URL: Uniform Resource Locator, or web address. Usually in the form of http://host.subdomain.domain Example: http://www.bls.gov

University Archives: University Archives, located in the *Rare & Manuscripts Collections* in Kroch Library, collects and preserves records of historical, legal, fiscal, or administrative value to Cornell University. Holdings include official records and reports of the university, its officers, and component parts; private papers of faculty, students, staff, and alumni; official and student publications; maps and architectural records; audiovisual materials including still photographs and negatives, motion picture film, oral history interviews, and audio and video tapes; and artifacts and ephemera documenting Cornell's history.

Vertical File: A collection of materials such as pamphlets, newspaper clippings, brochures, or pictures, which because of their shape and often their ephemeral nature, are filed in drawers or cabinets for easy reference.

World Wide Web: A graphical client-server information system that uses the Internet to access computers containing millions of hypertext documents.

Select Bibliography

Allen. F.P., Library expenditures of land-grant colleges and universities, 1928-1957. Lib. jour. 63:404-7, May 15, 1938.

Barcus, Thomas R., Carnegie corporation and college libraries 1938-1943 New York, Carnegie corporation of New York, 1943.

Bishop, William Warner, Carnegie corporation and college libraries 1929- 1938. New York, Carnegie corporation of New York, 1938.

Branscomb, Harvie, Teaching with books; a study of college libraries, Chicago, Association of American colleges and A.L.A., 1940.

Brumbaugh. Aaron J., Accrediting associations and the college library. Col. and research lib. 2:206-10. 276, June, 1941.

Butts. R.F., The college charts its course. New York, McGraw-Hili 1939.

Carnegie corporation of New York. Advisory group on college libraries. College library standards. New York, Carnegie corporation of New York 1952.

Carnovsky, Leon, Self-evaluation; or how good is my library Col. and research lib. 3:304-8, September, 1942.

Coney, Donald, and others, A survey of the Indiana university library. Chicago, A.L.A., 1940, (mimeographed).

Copeland, J. Isaac, The college library staff: a story of three centuries. Furman bull. (Furman university, S.C) 22:29-40, April, 1940.

Eells, Walter C., Needed developments in junior college libraries. Col. and research lib. 1:347-56, September, 1940.

Gerould, J.T., The college library building, its planning and equipment. New York. Scribner, 1932.

Gourley', James E. and Mohrhardt, Foster E., Teachers college libraries. Wil. lib. bull. 14:662-3, May, 1940.

Hirsch, Felix E., The use of the book collection in the teaching programme of a progressive college. Col. and research lib. 2:48-54, December, 1940.

Hunt, C.W., From normal school to teachers college. Col. and research lib. 1:247-50, June, 1940.

Kuhlman, A.F., The library and college education. Peabody jour. of educ. 19:196-208, January, 1942.

Kuhlman, A.F., and Iben, Icko. Report of a survey of the University of Mississippi library (Oxford, Miss.). University of Mississippi, 1940, (mimeographed).

Lester, Robert M., Development of junior college libraries. New York, printed for the information of the Trustees, 1937; *also in* Junior col. jour. 8:3-9, October, 1937. Includes Carnegie standards for junior college libraries.

Little, G.T., School and college libraries. *In* Dewey, Melvil, ed. Papers prepared for the World's library congress held at the Columbian exposition. Washington, Government printing office, 1896, p. 916-33 (U.S. Bureau of education, Report of Commissioner of education for 1892-93).

Ludington, Flora B., Evaluating the adequacy of the book collection. Col. and research lib. 1:305-13, September, 1940.

MacCracken, John Henry, ed., American universities and colleges. 2d ed. rev. and enl. Baltimore, Williams and Wilkins, 1932.

McCrum, Blanche P., A college library makes its own survey plan. A.L.A. bull. 31:947-52, December, 1937.

McEwen, Robert W., The North central association's 1943

survey of college and university libraries. Col. and research lib. 4:253-6, June, 1943.

McGrath, E.J., The evolution of administrative offices in institutions of higher education in the United States from 1860 to 1933. (Unpublished doctor's thesis, University of Chicago, 1936).

Randall, William M., The college library. Chicago, University of Chicago press, 1932.

Rosenlof, George Walter, Library facilities of teacher-training institutions. New York, Teachers college, Columbia university, 1929.

Shores, Louis, Origins of the American college library 1638-1800. Nashville, Tenn., George Peabody college, 1934.

Stanford, E.B., Honours work and the college library. Lib. quar. 12:221-45, April, 1942.

Walling, Ruth, Book requirements of survey courses. Lib. quar. 12:75-93, January, 1942.

Wilson, Louis R., The emergence of the college library, A.L.A. bull. 25: 439.46, September, 1931; *also in* School and society 34:483-92, October 10, 1931.

Wilson, Louis R., Purposes and scope of the yearbook. *In* National society for the study of education. Forty-second yearbook. Part II. The library in general education, ed. by N. B. Henry. Chicago, University of Chicago press, 1943, p. 3-12.

Works, George A., and Morgan, Barton. The land-grant colleges. Washington, Government printing office, 1939.

Index

R

S

T